Whose School is it?

the Democratic Imperative for Our Schools

A Book about School Governance,
Leadership and "The American Vision"

by Rich Migliore
Attorney at Law
Teacher at Heart

For information about permission to reproduce selections from
this book, write to permissions, Integrity Press,
1246 Dill Road, Havertown, PA 19083.

Library of Congress Cataloging-in-Publication Data
Pending—First Edition

Migliore, Richard W.
Whose School Is It? the Democratic Imperative for Our Schools

ISBN 978-0-615-18190-5
democracyineducation.com

Cover design by Craig Rogers
Text design by Sharon Bosler

A special thank you and credit to Dr. Martin Haberman,
Distinguished Professor Emeritus of Education at the University of Wisconsin,
for granting permission to reproduce his
"Dimensions of Effective Urban School Leadership."
His work and expertise is documented within the pages of this book.

The Symbolism of the Flag

The American flag that adorns the cover of this book is a picture of a huge mural painted on the side of a brick building on Delaware Avenue in Philadelphia, Pennsylvania. It has special symbolic meaning in relation to this book, the ideals America stands for and its inspirational nature to the author, Rich Migliore.

A mural painted on the side of a building is a speech right protected by the First Amendment to our Constituion. It is a prime example of the use of First Amendment rights to advocate for the protection of our ideals through the voice of the people which is a major theme that runs through this book.

This particular mural of our flag is entitled September 11th and was painted by Meg Saligman in response to the terrorist attacks executed against America on that day. It is one of the best known murals created through Philadelphia's Mural Arts Program and has been viewed by millions of Americans who have visited Philadelphia. It stands as a constant reminder to all Philadelphians of the ideals we stand for in America and our great city.

The author has driven by that mural every school day morning for the past two years and has drawn inspiration from it to complete this work. He hopes it inspires us all to remember those ideals and to make those ideals come alive in our schools as we attempt to create "The Great American School" for all of our children.

Painted on the wall of Philadelphia Warehousing & Cold Storage Co., Ray Tarnowski, President:

September 11th
© 2001 City of Philadelphia Mural Arts program / Meg Saligman
All Rights Reserved. Used by permission.

The Mural Arts Program (MAP) is the nation's largest mural program. Since 1984, MAP has created over 2,700 murals and works of public art, which are now part of Philadelphia's civic landscape and a source of inspiration to the thousands of residents and visitors who encounter them, earning Philadelphia international recognition as the "City of Murals." MAP engages over 100 communities each year in the transformation of neighborhoods through the mural-making process. MAP's award-winning, free art education programs annually serve over 2,500 youth at sites throughout the city and at-risk teens through education outreach programs. MAP also serves adult offenders in local prisons and rehabilitation centers, using the restorative power of art to break the cycle of crime and violence in our communities. For more information about the Mural Arts Program please visit www.muralarts.org.

Dedication

I dedicate this book to the following people who have been so inspirational to me:

First, to the schoolchildren of Philadelphia who have made my life so worth living....

May this book help make life in schools better and more productive so you may one day touch your dreams....

Second, to Marian, my wife, and my children, Dave and Danny, who have inspired me so much all through my life to stand up for what is right and who have sacrificed so much over the years for the schoolchildren of Philadelphia, their teachers and me. They have always stood behind me through thick and thin....

And I would like to acknowledge those friends and colleagues who have helped motivate me so much in their own sort of ways:

First, Deidre Farmbry, Philadelphia's superintendent of schools when the state of Pennsylvania took over our schools. She steadfastly reminded us to, "Focus on what is important—the children and their schooling. Do not get caught up in the turmoil that surrounds us." Her leadership and dedication will always be remembered as she stood so tall in the face of all the hysteria.

Second, all my Furness friends including Joanna Gocan who always "encouraged my heart" and reminded me to set my goals and keep on climbing until I reached them—and finish this book!

Third, all of my new friends at Mastbaum who continually asked me; "When is it going to be finished?"

And most of all, Joe DiRaddo, my colleague Reading teacher, critical friend and mentor forever; Dr. Davis B. Martin, Principal of University City High School, who was my father figure who instilled so much multicultural people-wisdom in me and still serves as my role model for the principalship; and all the friends and colleagues I have come to know and respect through the years....

A Special Thank You

A "thank you" to all the school board members and trustees of schools throughout The United States of America who serve our children and school communities, and a "special thank you" to the five School Reform Commission members who served first in Philadelphia, Chairman James Nevels, Sandra Dungee Glenn, James Galagher, Ph.D., Martin Bednarek and Daniel Whalen. You have served Philadelphia and our schoolchildren well and have entered a great arena of emotion and passion to embark on America's largest school reform initiative. May your and our work serve as an example of the greatness of America that always seems to emerge from the sincerity of our hearts and the depth of the American spirit.

We have all learned a great deal since the state takeover of Philadelphia's public schools and we all have a great deal more to learn. There is nothing more apparent from our efforts than the truth that we are all "life long learners" and what we are going through is a "process." It is actually the playing out of the "democratic process" that is a central theme throughout this book. It is the American democratic process that is founded in our Constitution that allows our collective greatness to emerge. We must embrace that process to serve our children and school communities well.

We all have much to learn from our forefathers about the democratic process of governance and leadership, but we might keep this thought in mind as we learn more about the democracy that founds our nation: Will we learn more about democracy, its process and its ideals by reading about it in our history books, or will we learn more about it by actually practicing it in our schools and school systems? It is my belief that nowhere is it more important to keep democracy alive and flourishing than in our schools. We must embrace its ideals and practices to achieve greatness in our schools for our children. Democracy is the sine qua non for great governance and leadership.

You have all done a monumental job leading our landmark reform initiative, and although we still live in a hotbed of controversy, the bottom line cannot be denied. Our standardized test scores in reading and math have risen significantly. Yes, we have "miles to go before we rest" for our test scores are still low in many of our schools, but we can celebrate our advances. Yet, we must still recognize and acknowledge our failures because it is through those failures that we find the path to ultimate success. The bottom line is that our schools are better than they were before.

For that, and especially for your undeniable good faith effort to reform our schools and entire school system, on behalf of the children, their parents and the professionals I lead, I thank you. May you all continue to individually, independently, and without reservation—**"vote your conscience."**

Sincerely,

Rich Migliore

Contents

Preface

We have important decisions to make for our children. As we face the critical crossroads in the new frontier of education, it is time for us, as the nation of America, to look in our collective mirror, review our values and decide what we want our schools and school systems to be for our children. America's elementary and secondary schools have come under scrutiny with many calls for reform of our public schools. We must decide together what we want our schools to do for our children, their parents, our communities, our towns and cities, our states, our country and ultimately our world. We must make them come alive for our children and us as a nation if we are to indeed have world-class schools. America must seek the goal of having the best schools in the world that set the conditions for the highest achievement and most well rounded educations for all of our children.

As we in America strive to create new designs for our schools that will allow and cause greatness in our schools to emerge, we look to new forms of governance of our schools, especially our public schools. Our schools lay the foundation for our America to prosper and lead the world now and in the future and it is the governance structures of our schools that lay the foundation for the organizational dynamics to happen that will make our schools all that they can be.

This book examines the various structures of school governance that have already emerged and are beginning to emerge from the think tanks of American educators and policymakers. It examines the ideals of governance we live by in America, our laws, and the best practices of leadership in our democratic society. It examines what is in place now and the consequences and results of what we are presently doing, and it examines the best practices of leadership through the lens of the research we have done in every arena that affects education and schools.

Yes, we have big decisions to make as the school reform movement continues to move forward through our nation. Our first decision is to decide just how we want to govern our schools, and as is set forth as a continuing and inescapable theme throughout this discourse, to achieve ethical and responsive governance we must first decide exactly *"Whose School Is It?"* While we do the analysis, we must always keep in mind the principles we stand for as Americans. We must always keep in mind the principles our children have died for in the protection of our ideals and our way of life.

There are several models of school governance that have emerged so far in our quest to reform the nature of our schools. They are examined throughout this book, and before you read the analysis and concepts set forth, you should ask yourself this question: Which model is most likely to set the conditions for great schools to emerge? Do we want our schools to be governed by any, some or all of these models?

- The traditional model found throughout America where the residents of a school district elect the board of school directors who in turn select a superintendent and govern the schools according to the pressures and voice of the community.
- The bureaucratic model that is found in our large urban cities and has an inescapable history of low performance where the school boards are most often appointed by politicians, a superintendent or CEO is hired, and an antiquated feudalistic system of governance is imposed upon schools.
- The school council model that creates a balance of powers approach similar to our Constitution where the school council becomes the legislative branch, the principal or CEO takes on the executive responsibilities of day to day operations, and the board of trustees becomes the supreme court overseeing and regulating the interplay of the two branches of governance. That "constitutional model" raises the issue of whether a constitution is a superior organizational document than a corporate charter.
- The charter school model where a coalition of founders or an individual is granted a charter to operate a school as a nonprofit corporation and creates a board of trustees through "appointment or election" and then runs the school according to the permeations of the charter and decisions of the founder, coalition of founders or subsequent trustees.
- The independent school model where teachers of a school district assigned to the school and parents of the children of the school are elected to the board of trustees who oversee the governance and leadership of the school. Community members of a variety of sorts may also be part of the mix of trustees on the board.
- The privately managed schools where a nonprofit or for-profit corporation is contracted to manage the school for a fee that goes to the stockholders and/ or officers of the management corporation. Can governance of our schools be ethically and constitutionally contracted away by a governmental body?
- The model advocated by the *New* Commission on the Skills of the American Workforce where schools of the future would be limited liability corporations[1] whose stockholders are the teachers who actually teach at the school. They foresee those schools to be professional organizations where teachers would be able to earn as much as $110,000.00 annually.
- The model represented herein as the "Hilltop Babe Ruth" model where parents and teachers who are enrolled or assigned to a school govern the school democratically through election of officers and trustees.
- Or, can we create other more viable and effective governance structures for our schools?

No matter what model we choose for our schools, we are still bound to the ideals and principles of governance set forth in the ***Constitution of the United States of America.*** We are still hooked to the reality that our schools are communities who work best when there is a common vision, a common mission, and a sincere collective endeavor for the benefit of the students, parents and community. It is also clear from all the research that our best schools are those where professional ideals and collegiality become the standard for interaction among all stakeholders and a professional learning community emerges. As we shall see throughout this book, the reality that always ultimately emerges when we speak of governance of our schools for the best interests of our children and the school community is—**the imperative of democracy for our schools.**

It is the ***American Vision*** and the American way of life. The ultimate truth is that we need **Democracy in Education!**

[1]While the New Commission speaks of limited liability corporations, the modern governance organization model is the limited liability "company" known as the "LLC." That model uses the term "member" rather than stockholder. Ownership rights under the LLC model vest in the members. The LLC is a model that combines elements of the partnership with the elements of a corporation that limits personal liability for those owning and managing the company. All corporations limit the liability of the stockholders for negligent acts of the corporate officers and employees. The LLC model offers great possibilities for innovative governance of our schools.

1

The Imperative

It is the "American Dream" that makes America—America! And it is the Constitution of the United States of America that "sets the conditions" that enable each of us to seek our dreams and have the real hope and opportunity to fulfill those dreams. It is the great equalizer of us all. For us to create "The Great American School" for all of our children, we must govern and lead our schools upon the very same principles and ideals. That is the only way to "set the conditions" for great schools to emerge!

There is an imperative for our schools—a democratic imperative. It is imperative that we turn to democracy as the governance structure of our schools.

Our children deserve great schools. They deserve inspirational leadership in their schools. They deserve great school communities. The only way to achieve great schools is through democracy. Our studies of schools, governance, leadership, and psychology, and how they affect the achievement and well-being of our children make it strikingly clear. We must change the governance structures of our schools to democracy if we are ever to instill greatness in our schools. That is **"The Democratic Imperative for Our Schools!"**

It is a simple paradigm of logic. Schools are communities. Communities need to be governed. The best form of governance known to man is democracy. Democracy creates participation that sparks the synergy for great things to happen in schools. Our school communities need to be governed by democratic principles in all their parameters if we are to create great schools. It is pure and simple.

We need to do it for our children, for our families, for our communities, for our nation and for civilization itself. Remember, our schoolchildren are compelled to attend school. They live in schools for much of their young lives and it is often their most significant community. Our children's psycho-social development and achievement both cognitively and affectively depend upon their total school experience. Nowhere else is it more important for our practices to pass the test of democracy. Nowhere else is it as important to give the community voice. Nowhere else is it as important to put up the ideas we teach and the practices that we hold to the scrutiny of open and honest debate.

This book is about governance of our schools and leadership for the twenty-first century. It is about the community of our schools our common mission and common vision. It is about how to choose effective leadership for our schools and the organizational synergy that is necessary to make all of our schools great schools that meet the needs of all of our children, our families and our communities. Simply put, **it is about democracy in education.**

This book is about the governance and dynamics of schools everywhere in America. The reform movement and the new frontier of education it has created is nationwide and it raises many issues of law and governance as we seek to facilitate a moral society. Philadelphia is the birthplace of American democracy and the ideals that mold our nation, so it is fitting for Philadelphia to serve as a "looking glass" for America's schools. Accordingly, much of its analytical focus is on urban education and the school reform movement as it plays out in Philadelphia, Pennsylvania, where the schools have been taken over by the state pursuant to Pennsylvania's *Education Empowerment Act* and an agreement between the mayor and the governor. The state has created the governing body known as the School Reform Commission (SRC) that has been charged with reforming the public school system in Philadelphia. In doing so, they have created new forms of schools and changed the landscape of public education which in turn raises a myriad of issues relating to the governance of our schools. From regular public schools to our charter schools that are being created everywhere in America, all public schools in whatever form need to be governed and we need to come out of the eighteenth century in our notions of school governance and into the twenty-first century.

We will look at the Philadelphia public school system, its bureaucracy, its charter schools, its privately managed schools, and its practices of governance to highlight and compare them to what is happening within schools and school districts every-where. The purpose is to look closely at what is happening in Philadelphia so all schools and educators that lead schools can look closely at their own practices and beliefs. The hope is to improve all schools in America for all of our children through "**the great debate**" of ideas and our ideals. In our comparison, we will look at the governance, leadership and leadership selection practices of blue ribbon schools and school districts. We will raise important issues for our policymakers and citizens to ponder as we look at the dynamics of human interaction within school structures. We will also look at new possibilities being raised by America's think tanks in our quest to create new school organizational structures.

The most important question is this: **How can we create a public school entity that is designed and governed to truly serve the best interests of students?** This school must be governed in a manner designed to serve only the educational needs of children and their communities and not serve the self-interest of any individual, nor any group of individuals, politicians or constituencies. **What form**

of governance shall we choose and what are the governance structures we will incorporate to ensure the appropriate and effective interactions between and among all members of that school community? We will look at that issue in depth in Chapter 2, entitled **"Whose School Is It?"** I will assert that, in the face of issues of school governance, we should all be asking ourselves these questions. We should be asking ourselves these questions in School Reform Commission meetings, in school board meetings, in our leadership team meetings at every level, in our universities and colleges, in our schools and in our homes—everywhere in America.

As we move through the focal points and ideas set forth herein, you will see a web of fact and law along with concepts of governance and leadership that will make clear the absolute necessity of turning to democracy as the governance structure and value system that we must embrace if we are ever to attain the ideal of great schools for our children.

While inclusive, democratic leadership ideals are taught in principalship programs and academies everywhere, in practice there is little democracy in education. In fact, most schools are governed in a manner that is devoid of almost all principles of democracy. And it is the effective lack of democracy in schools that destroys the requisite collegiality necessary to create the human dynamics that create great schools.

The most recent leadership training program for principals that I participated in was the Principals' Academy conducted by the School District of Philadelphia under the auspices of the School Reform Commission. It is an effort to promote the teaching and learning of good leadership skills and practices. Democratic, inclusive leadership and collegiality was rightfully promoted and we spent a good bit of time on the development of "professional learning communities" that give voice to all stakeholders in schools. But in reality I work in one of the least democratic school districts in America where most of us are afraid to voice our true beliefs for fear of retaliation and the apprehension that we will never advance in the bureaucracy if we are honest and vocal. And that is sad.

It is also strikingly ironic that presently in Philadelphia, Pennsylvania, the birthplace of American democracy, we arguably do have one of the least democratically governed school districts in America. I assert that provocatively in hopes of stirring up the debate that we need to have as a society. Have we lost our bearings? It is time for all of us, both individually and collectively, to stop and look in the mirror.

Democracy in urban school districts usually stops at the mayor's office and in Philadelphia, Pennsylvania, it stops at the governor's office because under the school takeover law and an agreement between the governor and mayor, the governor gets to appoint three out of five of the School Reform Commission members.

The mayor of Philadelphia gets to appoint two members. The citizens and school community members get to elect none.

The School Reform Commission (SRC) does operate with a certain degree of democraticity. It is a public body and does have open meetings that arguably meet minimum requirements of sunshine laws that require proceedings and deliberations to be in view of the public. But, exactly where the SRC stands on the **"continuum of democracy"** in its actual practices is an "open question." Especially since once the Chief Executive Officer is appointed, he operates with virtually unfettered power to do whatever he wants within the 200,000 person school district, and he usually does exactly that without any real checks and balances on the uses and abuses of power.

As we discuss in more detail in Chapter 2 on the role and responsibilities of trustees, the SRC members are "trustees" under the law, and therefore, have group and individual legal duties they must abide by. In the grand scheme of school governance in Philadelphia, their heavy burden is that they are **"trustees of democracy"** for the schoolchildren of Philadelphia, their parents, and the entire school community. As the law now stands in Pennsylvania, the SRC is in essence the "Supreme Court of the school community of Philadelphia." That is indeed an awesome responsibility.

All school boards in America, all boards of trustees of charter schools, and all boards of directors of schools of any kind have similar legal responsibilities. It is of paramount importance to all schoolchildren and school communities everywhere that they exercise those duties to the highest standards of democratic principles as embedded in the Constitution of the United States of America. Their futures, our futures, and the future of America depend on their doing so.

Just prior to the state takeover of Philadelphia's schools, then Governor Ridge contracted with Edison Schools to evaluate the School District and write a report. He spent nearly one and a half million dollars of taxpayers' money to have a corporate entity that wanted to do a corporate raid of the school district write a report. The self-serving and biased product was practically totally devoid of merit. However, it did highlight what we as insiders already knew to be the truth—**the "brain drain" that has transpired in recent years within the School District of Philadelphia has robbed our schools and our schoolchildren of many of our most talented educators.**

Why have so many great educators left our school district? Because of their frustration with the school district, its lack of professionalism, and the lack of any power and control over what happens in schools and what happens to them as professionals. We have had bureaucracy run amok in Philadelphia and the lack of democracy in our governance structures and practices within our district is disheartening and debilitating to those of us who have dedicated our professional lives to our schoolchildren and our school communities. What is happening in Philadelphia is also happening all over America.

Yes, we need to rebuild our professional learning communities within our schools. We need to "set the conditions" for our school communities to grow and flourish. The only way that can be done is through the establishment of democratic practices within our schools and within our school systems. Through our examination of school governance structures and their implications for leadership and organizational productivity, it will become quite clear—**democracy is imperative.**

In our analysis of governance structures of schools, we will examine the Constitution of the United States of America as it applies to our school system and look at the ideals it embraces. We will look at the Constitutional concept of equal protection under the law as embedded in the Fourteenth Amendment, and we will look at the issue of whether the Constitution has stopped at the schoolhouse door?

We will look at the issue of **"participative due process"**—the right of all students, parents, educators, school community members and community members at large to **"participate meaningfully in the decision-making processes of schools."** And we will visit the issue of whether the right to participate meaningfully in the decision-making processes of schools includes the right to meaningful participation in the selection or election of principals and other school leaders such as school board members, trustees of charter schools, superintendents and CEO's of any form. We will look at the issue of whether our present practices meet the **test of constitutionality.**

We will look at these issues both legally and pragmatically as we seek to learn how to plant the seeds that enable great school communities to grow and flourish in fulfillment of their common mission. We all have a stake in our schools and we all recognize our responsibility to fulfill the mission and ideal of equal education for all.

As part of that scrutiny we will look at the concept of school culture. We will look at what conditions cause school cultures to grow wholesomely and what conditions cause school cultures to become "toxic." We will look at the psychological and emotional effects of school climate and morale as they pertain to students and staff. Within that realm, we will look at the concept of and need for **"renewal"** as it psychologically effects schools as both a collective and individual phenomenon. The issue will emerge "whether there is a governmental and psychological need for term limits for principalships and school district leaders." Are term limits necessary requirements of democracy?

Within that realm I will raise two provocative issues: **(1) What do you think are the psychological effects on children who live in schools that are in a state of constant turmoil?** And, **(2) Toxic school cultures that are so devastating to**

our children and school communities are caused by the principals of those schools, and it is the feudalistic, autocratic governance structures of our school systems that create the conditions for that to happen and blindly supports it.

Does anyone really think that the adversarial processes that presently characterize many of our schools are good for our children? Do children thrive in homes where their parents and families are constantly fighting and bickering? What we know about children is that they thrive best in a warm, caring and nurturing environment—so do adults. We as a nation possess a vast knowledge of psychology. Why do we so often tend to forget it when we cross the threshold of our schoolhouse doors?

I believe the battle for the ideal of equal education and equal opportunity for all will be won as much through the exercise of our First Amendment right to freedom of speech than through any other avenue. Yes, there is a place for the lawsuit, but laws and lawsuits are won and lost on common notions of right and wrong. We, the American educational community, have not yet accomplished the ideals of **equality in education** set forth by our Supreme Court in *Brown v. The Board of Education,* 347 U.S. 483, 78 S.Ct. 686 (1954). The implementation of common notions and ideals can only be developed through the free exercise of speech and dialogue without fear of reprisal.

If our schools are to excel, we must learn to develop what is known as an "open climate" for discussion and debate of everything that matters in schools. That concept is essential for consensus building and it is impossible to develop a common vision and common mission without an open and nurturing climate where everyone can safely express their ideas without fear of reprisal. Everyone must be heard and respected in an environment of trust. For that voice giving process to rise to the level of **"true voice,"** there must be governance procedures that ensure those voices are listened to and given meaning. That can only be ensured through organizational structures that "give true power" to the community.

Great schools are characterized by a positive **"ethos."** Ethos is the "collective ego" of schools. In chapter 9, "The Psychological Perspective," we will look at that concept in depth. Here, let it suffice to say that a positive school ethos must be "nurtured from within" and that cannot happen without an open and nurturing school climate. The tone for that is set by the principal. Or it is destroyed by the principal!

That reality is also at work in the system itself. The CEO or superintendent sets the tone of openness for the system itself. The supervening governing body sets the policies and procedures that allows or disallows that to happen.

And yes, the logical sequence of democracy is that our educational leaders must be chosen through democratic processes. **It is an inalienable element of**

democracy that communities must choose their own leaders if they are to flourish. Yes, that pertains to the principals of our schools, also. A leader cannot effectively lead a group of people if he or she does not hold the support of that group of people. Period!

If a principal of a school, or a CEO of a school system, does not hold the respect and support of the school community, he or she is powerless to lead. There can be no inspiration. There can be no positive synergy. There will be little enthusiasm for what is done. There can only be mechanical compliance. There can be no greatness.

The right to vote is an essential element of democracy. The question is who gets to vote? And for what?

We now have school leaders who are imposed upon schools. Often they are imposed upon schools by people who have never even stepped foot within the walls of those schools nor walked among the people of those schools. They have never looked into the eyes and the faces and the hearts of the people that make up that school community. In Philadelphia, most of our principals are imposed upon schools by bureaucrats and powerbrokers who have not even taken the time to visit schools and speak to the students, parents and faculty. There certainly is not an articulated process that meets any standard of due care or ideal of professionalism, and we speak of giving voice to all stakeholders?

I submit that the processes, or shall I say lack of any viable process, we now use to choose our principals are blatantly negligent and violative of our constitutional notions of due process. I submit that they are totally devoid of any of the indicia necessary to meet the scrutiny of any test of the requirements of "participative due process." Choosing principals without the input of stakeholders is also arguably a "lack of due care" that legally constitutes negligence. Blue ribbon school districts take great care to ascertain the thoughts, ideas and feelings of every aspect of the school community as part of their principal and superintendent selection processes.

If our schools are to become great schools, we need to have **"inspirational leadership not impositional leadership."** In the words of the Harvard educator Pedro Nuguera (2005), "You cannot impose a culture on a school. You must cultivate it from within." Accordingly, you cannot impose a leader upon a school. A school community may collectively choose a leader from outside, but if an outsider is imposed upon a school, he or she has no initial leadership credibility and a steep mountain to climb to earn legitimacy.

What would you say if the president of the United States of America declared that he would choose the governors of the states and mayors of our cities and towns? Or, if he said he would choose a selection committee to decide who gets to run those communities? Or, if he said he would choose the senators and congressmen? You would say that is crazy. But that is precisely what we do to our school communities. And we wonder why they do not flourish?

Leadership is vital. The need for effective leadership in schools is well documented in study after study. The overriding question is what is the best way to get effective leadership in our schools? Do we really believe we can choose effective leaders without instituting democratic processes?

In answering that question we will visit the concepts of "legitimacy of leadership" and "leadership credibility." We will also look at the legal duties of boards of trustees, school boards and the School Reform Commission governing Philadelphia's public schools. The question there is: **"To whom does the School Reform Commission, the Board of Trustees of Charter schools and Chief Executive Officers owe their legal duty of loyalty, care and good faith? And what is the legal remedy for self-dealing and other breaches of those duties?"**

We will visit the essential issue of **"how shall we choose our school leaders?"** And we will meet it head on. In all of our leadership courses and principal training academies, we speak about the need to give students, parents, teachers and all community members a voice in the decision-making processes of schools. But without giving those constituencies true power within the organizational structures of schools and school systems, they have no real voice. It is a question of legitimacy.

Greatness in schools plainly cannot happen without democracy. **Democracy is the sine qua non for greatness in schools.** By the end of this discourse, that will be clear. Hopefully, you will be inspired to **stand up for democracy in education** and do the right things for the schoolchildren of America.

Go ahead, argue that democracy is not the best governance structure for schools. Argue that the present bureaucratic autocracy based on eighteenth century feudalistic practices is the best way to govern our schools. And I will point to the present status of our urban schools as proof that what is in place is not working very well. Show me one urban bureaucracy that is flourishing? The Philadelphia School District has been taken over by the state because of the crisis of our schools. It is not unlike all other urban school systems. The achievement test scores tell the truth. All of our urban school systems, bogged down by the politics of power, yield poor overall achievement test scores.

The data speaks volumes. **The least effective public schools in America are those found in our cities and they bear the least democratic governance systems in America.** While outstanding curricula and methodology are essential in successful schools, the most determinant indicia of successful schools is how the school community interacts between and among each other. That reality was made clear by psychologist James Comer in his trilogy of articles on the effective education of poor minority children (See, Comer, 1984, 1988, and 1996).

I will state the proposition here: **Public school success in America is directly proportional and correlational to the degree of democraticity in the governance practices of the school and its supervening governing body.**

That proposition is testable scientifically and I hope to "open the debate" on that issue. I hope it opens **"The Great Debate"** on school governance. I truly believe that we need a **"Renaissance in thought about our schools"** and we must move away from the feudalism of the past and learn how to set the conditions for the growth of great schools.

It is particularly important for our policymakers, educators and citizens alike to be aware and learned about what is happening in our schools as we move toward the institution of alternative school structures such as charter schools, partnership schools, independent schools, privately managed schools, and schools as limited liability corporations (LLC's) whose stockholders are the teachers who actually work at the school, etc. Our children's well-being depends on it. Our children's futures and the future of our society and nation depend on it, too.

We need to move toward schools that serve the children, our families, and the school community. We need to move toward servant leadership. And we need to realize that great schools and great school systems have school leaders that serve the community. Conversely, poor schools and poor school systems have school leaders who expect school communities to serve the school leaders. **Principal centered school governance is the worst form of school governance.**

As we take a hard look at what happens in our schools, I present numerous factual accounts of egregious and ridiculous events and circumstances that occur over and over again in various forms and are blindly supported by "the bureaucracy." We will look at what I call the "institutional illnesses" inherent in the bureaucracy, and I propose that the only cure for the institutional illnesses and the wrongs that they perpetrate against school communities and individuals within those communities can only be democracy.

Yes, democracy is the cure for the institutional illnesses plaguing our schools. The institutional illnesses that make our school system and many of our schools "unhealthy" organizations are what prevent our schools from being all that they can be. I once wrote a position paper to Deidre Farmbry, the Superintendent of Schools in Philadelphia who held us together during the state takeover, that what was happening within our organization were symptoms of an **"unhealthy organization"** and needed to stop. She agreed.

During this discourse, we will look at many of the actual events prior and subsequent to the state takeover, along with many factual accounts and stories of actual occurrences and events that happen in our schools now. Some of the stories may shock you. The names of many of the individuals are withheld so as not to embarrass anyone, as we are all human and fallible. The purpose of these stories is to show why we need to turn to democratic practices within our schools. Yes, there will be those within our district that will be anxiously turning the pages to figure out "who is he talking about." But I hope we can move beyond that to see the essence of the need for democracy in our schools.

The stories I tell will be true and factual. Sometimes they will seem Faustian, but nothing is made up. When I tell a story that may seem implausible, I will allude to this verification that I will now make. In the practice of law, when we write certain documents that contain statements of fact or factual accounts, we are under an ethical obligation to verify our facts. Here is the legal verification required by Pennsylvania law: "I hereby verify that the facts stated and contained herein are true and correct to the best of my knowledge, information and belief. I understand that any false statements herein are subject to the penalties of *18 Pa. C.S §4904*."

But let me be clear: **The reason I believe so much in democracy is that I believe so much in the people I have met and worked with elbow to elbow for over thirty years within the community of the School District of Philadelphia and beyond.** The people I have met and come to know during those years of service to the schoolchildren of Philadelphia are wonderful and good people. I have had the honor of working with students and adults of many cultures and I cherish the diversity I have had the opportunity to experience. They have performed miracle after miracle before my eyes time and time again. Our schools will one day be great schools because there are great people in all of our schools.

I have seen them perform in the face of great obstacles. I have seen them perform amidst great turmoil. I have learned to trust the inherent goodness of our collective community and that greatness, that goodness, will always rise and ultimately prevail.

I believe in the community of Philadelphia and the people of the school community of Philadelphia and its individual members. In every school there are knowledgeable people who care about children. I have faith in the community and I have faith in the individuals within it. I believe that in all schools in America, we have the seeds of greatness.

We just need good leadership. And we need good governance. **We, as a community, just need to be empowered to demonstrate our greatness.**

So let me conclude with a note that is strikingly poignant to the discourse at hand. In the year 2005, Senator Robert Byrd from West Virginia, slipped into a spending bill a provision that mandates teaching about the Constitution in all schools, colleges and universities. All schools were required to spend at least one day studying the Constitution on or near September 17th, the anniversary of its signing. In Philadelphia, the School Reform Commission designated that day as a district-wide "Constitution Day" and all schools were required to celebrate the Constitution in some manner.

I was honored to be asked to organize and lead the Constitution Day program at our school, Furness High School, in South Philadelphia. As part of the day's festivities, all schools were required to recite the preamble of the Constitution in concert. It was quite an inspirational experience as I asked our entire school with a Federal judge present and on stage to stand and recite in unison the preamble to our great Constitution.

And I ask you to stand and read it with me now:

> *We the People of the United States of America, in Order to form a more perfect Union, establish Justice, insure domestic Tranquility, provide for the common defence, promote the general Welfare, and secure the Blessings of Liberty to ourselves and our Posterity, do ordain and establish this Constitution for the United States of America.*

May I just add one more thought from the greatness of Abraham Lincoln and in honor of all those Americans who have given their lives for America in the defense of our great democracy—may I quote from his Gettysburg Address of November 19, 1863:

> *"...that we here highly resolve that these dead shall not have died in vain; that this nation shall have a new birth of freedom; and that this government of the people, by the people, and for the people, shall not perish from the earth."*

And may it not perish from our schools. Nor, may it not perish from the eyes and hearts of our schoolchildren and every member of our school communities.

2

Whose School Is It?

Whose school is it? That is the essential and ultimate question of school governance.

I originally got the idea for this book and its title when I attended the Nonprofit Institute presented by the Pennsylvania Bar Institute. The Pennsylvania Bar Institute provides professional development programs for attorneys in Pennsylvania so we can meet our continuing legal education requirements as laid down by the Supreme Court of Pennsylvania. I attended the program because I wanted to expand my law practice to the charter school arena and develop expertise in the area of school governance. The Nonprofit Institute was a two day symposium designed to help attorneys develop expertise for their representation of nonprofit organizations, especially nonprofit corporations.

It was there that a legal expert on the law of corporations first put to me the proposition that the initial and primary question of organizational governance is "whose organization is it?" It is the essential question of governance because it is in the answer to that question that we find the answer to the legal question to whom do trustees, directors, public officials and school reform commissioners owe their legal fiduciary duties of loyalty, care and good faith? That is also the paramount and essential question of school governance—**"Whose school is it?"** As we will see throughout this discourse, that is a very good question, and in the face of all that is happening to public schoolchildren in the new frontier of education and its alternative school structures—a very relevant one!

Charter schools in Pennsylvania and throughout America are by law nonprofit corporations. See, for example, *Charter School Law,* 24 Pa.C.S. §17-1703-A. The legal and pragmatic issues of school governance that arise in relation to their operations and the operations of other school management structures will be some of the great issues of our times within the realm of education law. The field is just beginning and it will grow. It will grow fast when two lawyers butt heads for control of charter schools.

The issues of school governance and fiduciary duties of trustees, directors and school leaders pertain not only to charter schools but to all school leaders including the School Reform Commission in Philadelphia, Pennsylvania, and similar bodies throughout the United States. They certainly apply to all boards of school directors everywhere and these issues become particularly tricky and problematic when we look at the legal duties of private managers of public schools. The laws and issues governing the fiduciary responsibilities of trustees, directors, and public officials apply to all schools in America. All school communities in America are legally and morally bound to be governed for the best interests of the children and their school community and not in the self-interest of any individual, group of individuals or coalition.

This section is a precursor to Chapter 7 where we delve into those legal issues and turn to advocacy for our schoolchildren, their families and the great professionals who teach our children. It is in that chapter where we take a hard look at how charter school trustees and CEO's can keep on the right side of the law and meet constitutional, statutory and ethical muster.

We will review in depth the legal and ethical issues of school governance, but what is most important is to keep our focus on the main theme of this book—**how to set the conditions for school communities to flourish and become great schools as they seek to fulfill their collective mission of appropriately educating our children to their fullest capacity.** School community synergy and the psychological and pragmatic conditions that create it are the most important aspects of great schools and we must keep that in mind.

But first, we all do need to understand the basics of the laws governing trustees and boards of school directors throughout America. It is in the understanding of those laws and their relation to our Constitution that is the underpinning of the democratic imperative for our schools. In our analytical process we will view some specifics of Pennsylvania education law as representative examples since all states function similarly and education laws throughout our country are basically consistent across jurisdictions.

One of the sessions within the Nonprofit Institute was presented by Donald W. Kramer, Esquire, a leading expert and author in nonprofit corporation law. The session he led was entitled "The Role and Responsibility of the Board of Directors and Trustees." He began by stating unequivocally that in order to represent and advise trustees and directors of nonprofit corporations you must first determine **"whose organization is it?"** That is an essential question because trustees and directors have legal duties to those whose organization it is. The legal duties trustees and directors are bound by are called **"fiduciary duties."**

We will focus our discussion here on the legal concept of "trustees" because the charter school law in Pennsylvania and elsewhere mandates that charter schools have boards of trustees. School Reform Commissions and boards of school directors everywhere have the same fiduciary duties although there are slight differences under the statutes and legal precedents between trustees and directors. The ethical and legal principles are basically the same and the laws governing fiduciary relationships are fairly well settled in every state in America.

The Pennsylvania *Charter School Law* also requires that charter schools in their governance documents must state **"the proposed governance structure of the charter school, including a description and method for the appointment or election of members of the board of trustees."** 24 Pa.C.S. §17-1719-A(4). The School Reform Commission members are also trustees under the law and their trust responsibilities are particularly heightened because the school takeover law grants them extraordinary powers and their decisions on charter schools are not subject to appeal. That provision that disallows appeal beyond the School Reform Commission imposed upon Philadelphia, because of the Fourteenth Amendment guarantee of **equal protection** under the law and the **due process** provisions of the Fourth, Fifth and Sixth Amendments, raises questions of the constitutional validity of the school takeover law itself.

The question that always remains is just who are they trustees for? And the answer to that question is in the answer to the question, **"Whose school is it?"** And in looking at the legal duties of the SRC there is the larger question, **"Whose school system is it?"**

It is "well settled law" in Pennsylvania and every state in America that trustees have legal duties to those whose assets they hold in trust. Those whom trustees hold assets for and on whose behalf and benefit they act are known as **"beneficiaries."** They are the beneficiaries of the trust. The beneficiaries of the trust are those to whom the trustees owe their fiduciary duties. The legal duties most often cited and litigated are the **duty of loyalty, the duty of care, the duty of good faith, and the duty to act in the best interests of the beneficiary.** See, for example, Warehime v. Warehime, 722 A.2d 1060 (Pa. 2000).

In the realm of corporate law and nonprofit corporation law, the trustees and directors have a legal duty to act in the "best interests of the corporation." Even in for-profit corporate law the modern view is that corporate directors as fiduciaries "are not limited to running corporations for maximum profit, but in fact and recognized in law as administrators of a **community system**" (Ratner, 1970). In the context of public schools the corpus of the trust is the school, its facilities, its assets, its budget, its organization and its governance structures, etc. The beneficiaries are most definitely the students, their parents and arguably the entire school community. The beneficiaries are not the mayor, the governor, the school board representatives, the chief executive officer, the superintendents, and especially, not the educational management organizations that wish to take over schools and run them for profit. See, *West Chester Area School District v. Collegium Charter School,* 760 A.2d 452 (Pa. Cmwlth. 2000), *affirmed by S.C. of Pa.,* 812 A.2nd 1172 (2002).

When a trustee, director, or public official acts in his own best interests and thereby receives personal benefit or financial gain it is deemed **"self-dealing."**

Self-dealing is a well settled breach of fiduciary duty that is actionable in law. A fiduciary who is found liable for self-dealing can be held accountable for damages to the beneficiaries of the trust or corporation or public entity. **In the setting of public schools self-dealing is not only a breach of fiduciary duty but it is clearly unethical.** Fiduciaries can also be held personally liable in negligence law suits for breach of the duty of care and also for the intentional tort of breach of the duty of good faith.

The Commonwealth Court of Pennsylvania in the case of *West Chester Area School District v. Collegium Charter School,* which was later affirmed by the Supreme Court of Pennsylvania, stated that a charter school's powers of management and operation are granted solely to the board of trustees of a charter school and can not be granted to a private management corporation who wishes to operate a charter school: "…that power is granted to the charter school's board of trustees who, as public officials, have a single purpose to promote the interests of pupils." 760 A.2nd 452 at p. 468. Whether the boards of trustees of charter schools or the School Reform Commission have legal duties to all members of the school community has not yet been decided in Pennsylvania and remains an **"open question"** under the law. **But in the modern view of the fiduciary responsibilities of trustees, directors, and public officials, the well reasoned opinion would undoubtedly fall on the side that they do have fiduciary responsibilities to act on behalf of and in the best interests of the total school community.** We all are stakeholders in what happens in schools—everyone in the school community has a stake in what we do.

The Superior Court of Pennsylvania summarizes the duty of trustees:

Perhaps the most fundamental duty of a trustee is that he must display throughout the administration of the trust complete loyalty to the interests of the beneficiary and must exclude all selfish interest and all considerations of the interests of third persons....

A trustee is under a duty to the beneficiary of the trust to administer the trust solely in the interest of the beneficiary. The trustee must exclude all self interest, as well as the interest of a third party, in his administration of the trust solely for the beneficiary. The trustee must not place himself in a position where his own interests or that of another enters into conflict, or may possibly conflict, with the interest of the trust or its beneficiary. Put another way, the trustee may not enter into a transaction or take or continue in a position in which his personal interest or the interest of a third party is or becomes adverse to the interest of the beneficiary. Warehime, 722 A.2d at 1064 *affirmed by S.C. of Pa.* (quoting George W. Bogart, *The Law of Trusts & Trustees* §543 at 217-218) (emphasis added).

The issue is one of conflict of interests and that is why we need the purification processes of democracy. Boards of trustees of schools and individual trustees whether on school reform commissions or school boards of any kind have clear legal duties and responsibilities to act in the best interests of students and the school community not in the best interests of anyone else, especially themselves. The only people who are well positioned to see and know if a leader, whether it be a principal, trustee or director, is acting only for his self interest are the people who live and work within that school community. No supervisor, group of supervisors or concocted supervisory procedures can possibly adequately purify the governance processes of schools—only true democracy can do that!

The grand conflict of interest issue for the School Reform Commission governing the School District of Philadelphia is to whom do they owe their fiduciary duties? Do they owe them to the governor who appoints three commissioners? Do they owe them to the mayor who appoints two commissioners? To the legislators? Or do they owe them to the schoolchildren of Philadelphia and their school communities? Certainly they do not owe them to the corporate entities that wish to "manage" our schools for profit. To be honest, from the inside view in Philadelphia, it most often looks like our government's clients are the corporations such as Edison Schools or Victory Schools that wish to "manage" our schools for profit. Let us keep it clear just who we owe our duties to—our students, their families and the school community. It is one of the major moral, ethical and legal issues of our times!

Within the realm of charter schools, the threshold question is to whom does the board of trustees owe their fiduciary duties? Do they owe them to the coalition of founders or others who have been somehow granted the power to appoint trustees, or do they owe their fiduciary duties to the students who attend their schools, their families and the school community? If we think the answer is that they owe legal duties to the coalition of founders, then give me a satisfactory answer to this question: Have we not then granted property rights to the individual founders or founder? Is that what our policymakers want society to do? Granting property rights in public schools to individuals or groups who are granted charters for schools is highly questionable public policy and is probably a constitutional violation. If school charters are set up where a single individual or a single group of individuals actually controls the appointment of trustees or controls the process for selecting trustees, they have control of the school and its governance. And, if that is the case, I question the ethics and the legality of such an arrangement for our public schools!

What is particularly concerning in the realm of charter schools is what I call the "Enron disease." The Enron disease is where a CEO of a charter school appoints the board of trustees. The board of trustees in turn grants the CEO whatever he wants. That is backwards governance and is arguably unethical. What happens is they usually appoint their friends who they can control. The CEO then exacts personal gain—like a high salary for himself! Or he creates a lease where he benefits from the lease. The lease scam has happened in Chester, Pennsylvania, and often in Philadelphia. See, *Commonwealth of Pennsylvania, Department of Education v. Chester-Upland School District Board of Control*, ___A.2d___, No.496 M.D. 2005, (Pa. Cmwlth. October 16, 2006). It is highly unethical and the legislature needs to put a stop to it!

Enron is a giant corporation that went bankrupt while the corporate executives were vacationing in luxury suites in the Rocky mountains and collecting million dollar salaries. The employees lost their retirement funds they had worked years to earn. The board of trustees was appointed by the corrupt CEO and his management cronies. They, in turn, approved the million dollar salaries and let the CEO run amok. The corporate community suffered. The corporation went bankrupt. That case is now being tried in Federal Court. In response to the Enron debacle, many experts in corporate law advocate for laws mandating greater use of democratic principles in the governance of large corporations.

The bottom line in a democratic society is that all public school leaders, trustees, directors, and school reform commission members owe fiduciary duties to the students, their families and the entire school community. To create great schools for our children, we need to keep that in focus and practice **"servant leadership"** and serve the total school communities we lead. We need to have governance by the people of the community for the people of the community. There is no place for government by the politically elite for the politically elite. **To serve the children and create great schools we must create governance structures that ensure their best interests are served and that positive synergy is created towards fulfillment of a common mission. To ensure that standard is maintained, those governance structures must be rooted in democracy and its great ideals.**

3

The Grand Hypothetical of School Governance

And that brings us to "the greatest issue in school governance": How can we create a governance structure for our public schools that "sets the conditions" for schools to become great schools and ensures the best interests of the students and the school community are, in reality, the guiding principle that governs our schools? What form of governance shall we choose?

Yes, that is the greatest issue of school governance. How to create a governance structure that "sets the conditions for great schools to emerge and sustain themselves" and ensures the best interests of students, their families and the school community is, in practice, the guiding principle governing our schools. The issue reduced to its essence is the question of what form of governance shall we choose so we can set the conditions for greatness in what we do in schools?

For great schools to emerge, we must facilitate productive collaborative endeavor. The community must work together collegially for a common purpose and produce a common vision of what outstanding education is and what it wants its school to be. There must be excitement and fulfillment in "what we do" and there must be a synergy that makes the collective endeavor of the community greater than the sum of all its individual members. There needs to be that chemistry among the people of the community—that magic that creates greatness.

For "that magic" to occur that makes schools outstanding learning communities, we need great leaders in our schools. **Leadership Matters!** It matters in every aspect of the schoolhouse. The principal leader of a school sets the tone for the community of a school and can either be the spark for outstanding organizational synergy or can debilitate the community. Either way the leader is the catalyst. **That is why the definition for leadership proffered here is "the ability to create positive organizational synergy toward accomplishment of a collective mission."** Leadership is paramount for a well functioning school community that meets the needs of all of its children. We are always hooked to the ever present issue: **"How shall we choose our school leaders?"** We need outstanding school leaders to achieve greatness in schools.

In answering the questions of school governance, we must answer other questions as well. How can we be sure to get the best possible teachers in our schools? How can we attract and keep the best teachers? How can we get great leaders

18

into our schools? How should we choose our school leaders? What should their powers be? What should the powers be for individual community members? How can we ensure that the highest standards of professionalism and collegiality are maintained? How can we ensure that parents and students have a meaningful and legitimate voice in what happens in schools? How can we ensure that teachers and the entire school community have a legitimate voice in what happens in schools? How about the community at large? Should they have a voice in schools? How do we ensure that the interests of all stakeholders are appropriately balanced? How do we ensure that there are effective checks and balances over the school budget and its uses. School budgets are typically in the millions of dollars. Who is the watchdog? What is the system?

These are just some of the issues of school governance. All issues of schools from the curriculum and methodology, to decision-making, and to enforcement of policy, rules and bylaws need to be weighed and balanced on the scale of justice and equity. There is a legal concept that fits our task and best states what we need to do—we need to **"balance the equities."** We must devise an effective system of governance to set the conditions for great schools to emerge!

That brings us to the "Grand Hypothetical of School Governance." It is a teaching tool designed to elicit thought and debate about school governance through analysis of the facts and issues of the scenario. It highlights what we all must focus upon as we take on the task of designing new governance structures for schools. It is especially important to all of us in America because the national movement is to redesign school systems and create school entities that better serve the people and promote a higher level of achievement for all. We should be discussing the issues everywhere in America—in our schools, in our colleges and universities, in school reform commission meetings of any sort, in board of school directors meetings, in leadership team meetings, in focus groups, in churches, in parent forums, in union meetings, in the corridors of our schools, and the corridors of our state capitals, everywhere!

The Grand Hypothetical of School Governance

Imagine you are engaged by the people of the "Community of the Land of Equality" to create a public school to educate our youth both cognitively and affectively in every way possible and to the fullest extent imaginable.

There is absolutely no already existing board of education or supervening governance body. You are completely free to design the governance of that school. You have a clean slate to write on!

This school will have 1,000 students from 713 families. The larger community consists of a population of 333,782 citizens within a state whose population is 18 million people. That state is situated in the United States of America. Assume it is already determined that the school will receive $7,000.00 per student enrolled in your school.

You may choose whether you are creating an elementary school, middle school, high school, or some other type of school such as a kindergarten through twelfth grade school.

The school must be governed consistent with the Constitution of the United States of America because of the Supremacy clause. It also must be governed by the mandate of the state Constitution that requires the state to create a "thorough and efficient" educational system and says nothing else.

You are free to create any form of governance for the school you wish within those confines except that the focus must be on "the best interests of the students." You must also assure through your governance structures that the school does not function for the self interests of any individual, group of individuals, or coalitions of any sort. You are also free to determine the governance structures of your school that determine how all stakeholders will interact between and among each other.

What form of governance will you set up and what governance structures will you create to ensure equity within the school community and ensure that the school community works collaboratively and collegially to create a common vision and work positively toward fulfillment of a collective mission?

Keep in mind that you must determine an equitable and fair process for choosing the principal or some other form of school leadership. You must also have a system for decision-making processes that will enable decisions to be made on such issues as organization of the school, curriculum, pedagogy, programs, course offerings, finances and budget, hiring of staff, evaluation of staff and programs, resolution of issues that may arise, employee and student discipline, etc.

This is your task and you are free to think as you will:

In accordance with the hypothetical, discuss all issues pertaining to governance of a school. Then create a form of governance and a governance structure that balances the equities of all the issues and ensures positive school community synergy toward accomplishment of their collective mission.

Also, keep these points in mind:

- You must choose a principal or some other form of leader or leaders but are not limited to traditional notions. For example, you may want to have a "lead teacher" or other form of principal leader.
- Term limits for leaders is an open question. You may have term limits in any variety of forms you think is best or none at all.
- You may or may not want to create a board of trustees or board of school directors to govern the school.

- You will need to answer the question, "How shall we choose our leaders?" What process will be used to select or elect the principal and other school leaders?
- You may choose to govern the school pursuant to a constitution, a type of charter granted by the state similar to a "city charter" or a nonprofit corporation design.
- If you choose a charter school format, you should consider that the charter school law in Pennsylvania and most states requires that the school be a nonprofit corporation and must have a board of trustees. In the organizational documents of the school under that law, you must state how the board of trustees is "elected or selected." However, you may also create a different kind of charter. You are not here bound by the charter school as a nonprofit corporation. You may want to have an alternative type of charter or even a constitution as your formulating and governing document.
- You must establish powers and authorities under any organizational design. So how will you divide up powers and authorities within your school? Who will have the power to make policy, enforce rules, resolve issues and disputes, etc?
- You may have a school council or any other governmental structure that creates a "balance of power."
- You must also determine and answer the question, "Who gets to vote and for what?" (Unless, of course, you determine the best governance structure is for a supreme being to install an omnipotent leader of some sort that has unfettered absolute power!)
- How will you give voice to all stakeholders?
- Which stakeholders will be "empowered" under your governance structures?
- Remember! Any governance structure requires that someone or some body handle the legislative, and executive duties and responsibilities. Do you want all those powers in the hands of one person or one group of people? Or do you want a separation of powers where those powers and responsibilities are divided into branches? Do you want to have a balance of power?

Afterword

Those issues and questions are precisely what I have thought about and studied for the last five years since the takeover of the School District of Philadelphia by the state of Pennsylvania. I have been pondering and discussing the answers to all those questions presented by the "Grand Hypothetical of School Governance." I have studied the state takeover of the public schools in Philadelphia and the issues of the new frontier of school reform that arise everywhere in America. I have tried to view the situation from every perspective. I have attended every forum I could and have read a multitude of books, articles, laws and court decisions about school governance, leadership and stakeholder participation and analyzed the issues from both a legal and personal point of view. I have attended every leadership development program I could and have visited and conversed with interest groups of many natures and tried to understand the perspectives of every aspect of our great diversity within our school communities.

I have learned a great deal from studying the new movement of school reform as it is happening throughout America, but where I have learned the most is by living within the community of the School District of Philadelphia. I have viewed the pros and the cons and seen first hand what is happening in our schools and have had great discussions with students, parents, grandmothers and grandfathers, teachers, civic leaders, school management company representatives, School Reform Commissioners, labor leaders, and school district leaders of just about every nature. Some of it is great stuff and some of it we need to change.

The conclusions I have drawn are presented here along with the facts and rationale that have led me to those conclusions. Everyone in America needs to join this discussion and the great debate for our search for greatness in our schools. School governance issues are in every school in America and we must all hold a magnifying glass to what we do in schools. Everyone must have a voice and that voice needs to be heard. What happens in our schools affects everyone in America—every child, every parent, and every citizen. It is the most meaningful discussion we need to have as a society!

4

Schools Are Communities!

The essence of great schools is in the community! We must understand that to the depth of all its meaning. Our children's welfare depends upon it.

Schools are communities. They are communities of people. They are communities in every way. The common denominator of great schools is that they are great school communities. It is the manner in which individuals of every level work together, teach together, learn together, provide services to children together, debate ideas together, make decisions together, implement initiatives together, support each other together, celebrate together and live together that makes schools effective or ineffective. Everyone in the community counts.

Effective school leaders and principals understand that. Ineffective principals and school leaders never get it. It does not matter whether the principal or CEO is implanted through the most autocratic manner imaginable or whether the principal is chosen through a truly democratic manner, he or she is still hooked to the reality that the school is a community and the success of the school is based on the success of the community in doing what needs to be done for children.

The difference between good schools and not so good schools is in the way individuals within the school community interact with each other (See, Comer, 1984, 1988, 1996). The essential ingredient for leadership of communities is the ability to get all of the community working together in pursuit of the common purpose. That is why the **definition of leadership proffered here is "the ability to create organizational synergy toward fulfillment of a common mission."** That is the essence of good leadership and that is the essence of good governance. Good leadership is inspirational in nature. Good governance fosters the emergence of inspirational leaders. When we look at what is good governance, we must look at the governance structures of the organization to determine if they allow and indeed "mandate" that the things we need to see happen within the school community actually do happen. That is the grist of this discourse.

Embedded in the definition of leadership as the ability to cause synergy within a school community is also the reality that principals can also cause negative synergy to occur within schools. I have seen it happen before my eyes in several school settings and we will look at the phenomenon of negative leadership, the debilitating consequences of negative leadership upon the school community and the emergence of toxic school cultures in Chapter 8. The social psychologist James Comer is the best known author who wrote about the difference between good schools and less effective schools being in the manner in which individuals within the school interact between and among each other (1984, 1988, 1996). We will look at participative models in more depth when we look at governance structures for schools, but for now, I cite his work in support of the thesis that schools are communities and we must understand that and treat schools as communities.

If we want to have great schools for our children we need to learn how to build great school communities. We need to learn how to "set the conditions" for school communities to grow into all that they can be. Fortunately, my practice in several different schools has shown me that there are the ingredients for great schools in every school. That is because there are absolutely great, caring, and devoted people in every school in America. We need to put our faith in them. We need to develop good governance structures to allow them, and in deed cause them, to interact in a manner that causes the requisite positive human interaction to fulfill a collective mission. And we need to foster the emergence of effective leaders that invigorate the community.

The premise herein that schools are communities will find little argument from the great authors and commentators about schools. All of the most read authorities on leadership of schools from Comer to Sizer to Deal to Haberman, etc., speak about schools as communities. The prominent authors about organizational leadership in the field of business organizations from major corporations to partnerships also speak of the need for a sense of community to enable the organizations to excel. As discussed in Chapter 2, the legal doctrine of the "corporate community" recognizes that organizations of people are communities of people. We pretty much have a consensus on the concept that schools are communities.

Because of the basic instincts and needs of man, any organization of people inevitably turns into a community of one sort or another. We will delve into that reality in more depth when we look at "the psychological perspective" in Chapter 9.

Central to the writings of our most cited authors on schools and school leadership is the concept of school culture. Yes, every school has a culture. All schools have basic similarities yet there are no two school cultures that are exactly the same. All schools have major ceremonies and celebrations but schools have celebrations that are uniquely theirs. Included in all of their writings is the notion that an essential element of good leadership is the ability to develop and lead the growth of a positive school culture. Terrence Deal and Kent Peterson expound upon the importance of cultural leadership including **"symbolic leadership"** in their book entitled *Shaping School Culture: The Heart of Leadership* (1999). Developing and changing school culture is a repeating theme in the literature of leadership and is a major strand of discussion topics in major principals' academies.

We cannot downplay the importance of culture in the performance of a school community. As Deal and Peterson accurately state as their thesis: *"The culture of an enterprise plays the dominant role in exemplary performance"* (p. 1). There is indeed, in every school, a culture that is uniquely its own, complex personal relationships, a set of folkways, mores, beliefs, norms, irrational sanctions, and a moral code based upon them (Waller, 1932; Deal and Peterson, 1999, p. 2). These complex entities do not develop overnight. Over time they develop, grow and become embedded as the essence of the community. "Cultural patterns are highly enduring, have a powerful impact upon performance, and shape the ways people think, act and feel" (Deal and Peterson, 1999, p. 4).

There needs to be another issue raised if we are to have an open, honest and comprehensive discussion of "culture change"—**the issue of whether the administrative culture of schools and entire school systems need to change?** The entire school system is also a community that has a culture. In fact, the very reason this book is being written is about changing the culture and administrative practices of school bureaucracies across the nation by focusing on the School District of Philadelphia and scrutinizing it as it moves toward new school reform governance models. One of the major themes we will raise later is how to change the **"culture of bureaucracy"** that stands in the way of the implementation of democratic governance structures that are a basic necessity of "setting the conditions" for greatness in schools.

A great philosophical question that needs to be debated both locally and nationally is the one being raised here: **Whether the bureaucratic governance structure is itself inherently flawed and incapable of producing good and moral governance of our schools?** And it is in the debate of that issue and the underlying issues that **"the democratic imperative emerges."**

One of the most poignant writings I have ever read on the subject of school as community came from an Asian parent whose child attends a multicultural school in Philadelphia. She wrote a commentary piece for Philadelphia's major newspaper, the *Philadelphia Inquirer,* about the difficulties her ten year old daughter was having in school and she wrote about how she helped her daughter resolve her issues by seeing her school as a community. The article, "Teaching My Daughter to See Her School as a Community," speaks volumes and sums up what we all need to do—learn to see our schools as communities.

We must understand that a school is a community in all its complexities and realities, and we need to govern our schools as communities.

Most of our schools in America are multicultural. There is much diversity in heritage, cultural background, religion, persuasion, etc., and the multiculturalism of our schools is growing. There is also much diversity in educational needs. The range of achievement levels, interests, cognitive needs, and social-emotional needs is great and the issues are complex. The complexity of our school communities is immense and so are the issues of governance and leadership.

The notion of schools as "professional learning communities" is being given much discussion in leadership circles. **The primary question is how do we develop our school communities into professional learning communities?** We probably have a near consensus on the idea that schools should be professional communities but we need to develop the "how" of building them and governing them. The "Small Learning Community" movement was prevalent during the last decade to develop the sense of "belonging" to a community. Some small learning communities were governed as completely independent schools-within-schools. **If we truly believe schools should be professional learning communities, then a common mission of schools would be to "develop a sense of community upon standards of professionalism." That is what we must learn to do if we are to have great schools!**

Yes, schools should be professional communities but the issue of schools as communities is not quite so simple. School communities are much larger than the professionals who run them, teach in them, and practice their profession and support services within them. The parents and their children who are the students are the major part of a school community. They are the clients and they are the beneficiaries of the "school trust." They are the ones our school leaders have a clear fiduciary duty to act in their best interests, and they are the ones who are most often excluded from participating in the leadership and governance of our schools especially in urban America.

May I raise this poignant and potentially controversial issue at this point: **It is only in urban America that parents and students are shut out of the democratic process of schools!** In America, the vast majority of suburban and more rural school districts are governed by "elected" school board members. In contrast, most large urban school districts have school boards that are appointed. They are usually appointed by the mayors of their respective cities. In Philadelphia and other urban school districts that have been victims of state takeovers, there are other appointment scenarios. The School Reform Commission in Philadelphia consists of three members appointed by the governor and two members appointed by the mayor. None are elected by the community. **That is an issue of "constitutional proportion." Why are urban school districts that are comprised of largely minority students and their families denied the right to vote for their school leaders. Is that not a violation of the equal protection clause of our Constitution?**

In democratically governed school districts, the community is far more cognizant of what is going on in their schools. If the constituents do not like what is happening in their schools and the school board members do not act appropriately, they "vote them out." In Chapter 7 on school governance when we look at that issue in depth, I will cite several examples of school communities doing just that in the face of controversies, but for now, let it suffice to say that in a democratic society we need to give parents, students and the larger community a legitimate and meaningful voice in what goes on in schools, including selection or election of the principals of our schools.

The third prong of the school as community issue is the larger community of citizens who do not have students who attend schools and do not work at the school. What is their role in the school community and what are the legal duties school leaders have to them? They pay taxes for schools. What is their stake in our schools and how do we engage the community at large? We certainly put a good deal of energy into creating partnerships with community organizations. What is their purpose and what is their role? The answers are not simple but it suffices to say, the community at large is part of the school community.

Those three constituencies of schools, the parents and students, the school staff, and the community at large, are known as "stakeholders" in the language of school governance. If schools are to become great, all those constituencies must be integral parts of the decision-making and governance process.

Think of all the issues that are present within the community of schools. They are all the issues of America and mankind! Yes, every issue that must be resolved in America must be resolved in the schools of America. And the issues are many times more sensitized in schools because they are powerful microcosms of American life. Emotions often run high as decisions are made. Values must be determined and used as guiding principles. Curricular and instructional decisions must be made and implemented; students must be supported socially, emotionally and psychologically; codes of student conduct must be enacted and enforced; budgets must be decided and acted upon; programs must be coordinated and implemented by groups of people; special education laws and regulations must be facilitated; multicultural issues must be dealt with; and heated issues must be resolved; etc. The missions of schools have become increasingly complex and the responsibilities of school communities are immense and extensive.

What we do in schools is of crucial importance to the students we teach, their families and the community. Many of the decisions we make can be determinative of our students' futures and the quality of their lives. What happens to kids in school contributes to their present happiness and may affect their happiness for their lifetime. Certainly the knowledge, skills, abilities, character and values we instill in our children during their school years affects them for their entire lifetime and may well determine their overall success in life. Some of what we do can amount to life and death decisions for our children. The magnitude of our collective responsibility to our schoolchildren is awesome in its essence!

For school communities to do all that they must do for our children, they must have a "community of purpose" and be well functioning in pursuit of fulfillment of that "collective purpose." The mission of schools is a "collective mission." There must be a "unity of purpose" and "common vision" for schools to excel. **It is the "collective endeavor of school communities" that makes schools great.** It is the way people work together within a school community that counts most. It is the way **"we"** do things for children that makes up the **"heart of a school."** And it is the **"heart"** that matters whether it is the hearts of individual children or the heart of any other individual within the school community, or the collective heart of a school.

Much has been said about the need of our school leaders and principals to have a "vision" for their school. **But let me state it unequivovally: It is not the vision of the principal that counts. It is the collective vision of the school community that counts!** There is no greater prescription for failure of school leadership than a new principal to go into a school and attempt to impose his or her vision upon a school. Instead, it is a new principal's task to lead the school community into developing or redefining its collective vision and collective mission. It is the standards and values of the community that matters. **It is not about the principal—it is about the school community and the children they serve.**

School communities and their values differ throughout America in accordance to the values of the larger communities they serve. The values of communities are always similar in nature, but never the same. Community values depend upon locale, demographics and a host of other variables. The values of communities within the bible belt differ in some salient ways than the values of inner city America. The values of the upper class, upper middle class, middle class, lower middle class and lower class all differ somewhat. So do the values of people from differing walks of life. The values of immigrant and minority populations may differ somewhat from the values of the majority population.

Our schools are increasingly multicultural and the value systems of school communities reflect that multiculturalism. In urban America there are magnet schools that attract students of families that have different wants, needs and aspirations. Some of those schools have themes that may attract students. Others are special schools that may cater to the academically talented, the artistically talented, special needs students, disciplinary students, etc. As our nation moves to educational management organizations and charter school scenarios, the need to understand the value systems of individual school communities also increases.

It is the value system of the school community that must be reconciled in any "vision" for that school and it is the community values that must be reflected in any "mission statement." The task of school leaders is to "lead the molding of those values into a collective vision." It is not the task of a school leader to determine his or her vision and then impose it upon the school community. It is the collective vision of the school community that counts. Yes, school leaders do help shape school visions, but they do it through their "power of persuasion" (Haberman, 1999).

The common notion that school leaders must be "visionaries" is misguided and mythical. I have been in education for just about thirty-five years now and have never met such a visionary. Everyone in a school has a vision of what schools and teaching should be. Whose vision is it that counts? Every school leader I have ever encountered who was so egotistical that they thought their view was better than anyone else's was a miserable failure at leadership. **Successful principals have "wisdom"—"people wisdom." They understand people and the community they serve.**

Every school has an **"ethos."** Every organization has an ethos. An ethos is a **"collective mentality"** that is very similar to the **"ego"** of an individual. **The ethos of a school is its collective ego that permeates the culture of a school.** We will take a more in depth look at the phenomenon of a collective ethos in the chapter on the psychological perspective of schools. For now as we look at schools as communities, we must also understand that not only are schools communities, but they all have an ethos that is unique to them. **Great schools have great ethos' about them.**

It is the ethos of schools that characterizes how effective the organization is in its totality. It characterizes "what we do for children." As Deal and Peterson point out: "In the late 1970s and early 1980s, the research on effective schools showed that these schools had a climate and ethos that was purposeful and conducive to learning (Levine and Lezotte, 1990)....The studies provided vivid proof of the power of culture." They go on to state that: "In a landmark British study, Rutter and his colleagues (1979) established school 'ethos' as a prime contributor to the academic achievement of students" (Deal and Peterson, 1999, p. 5). The evidence is conclusive that the underlying norms, values, attitudes, expectations and traditions embedded in school cultures strongly contribute to achievement gains.

Let me give a real life example: Manoa Elementary school is a suburban "blue ribbon school" in Havertown, Pennsylvania. My son had the good fortune to attend that school, however, when he was about to finish second grade, my wife and I were called in for a meeting with his IEP team. They recommended that he be held back. I did not necessarily agree at first. But then one of the teachers exclaimed, "All of our children are above grade level. Your son is not above grade level. It will hurt him psychologically to be with children he cannot compete with!" It took me about two and a half microseconds to agree to hold my son back. Why? Because I was not about to mess with that ethos! They had that notion as a collective mentality.

Manoa Elementary School has an ethos of excellence. They *believe* their kids are above grade level. The fact of the matter is that almost all of their students do score above the mean in standardized tests and they score near the top of collective achievement test scores in Pennsylvania. It is that ethos that helps cause the real excellence of the school.

Let us look at another school to illustrate one of the most important points of this book. I spent twenty years as a teacher and school leader at University City High School in Philadelphia. Close to ninety percent of its approximately 2,500 students receive public assistance. It was sometimes a great school and sometimes a troubled school, yet it always did great things for children. The school community proudly called itself "Uni" because it was always a crazy school. That was and still is part of its collective self image. That craziness and collective willingness to deal with anything that comes its way is part of its "ethos." The school community is proud of that and uses that ethos to survive as a group and still do wonderful things for children.

A point everyone needs to understand is that unless you live within the school community of University City High School, you can not possibly understand it! Believe me you can not. It has an ethos all its own. That is why we need to have democracy in our decision-making process of what happens in that school and who becomes the principal of that school or any other school in America. There is no one who can come from the outside and effectively lead that school unless he or she first assimilates into the culture of that school and learns how to lead it! No one can be sent to that school to "turn it around." The last time that happened to Uni, the "Joe Clark wanna-be" was sent packing in dismal failure! That principal was replaced by a principal who knew and understood the school community and the school transformed itself and became the leader of the "Small Learning Community movement" within the Philadelphia School District in the mid 1990s. We will look at that phenomenon and the phenomenon of toxic school cultures in depth in Chapter 8, entitled "Torch."

What we need to understand here is that we can never understand a school community unless we live in that school community. By "live" I mean work there for a sufficient period of time to become part of that school community. That is why we need to be governed by democratic practices including especially the choosing of our leaders! It is also why urban bureaucracies do such a poor job of choosing school leaders. They often eliminate the school community in that process. More on that later....much more!

Let me conclude this chapter with the example of Furness High School in South Philadelphia that illustrates the point that great schools, no matter where and how situated, are great because of their sense of community and school ethos. They are great because of the relationships and friendships that are built among the community. They are great because of the relationships the teachers and support staff build with children and their families. Those positive relationships and the warm and caring atmosphere that permeates the school is what enables the school to succeed in so many ways. Everyone who walks through the front door of Furness feels the warmth of that atmosphere and usually comments about it. It is something intangible that is built over time. It is about caring about each other and the children we serve.

Furness is not unlike most schools in America. The student body is very multicultural and diverse. There is a very good mix of African American, Asian, Caucasian, Latino, and students from a wide variety of countries including India, Guyana and Jamaica. Most students come from working class families and a good number come from distressed families. The academically elite go to magnet schools and do not attend Furness, but an overload of special education students do. It has been said, "We teach whoever walks through our doors."

Three of our traditions, traditions that are present in probably every school in America, illustrate the power of the bonds of relationships within the school community. First, our Senior/Junior prom was especially warm and beautiful this year. Almost every teacher and support staff member attended. As I observed our students interact with each other, I was amazed by the warmth and "oneness" of our students. I was also amazed at the bonds of caring I saw between the adults and the students. The wide-eyed greetings, smiles, hugs, excitement at the classy way everyone was dressed, and the "Can I get your pictures!" permeated the atmosphere. The atmosphere was totally heartwarming and beautiful to see. It is moments like those that give us fulfillment as professionals.

That bonding between and among students, between and among adults, and between and among students and adults translates to the essence and power of the school's culture and its ethos. And it is that ethos that enables the second tradition to be so heartening and gratifying—graduation day! Many of our students have gone through trials and tribulations just to make it to graduation day. They were nurtured and prodded through their adolescence by the adults and peers that cared about them. Along the way, the students do become educated and deserving of the walk down the aisle. The fruit of our collective labors is often a result of little miracles involving families, parents, grandparents, caregivers, mentors, teachers, support staff, administrators and everyone within our school community.

But what is enlightening, is viewing the totality of the culminating graduation ceremony. Teachers, support staff and administrators rush around heroically to put the thing together, and it results in a wondrous ceremony of success and togetherness. The satisfaction and affection towards each other and the warmth of the atmosphere speaks volumes of what we do and what we are as a school community. It is our final report card! The heartfelt hugs and kisses, and the sparkle in the eyes of students, parents, teachers and everyone that has a place in the **"school family"** tell the story. The ceremony, its meaning and splendor is simply a thing of beauty.

The third part of this illustration shows the power and pervasiveness of the bonds of relationships and friendships that, over time, develop within the community of schools. The end of year party often becomes a retirement dinner. The year ended with the retirement of several significant members of the school family who played major roles in the school culture. A friend of each retiree had the honor to speak about the exploits of the individual. The roasts always turned to more serious acknowledgements of the wonderful little things the retirees did for people and children of the school. How they brought in food and clothing for needy children, how they supported children or adults in trying times of tragedy, or how they were just a friend when someone needed a friend, etc. Most speakers had emotional difficulty keeping their composure and several did break down in tears as they expressed their admiration for their colleagues and their sense of prospective loss. It spoke volumes of the essence of the school community. It is that closeness that enables the community to do great things for children.

The point is that Furness High School is typical of schools throughout America and the world. They have a culture and ethos and it is the ethos of a school community that counts. It is the ethos of caring, the ethos of achievement, and the ethos of collegial endeavor that counts in schools.

It is the community of schools that determines its success in educating our children and providing them with a wholesome school experience where they can grow, achieve and prosper as human beings. To create great schools we need to learn how to build great school communities. The foundation for building school communities lies in the governance structures of schools, and if we are to learn how to build great school communities, we need to learn how to create governance structures for schools that "set the conditions" for the requisite organizational synergy to happen.

Our children deserve that and so do the adults that pour their hearts into our children.

5

Leadership For the Twenty-First Century

Great leadership is inspirational. It is about creating excitement and energy in the hearts and minds of children and adults so great things happen within the community.

Leadership for schools of the twenty-first century is about serving the community of the school. It is inspiring the hearts and minds of children and young adults to excel and fulfill their potentiality. It is inspiring the school community to work together for the welfare of students, their parents and the community as a whole. It is the encouragement, caring about those we lead and the integrity of what we do that enables great leaders to lead. Effective leadership for schools builds the community of our schools, builds a common purpose, and most importantly, builds the sense of oneness of the collective ethos and the "we" of what we do.

Great leadership is of, by and for the community. It must be. After all, "Whose school is it?" Why does it exist? Who exercises the responsibility of making it work for children? And ultimately, who are supposed to be the beneficiaries of "the public trust of schools?" A school community exists to educate children and fulfill the ideals of education. It is the entire school community that facilitates the process of education and provides all the services to children that enable and inspire them to succeed. It is a collective enterprise. It can be no other way if we are to do all we need to do for children, and their families. The job of schooling is just so immense, complex and never ending and the synergy of schools must always be renewed, regenerated and sustained if we are to have great schools for every child all the time.

Leadership for the twenty-first century is collegial and collaborative. Schools are filled with professionals who must be trusted and empowered to be professionals. Every school in America has a multitude of great people and outstanding leaders who can be trusted to do the right thing for children. The leadership those leaders need is facilitative and enabling. The notions of good leadership for the modern age are rooted in our notions of democracy that are part of the culture of America. The tremendous body of research of the past century on effective leadership underscores that proposition.

Modern views of leadership focus on the concept that good leadership serves the community. The notion of "servant leadership" has entered modern thought on the best practices of leadership because of the increasingly common understanding that if organizations are to fulfill their collective mission they must function well as an organization and a leader exists for that purpose—to facilitate the successful collective endeavor of the organization. Robert Greenleaf was the originator of the concept of servant leadership and wrote: *Servant Leadership: A Journey Into the Nature of Legitimate Power and Greatness* (1977). He believes effective leadership emerges from a desire to help others.

It is not the other way around. The community does not exist to serve the leader. The leader exists to serve the community and the community exists to serve the purposes of the existence of the community. If we are ever to have great schools for our children and reach the ideal of having great schools for every child, we need to understand that. No longer can we cling to the feudalistic practices of the past that are based on the archaic "master-servant" relationships of an era long gone. We must as an educational community grow beyond and above that if we are to attain our collective goals.

In the process of our collective intellectual growth, the educational community has recognized the dichotomy of management vs. leadership. It is the realization that the outdated industrialization of schools into the domains of labor and management just does not cut it in the development of good schools and the creation of ownership of what we do and the formation of a unity of purpose. There must be more. The adversarial relationships that emerge from management vs. labor and the entrenched thought that is embedded in our school cultures because of that history must be overcome if we are to indeed create the common mission that is so important to the development of the community of organizations.

It is an essential theme of this treatise that there is an additional element to that dichotomy and any organization's success is really a trilogy of management, leadership and governance. The third prong of governance has just been brought to the forefront in recent years and the arena of school governance has grown quickly with the advent of charter schools, educational management organizations and other forms of innovative school governance structures. The issues of governance of schools will have to be dealt with by America's governmental and legal systems. Those issues can no longer be avoided. Governance will be discussed in depth in the next chapter. It will not go away.

While this chapter is about leadership, we must first understand that we do not get to leadership unless we have a certain degree of good management. If our schools are chaotic, out of order and books, materials and supplies are missing or mismanaged, we will never get to leadership. In fact, when we get to toxicity in schools we will see that toxic school cultures are often caused by poor management of the basic necessities of schools—law and order along with the essential basic resources and materials to "do our jobs."

Leadership today must be focused on the inclusion and involvement of all stakeholders in education. Everyone seems to be getting into the act of education and that is good. Everyone needs to be in the act of education if we are to do all we need to do. **Leadership is a process.** It is a process between people. It is a process of involvement. It is the process of giving voice to all stakeholders and constituencies and sincerely acting upon those voices. It is the process of creating a common vision and collective mission and then going about fulfillment of that mission. Goals must be collaboratively created and attained. Collective risk must be taken, and if failure ensues, that failure must be collectively overcome.

As we review the outstanding studies of leadership and our most effective leaders, we will see the manifest importance of inclusive leadership. It is only through building a sense of belonging, a sense of team, a sense of family that we build success and achievement in schools. The quality of leadership does affect student achievement (See, Marzano et al, 2005). It affects everything that happens in schools.

The leadership process that is imperative for greatness in schools is the democratic process! It is the democratic process that gets everyone involved and creates "ownership." Every author on school leadership speaks about the need for "shared leadership," inclusivity and ownership for teachers and support staff to "believe in what we are doing." Most experts believe in the concept of **"teacher empowerment"**—the need to empower teachers to rise, make decisions, and act accordingly in a collegial manner. Only when a school community believes in what they are doing will they make it work. Only then will they go the extra mile. That is an inescapable truth of followership and commitment to task. It is why armies win wars!

It is also the democratic process that creates synergy in the organization. Synergy is the "collective energy" that makes the whole better than its individual parts. We all can do things well individually but we all can do things better when we work together and create excitement for what we are doing. It builds cohesiveness and the desire to fulfill the common purpose of the organization and reach common goals.

That is why the definition of leadership ability proffered here is **"the ability to create organizational synergy toward fulfillment of a collective mission."** It is inspirational in nature. And that definition is inclusive of the reality that poor leadership can destroy that synergy. In fact, poor leadership can destroy a school. Poor leadership creates toxicity in school cultures, that in turn, harms children. It harms every person in that school community by killing the joy of coming to work every day and working with those wonderful children that we all come to love. We are always hooked to the reality that great leadership is invigorating! And poor leadership is debilitating.

In his book, *What Great Principals Do Differently: Fifteen Things That Matter Most* (2003), Todd Whitaker speaks about the power of praise and the fact that we can never have too much "nice" because it energizes people and inures to the benefit of students through a positive school climate and atmosphere of dignity, respect and mutual cooperation. He states: "Principals who consistently model their expectations for how people should be treated give their schools a valuable gift—a gift that, in time, everyone in the school can give to each other" (2003, p. 26). **He goes on to say quite profoundly: "If everyone in a school is treated with respect and dignity, you may still have nothing special. However, if everyone in a school is not treated with respect and dignity, you will never have anything special. Of that I am sure."**

The Coalition of Essential Schools, led by Ted Sizer who wrote a trilogy of books, *Horace's Compromise, Horace's School and Horace's Hope* (1984, 1992, & 1996), promotes ten principles that they have concluded are essential for good schooling. One of those principles is democracy. Why? Because they recognize the importance of democratic ideals to good schooling and ensuring that the right things are done for children. Remember, all the issues of America are the issues in our schools, and then some. Later in this chapter we will look in depth at the necessity of developing and maintaining an **"open climate"** in schools where the ideas of education can be freely discussed and debated with respect and without fear of reprisal or retribution. **It is only through an open climate for discussion and debate of all ideas that we can determine what really are the best practices in education. Our children deserve that.**

In education, the notion of a principal's cabinet is giving way to the concept of the "leadership team." The makeup of the leadership team depends on the structure of the school. For instance, whether the school is broken down into units of small learning communities, departments or other organizational strategies largely controls who are on the leadership team. It is common thought that the leadership team should be as inclusive as possible including even the janitorial team leader. In Chapter 8, we look at one visionary leader who turned a troubled school around by first inviting everyone in the school to be on the leadership team. A whole bunch of great school leaders did rise up and join that team and it created so much positive energy that the school did turn itself around.

The modern view of principals today is that they must be leaders of leaders, but it goes deeper than that. The principal is a leader of teams who in turn become the leaders of other teams and so on throughout the school community. The role of the principal within that dynamic becomes more of a "persuader and a consensus builder." Persuasion and consensus building really becomes an art form more than just a skill. Great leaders have that ability. An essential element of consensus building is that everyone must be given the opportunity to express their opinion and be heard, sincerely. Then, ideas must be molded into action plans, the action plans must be implemented in consistency with the embraced ideas, and the results must be assessed by examining data and listening some more. Leadership is a team sport.

We can not forget that there is also an "administrative team" consisting of the principal and his or her assistant principals or vice-principals as they are often called. They also need to work collaboratively as a true team. That relationship must be more than mere delegation—the delegator/delagatee relationships of the past must give way to collaborative relationships for the twenty-first century. And we cannot overlook the role of parent, community and student groups in school leadership.

School councils are prevalent throughout America in an effort to make school governance more democratic. They have leadership responsibilities also and are often comprised of the most respected individuals among the school community if they are selected or elected through a democratic process. They normally include, in addition to an administrator and teachers, parent representatives, local community representatives, and in high schools, students. We will look at school councils in depth in Chapter 7 on governance.

And we must never forget that the most important group principals need to lead are the students. Yes, leadership for the twenty-first century must focus on the students, and I do not mean demanding that the teachers be "student centered." I mean principals must get out into the hallways and classrooms and inspire and motivate students. They must "lead the students." Today's principals, to be inspirationally effective as instructional leaders, must be involved. They must get into classrooms for more than just observations. They must demonstrate and model good teaching by taking over a class now and then. They must challenge students to read, study and become. Never forget that the whole purpose of schooling is achievement. To inspire high achievement, principals and their assistants, while they are in school, "must live among the students."

Great leadership for schools includes great leadership of students. That is why the small schools movement is so important. It is so much easier for a principal or assistant principal to inspire students in small schools, because to inspire students, one must build a relationship with the students. And that relationship must go through a process of bonding. All relationships are emotional and psychological. Great principals build great relationships—that is their power (See, Whitaker, 2003, p. 30).

Visibility is the key. And I do not mean visibility in a critical, supervisory sense. I mean visibility in an encouraging, invigorating and facilitative way. Facilitative leadership is essential. Good leaders "facilitate happiness" that leads to facilitation of success and inspires fulfillment of the mission on an every day basis. They do that through encouragement, nurturing, coaching and genuine helpfulness.

Principals and all school leaders must be **"instructional leaders."** That is a realm of leadership that is essential to developing successful schools. It is also why the concepts of **"the lead teacher"** and **"the professional learning community"** have emerged in educational leadership thought. It is centered on the concept that teachers are professionals and should be empowered to function as a professional team. Most authorities on leadership conclude that democratic leadership is superior to autocratic leadership. I submit, that in schools, democratic leadership is far superior to autocratic leadership. **If teams of professionals are to actually be teams of professionals, there has to be collegial practices and decision-making must be collegial in nature. Only democracy can do that. Democracy is the sine qua non for collegial practice. That is another reason why it is imperative to embrace democratic ideals for schools.**

For a principal or any school leader to be an effective instructional leader, they must be respected by the school community for their knowledge of pedagogy. That respect must be earned. Instructional leadership credibility is earned or lost during discussions of pedagogy, and organizational design for instruction. The community will readily see the principal's expertise or lack of expertise, style, mentality, and inclinations. Every eye is on the principal, especially a new principal evaluating everything he or she says and does. They will see whether the principal means to impose his or her views upon the faculty or whether he or she will facilitate the values clarification of the community and lead through persuasion and appropriate analysis and discussion of data. They will see very quickly whether the leader is a "me" person or a "we" person. If a leader is a "me" person, his or her capacity to lead is severely diminished. You cannot impose followership—it must be developed and earned. It must be earned with rolled up sleeves.

Sometimes good principalship requires the principal to **"stand back and lead."** That is how Dr. James Lytle of the University of Pennsylvania turned around Philadelphia's University City High School (See, Chapter 8 for a detailed analysis). He restructured the school into small learning communities that functioned as completely independent schools-within-a-school. Then he allowed them to organize themselves as they thought best, lead themselves, and govern themselves. It created excitement and productive energy that I had never before seen in my twenty years as a teacher and school leader there. That is known as "laissez-faire" leadership and it can be used affirmatively.

Now let us turn to what the experts say about leadership. Everything I have said above is supported by the evidence I will now visit and cite below. In school districts around the country there seems to be a mantra for "research-based" instructional practices. If we are ever to truly get there, we must first go to the evidence on leadership strategies.

What the experts say about leadership:

There have been thousands of studies about leadership and hundreds of books written on the subject. While we know so much about leadership we still know so very little. Everyone who pens a book or an article on leadership purports to have found the essentials, but none of the authors have found the same things so where is our consensus? Some authors say leadership can be taught and learned, but others say leadership ability is gained through life's experiences and must be developed through experience. What makes a leader effective? The answer is an "open question" but there is one fact that is always going to be the truth—**leadership will emerge.**

In the summary of the modern literature on leadership, we will focus on several authors and a few books about leadership that are used in today's graduate schools that provide courses and programs on leadership and organizational dynamics in education. They are representative of the literature on leadership and it must be reminded that there is no substitute for reading for yourself the works cited here and other books and articles on leadership. There is a great wealth of knowledge and ideas out there and we need to seek it, assimilate it, own it, and bring it with us to our schoolhouses. Life long learning and freedom of thought is integral to the democratic process.

While there is no pure consensus on all the elements of good leadership, there are recurring themes in the literature. We must be aware of those themes, they have been with us since the beginning of civilization and they are not going away.

One of the most salient recurring themes and the one element that in my experience has proven to be the most important element of effective leadership is **"trust formation."** It could very well be the most important ability of great leaders. Without trust, a leader is powerless to lead. They can "manage" to some degree, but they can never "lead" to any effective extent. They can never build the organizational synergy necessary to make the group better than the sum of its individual parts. Trust is a basic need of man. And trust is a basic need of everyone in the school community, children and adults.

James Kouzes and Barry Posner have studied leadership for more than two decades. They have collected thousands of best practice leadership case studies, researched the practices of some of our nation's best leaders when they were functioning at their personal best, and analyzed tens of thousands of leadership assessment instruments (Kouzes and Posner, 2003). Their research visited corporations, government, and private organizations. I cite their works first because there is a movement in America to try to impose corporate governance and leadership strategies on the educational establishment and if we are to do that, we need to understand that the best practices of corporate leadership are also the best practices of leadership in government, school systems and schools. Good leadership practices are good leadership practices everywhere and anywhere.

Encouraging the Heart
Kouzes and Posner

Kouzes and Posner authored three especially excellent books, *The Leadership Challenge, Credibility, and Encouraging the Heart* (2002, 2003a, & 2003b). They also wrote *"Leadership Is In the Eye of the Follower"* (1986), an outstanding article that reviewed their findings after a five year study of leadership that included the study of over 10,000 managers nationwide and the perceptions followers have of leaders. They concluded that leadership is as much about followers as it is about the leader. They found it to be a reciprocal process between people. Much of what I say here is taken from their recent book *"Encouraging the Heart"* and I encourage your heart to read it thoroughly.

They state unequivocally: **"The foundation of leadership is credibility"** (p. 29). That is an important idea to remember, especially so, because the concept of **"leadership credibility"** will be an important focal concept when we look at school governance in the next chapter and visit the question, "How shall we choose our principals and other school leaders?" **Unless we choose our principals in an open, honest, fair, democratic and ultimately credible manner, leadership credibility is always difficult to earn.** It matters how the followership views the process of determining who is the leader. In schools, we are talking about the entire school community. **It must be seen as a valid and credible process. Credibility is everything. Inclusivity is a necessary element of credibility.**

Of utmost importance, the leader must be seen as credible by the followers. Kouzes and Posner state: "It seems there are several essential tests a leader must pass before we are willing to grant him or her the title of 'leader'." In their study, "honesty" was cited more often than any other leadership characteristic. Is that person truthful? Ethical? Principled? Have high integrity? Does he or she have character? In their discussions with respondents they found that the *"leader's behavior"* provided the evidence. "Regardless of what leaders say about their integrity, followers wait to be shown" (Kouzes & Posner, 1986).

A leader's integrity of word and deed is of high importance. Interestingly, the word "integrity" was found to be the most looked up word on internet dictionaries! Kouzes and Posner say that, "Over and over again people tell us credibility is 'doing what you say you will do.' Leaders set the example for others. They practice what they preach" (2003b, p. 29). If leaders do not keep agreements, make false promises, cover up things they do that are not right, act in secrecy, or display inconsistencies between words and actions, they are seen as dishonest and not worthy of following. And as Kouzes and Posner poignantly state, "On the other hand, if a leader behaves in ways consistent with his or her stated values and beliefs, then we can entrust to that person our careers, our security, and ultimately even our own lives" (1986).

They cite another of their studies that showed that the element of trustworthiness is essentially a basic necessity of effective leadership. In that study, they found that of all the behaviors describing leadership, **"The most important single item was the leader's display of trust in others"** (1986). Irwin Federman, a venture capitalist and CEO of computer chip-maker Monolithic Memories once said, **"Trust is a risk game. The leader must ante up first."**

Psychologists tell us trust is a basic human need that results from our most basic instincts. We all need it all the time. Trust is a matter of basic human security that we learn as infants. We all need to be secure in the world around us if we are to grow and thrive as human beings. We cannot function on a nerve's edge keel. That will always be true because of our psychological and emotional make up as human beings. We must trust in the world around us and that trust comes out of nurture. A leader who is trusted by those he or she leads will be successful even if that leader is a novice. A lack of experience and knowledge will always be overcome if the leader is trusted and respected by the followers. They will gladly do the leading. And as we will see later, the best thing a leader can do is say to his followers, "Go ahead—lead!"

But an ultimately important concept that must be remembered is that **"trust must be earned."** It is initially granted with wary eyes, but it will be either earned or unearned rather quickly. The leader's character will be intensively scrutinized by the followership. "Character" may be the most important facet of good leaders, and as Dr. Haberman says, "Character is manifested by one's ability to give and get respect" (1999).

When we pass the test of trustworthiness we are granted respect. We are granted leadership credibility in the eyes of our followers. Our principals as school leaders are always initially granted positional respect because of their position authority, but it is in the use of positional power that earns respect or disrespect. When a leader has earned his respect, great things can and usually do happen with a school. When a leader fails to earn the requisite respect, he or she loses the faculty and entire school community. When the leader loses the support of the followership, he or she is powerless to lead.

As Gorge DiPilato, a president of the PA Commonwealth Association of School Administrators, once said to a group of prospective principals, "They better respect you for what you do! And if they don't, you are finished." And as we will see when we visit the phenomenon of toxic school cultures, it is the lack of mutual respect between the leader and his or her followers that begins the vicious downward spiral into toxicity.

Encouraging the Heart (2003b) is a recent book by Kouzes and Posner and represents what they have learned from over two decades of intensive study of leadership. We, the educational community of America, would do well to take cognizance of what they say. **To them, leadership is creating "vitality and enthusiasm" in the hearts and minds of those we lead. It is a "chemistry" based on "affection, caring, and even love."** It is a relationship between people, and they urge you as readers of their work, to keep in mind their basic message: **at the heart of effective leadership is genuinely caring for people** (p. 14). We must never forget that bottom line.

They cite a study by the Center for Creative Leadership (CCL) in Colorado Springs that found that the number one success factor for success in the top three jobs of large organizations is "relationships with subordinates" (Kouzes & Posner, 2003b, p. 5). **They found that what distinguished the highest performing managers from the lowest performing managers was not a high need to express control.** They found that the single factor that differentiated the top from the bottom managers was that the highest performing managers scored highest on affection—both expressed and wanted. They state, **"Contrary to the myth of the cold-hearted boss who cares very little about people's feelings, the highest performing managers show more warmth and fondness toward others than do the bottom twenty-five percent. They get closer to people, and they're significantly more open in sharing thoughts and feelings than their lower performing counterparts"** (2003b, p. 9).

It is not that these managers did not have a rational, thinking part of their make up that enabled them to handle their responsibilities competently, it is that those factors did not explain why managers were high performers. What does explain the results is that **"leadership is an emotional connection"** between leader and follower and a leader's need to have power, control and influence over others was not the determining factor of effective leadership. Openness and affection clearly pay off when it comes to being an effective leader. But it must be genuine (See, Whitaker, 2003).

Kouzes and Posner state it best: "We've all heard the dismissing comment made by many in the managerial ranks that 'I don't care what people think of me.' Well, it may be true for them, but it's not true for the best leaders. The best leaders want to be liked, and they want openness from other people. Not caring how others feel and think about what we do and say is an attitude for losers—an attitude that can only lead to less and less effectiveness" (2003b, p. 11).

They go on to say, "The secret is this: we all do really want to be loved." They quote Irwin Federman, a renowned CEO and venture capitalist, who states, "You don't love someone because who they are; you love someone for the way they make you feel." It is Federman who speaks about leadership as "chemistry" that exists between great leaders and those who follow them. He speaks as love as a necessary ingredient, one that is rarely appreciated because we underrate the role of our feelings. He also criticizes what he calls "the conventional thinking" that "management is not a popularity contest.... I contend, however, that all things being equal, we will work harder and more effectively for people we like. And we like them in direct proportion to how they make us feel" (Kouzes & Posner, 2003b, p. 11).

Leadership is an interpersonal art. It cannot be exercised from a distance because it is an interpersonal relationship. It is a consequence of building relationships whether positive relationships or negative relationships. Leadership capacity may very well be correlational to relationship building capacity. It is "managerial myth" that says we can't get too close to our associates. Kouzes and Posner believe that to be fully trusted, we must be open—not only to others, but *with* others. "When we are open, we make ourselves vulnerable. But this vulnerability makes us more human and more trusted" (2003b, p. 85). "There is a growing body of evidence that "emotional intelligence" can be more important than IQ in predicting success in organizations—or in life, for that matter" (p. 10).

In a famous study by Lawrence Lindahl, highest on the employees list of intangible rewards were (1) feeling appreciated, and (2) feeling that they were being informed about things that were happening (Cited in Kouzes & Posner, 2003b). They wanted to be listened to. "We all have these needs to feel that we matter, to feel that those with whom we work appreciate what we have to give and that they value us enough to let us know what is going on" (p. 13). It goes significantly deeper than that in schools—**everyone wants to be "part of" what is going on. That is why "to give voice" to the school community and every individual in it is so important. It creates meaning and dedication to what we do together.** But it must be a true voice. If we just pretend to give voice and do what we want because as the boss we can do that, it will cause disenchantment and a definite lack of motivation and commitment to task. It will create negative synergy within the school.

Let me sum up the work of Kouzes and Posner so we are clear on what their years of study of leadership has revealed to them. According to their research, "The majority of us admire leaders who are honest, competent, forward-looking, inspiring, and ultimately, *credible.*" **"Credibility" is the foundation of leadership!** And in *The Leadership Challenge*, they detail what they have found—that when getting extraordinary things done, leaders: (1) Model the Way, (2) Inspire a Shared Vision, (3) Challenge the Process, (4) Enable Others to Act, and (5) Encourage the Heart.

It is definitely my experience that what they say is true: "It is impossible to escape the message here that if people work with leaders who encourage the heart, they feel better about themselves. Their self-esteem goes up. These leaders set people's spirits free, often inspiring them to become more than they ever thought possible. This, indeed, may be our ultimate mission as leaders" (2003b, p. 12).

Our task as leaders is to help every individual within our schools reach their fullest potentialities—first, our students; and second, our staff, because what they do affects our students so much. They are the key, not us as leaders. And third, everyone else in the entire school community must be encouraged because they serve our children, too.

It all revolves around **truly caring for people.**

"Star Principals Serving Children in Poverty"
Martin Haberman

Dr. Martin Haberman is a Distinguished Professor Emeritus of Education at the University of Wisconsin. He has studied education and teaching for over 40 years and has developed more teachers for students who live in poverty than just about anyone in education. His most widely known program is the National Teacher Corps. He has studied administration and effective principals during those years and has developed his own Principals' Academy to teach and develop leadership for school administrators. He has also developed his "Star Urban Administrator Questionnaire" that assesses thirteen dimensions of effective urban leadership. He has established the Haberman Educational Foundation to promote his ideology and helps over 40 urban school districts assess and choose their teachers and principals.

While Mr. Haberman focuses on urban educators, what he says about leadership and best practices for principals is also true for suburban and rural schools. He differentiates effective and ineffective principals from what he calls "star" principals. In his book *Star Principals Serving Children in Poverty* (1999), he does add some important research-based concepts to the discussion of school leadership for the twenty-first century. His ideology and notions of the importance of "dealing with the bureaucracy" warrant review.

Dr. Haberman uses the term "star" to indicate the behaviors and ideology of principals who are more effective (p. x). He points out that there are "no effective urban school districts" and that all large school systems are failing to some substantial degree. Yet, he does say that there are highly effective schools within every urban school system. He states that the principals of these schools succeed in spite of the bureaucratic conditions imposed upon them by states and school districts.

Haberman believes, "The ideology is a value-laden system of beliefs caught and developed by life experiences rather than *taught* in graduate courses of school administration. He believes that training of administrators does help, but it will only "take" with individuals who already accept the ideology.

Haberman believes school leadership has two goals: to "elicit voluntary commitment to shared purposes" and to "create the conditions" of work that will enable staff, teachers, and children to be successful. He states that leaders become more effective when they concentrate less on being the boss and more on creating the conditions under which school personnel perform their duties with fewer impediments. He understands that ultimately a principal and school will be judged by student achievement.

What Haberman adds to the body of leadership for educators is his notion that effective school leaders develop **"community of purpose, team building, and commitment to task."** It is the **unity of purpose** and the establishment of working teams that allows for success in schools. He believes everyone, especially the principal, needs to be a **"responsible participant"** in the process and everyone needs to be **"product oriented."** He also recognizes that the establishment of trust and rapport is an essential element of that process and that staff members must have a voice in every aspect of an initiative for it to be their own.

Haberman believes the most important power of a principal is his or her **"power of persuasion."** He states that star principals **"eschew coercive power"** because they only beget **"hollow forms of compliance."** In reality, principals cannot force anyone to do anything. The ideology does embrace democratic decision-making and collegiality, and goes on to say: "The notion that the principal can function as an independent decision maker is dangerous. The more important the issue, the greater the likelihood that the principal will need additional information and wider consultation with others" (p. 67).

Of particular importance to note is that Haberman concludes that effective principals are responsible participants in all aspects of the process of schooling rather than being **"mere delegators."** This is an important concept because delegation of duties and responsibilities is so prevalent today in the practice of administrators, and if a principal is seen as delegating all their work and responsibility to others, he or she is seen as lazy and ineffective by the followership. In one assistant principal's position I held, one of the teachers said to me, "The way she runs the school is have you do it!" This is an important distinction with the advent of "distributive leadership." Distributive leadership is one thing and "distributive delegation" is quite another. Mere delegators are never respected by the school community and they are not leaders in any sense of the word. If a principal delegates all of his or work to subordinates, then who is running the school?

As part of the principal's responsibility to participate, the principal must see his or herself as responsible for everything that happens in schools. In his

"Responsible Leader vs. Delegator" dichotomy of his "Dimensions of Effective Urban School Leadership Assessment Questionaire" Haberman asks, "Does the respondent understand and accept the role to be primarily one in which s/he will be the responsible authority for performing major functions, or does s/he believe the leader's role is primarily one of delegating as much as possible to others and overseeing their work." The correct answer is that a principal must "be the responsible participant performing major functions." There is only so much a principal can delegate to others before they are seen by the followers as shirking their responsibility to perform their share of the work. **Leadership cannot be delegated. It must be shared! That is a psychologically important concept to understand.**

In his questionnaire he also explores the prospective leader's belief whether he or she will be personally accountable or seek to only hold others accountable. That is his "Personal Accountability vs. Others Accountability" dichotomy. Haberman's studies lead him to conclude that effective principals are responsible participants and hold themselves accountable. Ineffective principals seek to delegate and hold others accountable. I call the latter the "King on the Throne" syndrome, and it is not only ineffective, it is a counterproductive and disheartening practice. In most bureaucracies it is an institutional illness.

Haberman's summary of his 13 domains of effective school leadership can be found in the Appendix. His domains are worth reading and noting and his foundation for advancing his ideology does some excellent work helping school districts choose prospective principals with personal characteristics that are likely to yield positive school community synergy (See, Haberman Foundation, 2007).

Another idea that is important to note is his notion that effective principals in urban systems are those that can deal with the bureaucracy effectively. He remarks, "Indeed, the more detached the individual school becomes from the chaotic central bureaucracy, the greater the opportunity to be more responsive and effective" (p. 70). This will be an important discussion topic when we get to school governance and we visit the central vs. local governance argument.

As we discuss those issues, remember, charter schools were legislatively designed to govern themselves independently of the central bureaucracy! They were also designed to empower teachers, parents and community members at the local level. The concept of **"teacher empowerment"** and **"community empowerment"** have been with us for a long time. Haberman believes that, **"Parents, caregivers and the community need to be involved in the life of the school as participants with voice, input and even power."** And it is the question of giving parents, staff and community members **"legitimate power"** within the governance structures of schools that will be an issue at the heart of school governance.

In conclusion of this summary of Haberman's work, let me use his words: **"In some schools, principals still hold all of the power and make the final decisions. Everyone votes and then the principal decides. This traditional model will not work in the 21st century; parents, caregivers, and community members expect to be heard"** (p. 90). So do the teachers, and in high schools, how about the students?

Leadership & Student Achievement

Whether leadership influences student academic achievement is an essential question and there have been many attempts to link leader effectiveness to student achievement. There is a large base of research conducted over many years that consistently supports the proposition that the leadership capacity and specific behaviors of the principal affect student academic achievement both positively and negatively. Certain leadership behaviors and competencies have been found to cause positive student outcomes and many researchers have attempted to identify specific characteristics of principals that result in high student achievement.

Kathleen Cotton has done a comprehensive analysis and synthesis of much of the best research in the field (2003). She found that there are two lines of inquiry: First, what she calls the "effective schools research" that repeatedly identified a common set of principal attributes that appeared to facilitate the success of the high achieving schools. Those attributes included high expectations for students and staff, a safe and orderly environment, resources focused on achieving key objectives, regular monitoring of student learning progress, and instructional leadership on the part of the principal. The second line of research focused on the principal's involvement with the instructional program and his or her ability to provide effective instructional leadership. Similarly to Haberman's research, she found that a large part of effective instructional leadership is the ability to "gain schoolwide commitment" to clear learning goals, largely through the involvement of staff and community members in decision-making—**the democratic process!** Effective principals were found to have a high capacity for building positive interpersonal relationships and modeled the behaviors they expected from those they supervised. "Modeling the way" and "building relationships" are recurring themes in the literature—are they not?

Robert Marzano, Timothy Waters and Brian McNulty conducted an extensive "meta-analysis" of the research on school leadership spanning 35 years to answer America's call for "research-based" practices and school leadership that translates into student achievement (2005). They found a positive correlation between the leadership behavior of the principal and the average academic performance of the students in the school. They conclude that the leadership behavior of the principal does significantly affect student achievement, and they point out the obvious: whether a school operates effectively or not significantly increases or decreases a student's chances of academic success.

Marzano et al differentiate the practices that result in what they call **"first-order change"** and which practices are necessary for **"second-order change."** First-order change focuses on "managing the daily life of schools." Second-order change is deep change that significantly alters the practices within schools.

Marzano et al explain the basic dichotomy thusly: "First-order change is incremental. It can be thought of as the next most obvious step to take in a school or district. Second-order change is anything but incremental. It involves dramatic departures from the expected, both in defining a given problem and in finding a solution" (2005, p. 66). They describe the difference between first and second-order change as that between "incremental change" and "deep change" (See, Waters, Marzano and McNulty, 2004a, 2004b). "Incremental change fine-tunes the system through a series of small steps that do not depart radically from the past. Deep change alters the system in fundamental ways, offering a dramatic shift in direction and requiring new ways of thinking and acting" (p. 66).

Their analysis revealed specific behaviors related to principal effectiveness and developed what they call the 21 responsibilities of the school leader. They state that all 21 responsibilities interact in first-order change but leadership for second-order change is related to seven of the responsibilities in their factor analysis: (1) Knowledge of Curriculum, Instruction and Assessment, (2) Optimizer, (3) Intellectual Stimulation, (4) Change Agent, (5) Monitoring/Evaluating. (6) Flexibility, and (7) Ideals/Beliefs 2005 (p. 70).

Their factor analysis of effective leadership practices using the scientific approach of meta-analysis represents a significant endeavor to make the analysis of leadership **"research-based."** In the light of all the research, we can come to a reasonable consensus that **leadership matters!** It matters very much.

Local School District Principal Competencies

Most urban school districts use either a leadership assessment tool or develop their own set of competencies and abilities they look for when they interview prospective principals. Just about every author or group who have studied leadership develop their own leadership assessment inventory that they claim can be used to interview and assess the leadership ability of the interviewees. The problem with that as we look at the big picture of leadership is that every assessment instrument differs. So who has the correct one? And the answer to that is obvious: there is no correct one because the phenomenon of great leadership is just too vast an ocean and great leaders have been found to be just so many different kinds of people.

As an example, let us look at the School District of Philadelphia. Ever since the takeover of the school district by the state of Pennsylvania, the school district has been managed in an extremely centralized and autocratic manner. The leadership that was in place at the time was "jettisoned" by the new CEO, Paul Vallas, who put his own people in leadership positions. They eliminated the **"site selection"** of principals where a team of teachers, parents, and in high schools, students selected the principal, and replaced it with a centralized selection process. They first used Haberman's process based on his thirteen categories where prospective principals were interviewed by two or three interviewers who analyzed what was said according to Haberman's principles.

The prospective principals who "passed the test" were either given principalships and sent to schools or admitted to the newly formed "Principals' Academy" that was developed internally. From there, principals were "assigned" to schools without any input from the school community. Assigning principals to schools without input from the school community is what I call **"impositional leadership"** which will be a significant issue of discussion when we get to the governance of schools, but for now, let us just look at that process. The central administration must not have found success with that model or Mr. Haberman was charging them too much money, because shortly thereafter they developed their own set of competencies.

The School District of Philadelphia has developed a partnership with the Microsoft corporation and has recently built the "school of the future." Microsoft has a set of competencies they use to help choose their leaders so the school district used their competencies as a basis for their own. They whittled the competencies down to a final 12 that they have determined are the most important from nearly 70 competencies they started with in the analytical process. Their original draft had another 22 competencies that are also important leadership domains. Those competencies can be found in the appendix.

The problem with that philosophy of choosing principals is that in description of those competency categories are several sentences of description that use adjectives that actually add more concepts to the analysis. When all is said and done there are over 1,000 concepts to keep in mind during the process. Whether two or three interviewers can possibly competently do that in a one half hour interview is highly questionable at best. When we get to the psychological perspective we will see that the minds of man and woman do not work like that. Psychological studies of the subjective realities of the psychological nature of man show us that people choose who they like on more irrational terms even if they try to be objective.

While such processes can be of some use in the determination of our leaders, they are no substitute for democratic practices. Again, what would you say if our mayors of our towns and cities, our governors, our congressmen and our senators were selected in that manner? You would say that is crazy? Why should we do that for choosing our leaders of our school communities?

What is vastly more important is that the followership view the leader as capable and possessing the ability to lead *them.* They must see the process as **credible.** The only way that can possibly happen is if the followership is included and participates in the process of choosing their leaders. You cannot get that **chemistry of leadership** that is necessary for outstanding leadership and outstanding schools without including the school community in the process. It just does not happen any other way.

Leadership is too complex a phenomenon and effective leadership is based on just too many variables. Emotion and psychology play a huge role and so does compatablity with the leader and the community he or she leads. As Kouzes and Posner point out, emotional intelligence may be the most important factor of leadership. And emotional intelligence can only be tested in the battlefield of leadership. A whole lot of people can give politically correct answers in an interview only to falter in the field.

Leadership Styles

Leadership style theories have been with us for many years probably since the beginning of civilized society. Traditionally, leadership styles have been visualized along a continuum from "laissez-faire" to "autocratic" with "democratic" being in the center (See, figure 5.1). Autocratic leadership has also sometimes been called "heroic" leadership. While we can classify styles in so many ways and place them along that continuum, the reality of the matter is that there are as many leadership styles as there are personality styles.

Daniel Goleman, a leading researcher on corporate leadership, reviewed a recent research study on leadership styles of effective executives in an article for the *Harvard Business Review,* "Leadership that Gets Results" (2000). He claims the research found six distinct leadership styles that are all used by effective leaders. Goleman asserts that, "New research suggests that the most effective executives use a collection of distinct leadership styles—each in the right measure, at just the right time. Such flexibility is tough to put into action, but it pays off in performance. And better yet it can be learned" (p. 79).

The article by Goleman, who is also the author of *Emotional Intelligence* (1995), is based on research by the consulting firm Hay/Mcber which draws on a random sample of 3,871 executives selected from a database of over 20,000 executives worldwide. They determined six leadership styles: (1) coercive, (2) authoritative, (3) affiliative, (4) democratic, (5) pacesetting, and (6) coaching. Goleman's team of Harvard researchers set out to "gain a more molecular view of the links among leadership and emotional intelligence, and climate and performance" (p. 81). That team of researchers conclude that: "Leaders who have mastered four or more of the styles—especially the authoritative, democratic, affiliative, and coaching styles—have the best climate and business performance" (p. 87).

They describe their six styles of leadership in this poignant manner: "What are the six styles of leadership? None will shock workplace veterans. Indeed, each style, by name and brief description will likely resonate with anyone who leads, is led, or as is the case with most of us, does both. Coercive leaders demand immediate compliance. *Authoritative leaders* mobilize people toward a vision. *Affiliative leaders* build consensus through participation. *Pacesetting* leaders expect excellence and self direction. And *coaching leaders* develop people for the future" (p. 80).

Their work represents an interesting view of leadership but in no way is it exhaustive or determinative. All of us have a little of each style in us and there are thousands more adjectives to describe leadership personality.

A classic study of leadership styles was done by Powers and Powers (1983) and they looked at the autocratic style in particular. Their findings are particularly pertinent especially when we look at the inherent nature of bureaucracies and their over reliance on autocratic leadership. **They concluded from their research that an autocratic leader's behavior will only be accepted "as a necessary burden" if that leader is seen as "especially competent." If not, "his or her tenure in office will be marked at least by hard feelings and discord and at the most by hatred and fear that can paralyze the operation he is supposed to make more efficient by his management"** (p. 26).

This quotation is especially poignant about autocratic leadership and right on point when we look at the phenomenon of toxic school cultures:

> When heroic leadership is the dominant mode, a number of undesir-able and dysfunctional consequences are produced. Heroic leaders must maintain control over others since to lose that power entails a loss of ability to give orders that will be obeyed. Coercion, threats and power plays are common and they often engender feelings of resentment and acts of confrontation. As one respondent in our study of administrative style and student performance stated. "The top-down style of manage-ment alienates us. There is a real 'us {Administration}—they {teachers}' mentality. We are not working together to benefit students. We are locked in an adversarial relationship." Another respondent wrote, "Ignoring and not listening to teachers' ideas and concerns...does not allow for creative and innovative teaching, thus students do not get the benefit of a happy rejuvenated teacher—one who is constantly learning and improving." Another teacher said that the authoritarian leadership in her school "{gives us} a depressing feeling of hopelessness and neglect."

The autocratic, authoritarian, "King on the Throne" leadership mentality is really not leadership at all. It is poor management and leads to negative synergy and a definite and debilitating down-spiral of interpersonal relationships within a school or any organization for that matter. It is so prevalent in bureaucratic school systems it is "an institutional illness" that is part of the mentality of **"unhealthy organizations."** The collective ethos caused by that mentality ultimately leads to a destructive atmosphere and school climate. And what do you think is the effect on children who must attend a school like that and live there for much of their day?

At the opposite end of the continuum is laissez-faire leadership. It does have its positive uses as I alluded to earlier in a situation where a school turned itself around, but any school or organization left alone without a viable governance system is destined for difficulty if not ultimate failure. Usually, according to "chaos theory" the universe will organize itself—or the organization will organize itself into some sort of a system for getting things done.

There is a substantial caveat for laissez-faire leadership: If there are no clear procedures for decision-making, supervision and feedback, it can lead to struggles among competing subordinates to exercise power and establish leadership based on referent power (French and Raven, 1959). That situation can draw members of an organization into a "continual series of conflicts among competing factions and sap energies that could otherwise be directed toward professional activities. It tends to leave members of an organization adrift with feelings of frustration and low group unity and morale, and it makes the organization vulnerable to power plays" (DiPilato, 1995, p. 66).

At the center between autocratic and laissez-faire leadership lies democratic or "participative" leadership. A participative leadership style is grounded in a "behavioral model" of leadership. "A participative leader is flexible and able to exercise leadership skills as the context dictates. Moreover, a participative style relies on noncoercive sources of power, especially expertise, persuasion, reason, and rewards. Positional power is generally of limited consequence to the participatory leader, particularly because he or she has as one major objective—the delegation of power and sharing the responsibility when appropriate" (DiPilato, 1995, p. 66).

The essence of participatory leadership is the sharing of power and authority. It is delegating power and authority. It is teacher empowerment! It is not delegating administrative work and it is not creating a committee to create a plan that meets the principal's preconceived specifications. Again, that is a caveat of what is known as "distributive leadership." Too often it becomes "distributive delegation of the principal's work load." In that event the principal loses his or her credibility. Hard work must be modeled by the leader. So must sincerity be modeled. Everyone is watching.

There are basically four dimensions to the participative leadership style: (1) involving others in creating and communicating a vision, (2) building trust and organizational commitment, (3) utilizing the organizations expertise, and (4) developing the organizational team.

Of course, there are times when highly autocratic leadership is necessary. When a crisis occurs, a leader must act swiftly and decisively and the followership looks to the leader for that behavior. In the daily course of running schools there are hundreds of decisions that cannot be made as a group because there just is not enough time. That is why in our American constitutional governance structure we have the executive branch. Someone must execute the policies and rules of schools. Someone must "run" schools on a daily basis and anyone who has ever worked in a school knows that the pace is excruciatingly hectic. There always is the need for balance.

In the final analysis we all have our own personal leadership style that we have learned and developed over time for whatever psychological or practical reasons. Knowledge of various leadership styles and when to use each one will help us become more effective leaders. The complexity of the nature of leadership style and the emotional and psychological mechanisms underlying our behavior and interpersonal effectiveness is a matter within the realm of psychology, but we all must be aware of ourselves and our actions and the effect it has on ourselves and others. Our success in leadership depends on it.

The Necessity of an Open Climate

In our discussion of leadership and the reality that our schools are communities, we have used such terms as collegiality, voice, and trust. For those things to actually happen in schools there must first be what is known as an **"open climate."** Without an open climate for discussion and debate of the ideas and issues of education, there can be no greatness in schools.

For us as a community to do all that needs to be done for children, we must first establish a **climate and atmosphere of trust and security** so that everyone within the school community feels free and safe to express their opinions and beliefs without fear of reprisal. The evidence is clear—there needs to be participation in all that we do if we are to develop the necessary commitment to task that can only result out of collective ownership. If we want to make it happen for children, we must do it together.

Participation in the process must occur. If people are afraid to participate or they feel that it is useless to participate, they will fade away into their own classrooms and work in isolation. They will just do what they can for those students who happen to be in their classroom. Good things will occur, but great things will not.

Schools are communities because man is a social being and has basic needs to belong to the group—or more appropriately said, man has a need to belong to the family. The need to ***belong*** is a primal instinct that is in us all. So is the need to be and feel safe. Everyone also has a need for ***esteem*** and ***acceptance.*** Everyone in schools from the children, to their parents, to the teachers and support staff have basic human needs and for everyone to do their best we must first establish a **"secure climate"** for collegial endeavor. It is necessary for the whole to be greater than the sum of its parts. We can not help people rise and become better unless we first establish trust and the climate of trust.

Participation is a must and I believe that we all as members of our school communities and American society have a right to participate in the process of schools and its decision-making. I call that **"participative due process"** and can well argue that is both a statutory right and a constitutional right of all Americans. I also believe it is a **duty and obligation** of school community members to participate in what we do. As professional employees, it is our individual "professional responsibility" to participate in the processes of schooling. And lastly, I believe it is a collective professional responsibility to create valid mechanisms for ensuring everyone can be involved in that process. It is a basic human right.

For principals, assistant principals, teacher coaches and other school leaders to be successful **instructional leaders** there must first be an atmosphere of trust and humanity. For a colleague or superior to walk into another person's classroom, observe what is happening, and discuss the lesson with the teacher it must be done in a positive and trusting manner. Otherwise, the observer or colleague will be shut out. That is basic human psychology. When a supervisor enters a classroom, sits in the back, and starts writing things down in a critical manner, all positivity is lost.

For us to improve as teachers and educators we must discuss everything we do. We must debate best practices. We must debate curricular decisions. We must discuss and debate diversity issues. We must debate discipline issues and enforcement of rules. We must do a thousand different things and we must determine what we think and believe is the best way of doing things. That can only be done through our interpersonal interactions and that is why it is so important for leaders to establish positive relationships with subordinates and everyone in the school community. What we do together inures to the benefit of children in one way or another.

For an atmosphere and climate of collegiality to exist, everyone in the school must be treated with dignity and respect at all times. That is why it is so important for principals and all school leaders to **"model the way."** They set the tone for the school. If a principal or leader talks down to people, acts like he or she is better than them, or speaks to them negatively, he or she loses his capacity to lead.

Everyone must feel free to express their ideas without fear of reprisal. They must feel free to disagree and stand up for what they believe. That right and need must be recognized and supported by the leader. It is part of consensus building that everyone must be heard and listened to. It is an essential part of making our schools better. The operative word in consensus building is "building." Consensus must be built and that is a leadership art. The sense of "we" must be built through relationship building—and community building.

In bureaucracies, and schools within them, reprisal often runs rabid. Anyone who has worked for large school systems can tell you many a story about reprisals they have felt and Faustian behaviors of superiors. Some of the things I have personally witnessed are shocking and that is why I believe we need to turn to democracy as the purification process for our schools and school systems. If we are going to have great schools, we need to cure our systems and schools of the destructive practices of bureaucracy.

We will get to the subject of institutional illnesses later, but let me just tell one story that illustrates the systemic nature of fear of reprisal:

I am a member of the Asian American Educators association in Philadelphia. One day at a meeting the topic of discussion was how to get the concerns of Asian educators and Asian students addressed by the school system. I asked the question of how can they ensure that their voice is heard and acted upon in a sincere manner. We discussed the realities of dealing with the system and its uncaring bureaucracy.

The conversation turned to my belief that not only should schools be led democratically but that they should be governed democratically. She became excited during our discussion because she believed what I said was true. She was especially interested in the fact that I was writing this book, but almost immediately she raised this question: **"But what will Paul Vallas, the CEO, and the downtown administrators do to you for writing your book?"** That is sad!

What a sad statement that is on the state of affairs in our school district. What is really sad is that it is the state of affairs in many school districts across America. And this is in America and I practice education in Philadelphia, the seat of American democracy. The First Amendment still contains the right of free speech. If we have to worry about reprisal from our superiors for speaking and writing what we honestly believe, where is our right of free speech? There is no greater place in America where the right of free speech needs to be protected than in our schools.

The fact of the matter is that I have made the choice to speak what I believe even if small minded people do try to hurt me personally for what I say. I have chosen to stand up for children, their parents, their teachers and everyone in the school community to say, "Hey, we all have the right to meaningful participation and say in what happens in schools. That right includes the right to be part of the process of choosing our principals and other school leaders." I chose to take that risk and do so out of the love of the students, their parents, and the teachers that I have developed over the years.

We have a sign on the wall at Furness High School. It says, **"If you don't stand for something, you stand for nothing."** My superiors may be able to take my position from me or stop me from advancing in the bureaucracy, but there is one thing no one can ever take away from me or anyone else who has spent their lives in schools. No one can take the love, friendship and respect I have earned from the students, their parents, their teachers and support staff within the school communities that I have had the good fortune to become part of over the years.

We all need to have a voice in what we do. There is no other way to have great schools for our children. The future of our country depends on it. The future of us all depends on it.

6

Hilltop Babe Ruth
A Lesson in School Governance

I knew for a long time that my local community athletic organization functioned far superior as an educational organization than any public school I have ever known. It is a lesson that everyone who has anything to do with education in America should learn.

Hilltop Babe Ruth stands as a model of democracy in school governance. It is a community organization whose mission is to provide Spring and Summer baseball and softball instruction, coaching and competition for over one thousand children who live in or near Haverford Township in Pennsylvania. Its governance structure is completely democratic and the parents, coaches and community volunteers do a far superior job of collectively running their organization for the benefit of children than any school I have been associated with throughout my professional career in education. It is a lesson in outstanding educational community for it is in the community of schools that we find the key to outstanding schools.

As American education moves toward different kinds of governance structures for our schools, it would do us all well to look at its simple structure and the organizational dynamics it produces. Hilltop Babe Ruth is in reality an educational organization that essentially does everything we do in schools and does it in such an amazingly efficient way. The result as we see the intellectual and emotional growth and achievement of our children, is a thing of beauty every year. It renews itself and perpetuates itself continually as it grows and develops itself along the way. It is a successful educational community we should look to as a model of effective school governance.

Any parent or guardian who signs his son or daughter up for participation in the youth athletic program of Hilltop Babe Ruth is a member of the organization. Each year there is a meeting held where the board of trustees is elected for a term of one year. Any parent member or coach of a team who attends that meeting may cast a vote for the board of trustee positions. The board of trustees then votes for the president of the league who is normally a member of the board of trustees and is elected for a term of one year. The board of trustees makes the decisions pertaining to its governance, rule making procedures and management of the organization. The president carries out the management of the organization and provides essential leadership. Everyone helps.

What Hilltop Babe Ruth does is essentially the same as what every school in America does. It teaches children how to do something that is determined by adults to be of importance to them and their development as human beings. It provides children of different ages with learning experiences that builds knowledge and develops them intellectually, athletically, socially, and emotionally. It provides both cognitive and affective education for the youth of their community exactly the same as any school in America.

Along the way it chooses and assigns coaches who teach baseball or softball and all the stuff that goes along with that mission. Collectively, they develop leagues for internal competition and develop teams for external competition. They create rules for operation and fulfillment of their mission and essentially govern themselves. They do that under the supremacy of the national Babe Ruth Association and follow the rules enacted by that superior organization as they pertain to the local association.

In the continual growth and development of the association, the parents and coaches do essentially the same things as schools, their parents, teachers and school districts do throughout America. They develop organizational structures in terms of leagues for every age group. They determine procedures for choosing and assigning children to teams and for selection of coaches and coordinators for the effective functioning of the organization. They collect funds, create fund raising initiatives, purchase uniforms and equipment, and apply funds where and how they can be effectively used to bring to fruition the purposes of the organization. They audit the books regularly with several overseers of the process.

Like schools and school districts, they acquire rights to land and use of fields through use agreements, rentals and purchases. They build facilities, fields, add fences, maintain all assets, and as the number of participants increases, they seek new and additional fields and facilities to improve the program for children.

They seek out and facilitate professional development of its teaching and coaching staff in the form of instructional clinics for their coaches, parents and players just like schools do. They evaluate their coaches and programs and assess their effectiveness. When necessary, they change programs or discontinue them entirely. They decide whether to keep or dismiss coaches based on their performance and handle complaints from parents. There is a democratic procedure for bringing complaints to the board of trustees during open meetings and they resolve disputes in a very positive manner.

There are regular meetings of the board of trustees and when necessary they call special meetings to resolve any issues that arise. It is a completely open and democratic process that would make Ben Franklin and Thomas Jefferson proud. The result is a healthy robust organization that functions as a true community for the benefit of children and the community it serves. It grows as an organization and continually improves itself.

Everything Hilltop Babe Ruth does can be analogized to schools in terms of creating classes, assigning students and teachers to classes, developing courses and curriculum, and creating instructional organizations within the major organization along with educational programs for children. The traveling teams and tournament teams are no different than the creation of advanced placement courses or star classes to challenge those who excel. There are also teams and player participation rules made for even the less gifted to wholesomely participate in the program.

Keep this simple democratic governance structure in mind as you read the succeeding chapters on the governance of our public schools and view the realities of the governance of regular school district schools, charter schools, schools managed by educational management organizations and independent schools. Hilltop Babe Ruth stands here as a lesson in the effective governance of an educational organization. It is a completely democratically governed organization where the parents, coaches who are the teachers, and community members run and govern the organization in a collective manner and actually do fulfill their collective and common mission.

It is an important example to consider and keep in mind as we begin to answer the questions raised by the Grand Hypothetical of School Governance. Charter schools in America are most often designed as independent educational organizations and the question of how they are governed will be some of the major issues of our times. The proper governance of America's increasingly growing school districts and the individual schools within them raise issues that will never go away. There are also other school governance organizations such as the independent school model that must be fully considered as our nation increasingly moves to alternative forms of schools and school governance.

The model of organizational governance represented by Hilltop Babe Ruth is very similar to the recommended model of school governance proposed by the *New* Commission on the Skills of the American Workforce that spent two years researching education practices and achievement worldwide. The commission was comprised of many of our leading Chief Executive Officers of our greatest public and private organizations and institutions both educational and non educational. In their report, *Tough Choices Tough Times* (2007), they proposed that schools of the future be limited-liability corporations run by teachers who are the stockholders who have complete control over every aspect of the school and are actually employees of the state. I would just add to that rubric that parents and the local community must be full partners in the governance process.

The models of school governance represented by Hilltop Babe Ruth, the *New* Commission, and our charter school laws require central administrations and state departments of education to take on a new role and position in the rubric of school governance. They must become enablers that support and fund the schools of the future, and they must become the overseers of schools that provide the resources and partnerships that fertilize the processes of schooling. No longer can we look to the bureaucracies of the past to implement education from afar. Effective leadership does not work that way and neither does effective governance. The *New* Commission concluded that the problem of education is not with our educators. It is the system in which educators must work (2007). If we are to truly reform our schools, we must first reform our school governance processes that enable schools to excel in their organizational dynamics.

Yes, there are hard issues and hard questions we must answer for the good of our children and the good of America. Keep in mind the example of simple and effective democratic governance represented in this chapter as we dive into the issues of school governance and examine how to implement **"governance and leadership for the 21st century."** Charter schools, independent schools, and other forms of school governance are being explored in America in the hope of finding better ways of education for our children. Doing great things for children and creating great schools for our children and their school community begins with the governance of our schools.

In the next chapter we will explore in depth the issues and realities of the governance of our schools. In the process we will take a hard look at the positives and negatives of what we are doing now and lay bare many of the improprieties and ridiculousnesses of our bureaucratic governance structures that stand as dinosaurs of the past and prevent the very collegial and collective endeavor that is necessary for great schools to emerge. We know too much about psychology. We know too much about leadership. We know too much about governance to cling to the feudalistic ways of the past. We must grow in our notions of school governance if we are to meet the needs of all of our children and serve them and their school communities to our fullest capacity.

All the while, I do not want you to lose perspective of how democracy has the power to **"set the conditions"** that allows our schools to become true communities working together for the best interests of children. **The promise of alternative forms of school governance lies in the promise of democracy!**

We may be somewhat blinded as we jump into the bramble bush of issues related to our schools, but when we emerge we will see so clearly—**the democratic imperative for our schools.**

7

On the Governance of Our Schools and the Imperative of Democracy

I read our high school American History textbook, The American Vision, and you know what I learned? It is amazing how much our nation's founders knew about school governance for the 21st century!

Schools are communities and the best form of governance for communities in America is democracy. We cannot escape that reality.

Then why are we still using an eighteenth century autocracy as the model of governance for so many of our schools and school districts? It is the 21st century and what we have learned about leadership is so much better than what autocracy can ever give us. Our students, our parents, our teachers, our communities deserve the best practices. **After all, whose school is it?**

Schools are undeniably communities. They are groups of people that interact for the common good and purpose of acting in community. They are just like our towns, cities and states. Their only real difference is that the adults that run them and govern them have the legal duty to act collectively in the best interests of students and it is through that rubric that our children, their parents and our total society reap the benefits of equal education for all. But we must always remember it is what we do for our children in schools that really matters.

Go back to chapter 3 and revisit "The Grand Hypothetical of School Governance." Look at the issue: "How can we create a governance structure for a public entity known as a public school that ensures the best interests of students and the school community is, in reality, the guiding principle that governs our school. Integral to that is the sister question: **How can we "set the conditions" for great schools to be born or emerge and maintain themselves as great schools through the years? That is the mission of school governance.**

We have already reviewed what good leadership practices for schools are in the opinions of those who have intensively studied leadership, and we probably could come to a consensus on what good schools are if we came together, debated all the issues in an open and collegial manner and drew some conclusions together and acted upon our common agreements. So how do we create a system of school governance that causes and ensures all that needs to happen in schools does happen? As architects of the social system for schools, that is our task, and it is how our founding fathers created America—they set the conditions for our country to grow into the greatest country in the world through the democratic process set out in our Constitution.

What was your answer or what was your discussion group's answer for the "Grand Hypothetical of School Governance?" What form of governance did you choose for your school? What were some of the issues that arose in your discussions or your thought processes? Did you come to a consensus? How did you resolve the issues? What structures did you put in place to ensure everything works and keeps on working and that fairness and equity is ensured? No easy answers are there?

But this I am sure: How many of you chose schools to be governed by a supreme being with unfettered, autocratic power to do what he or she wants. I will bet the answer is close to **none!** But that is the authoritarian school format that was handed down to us through the ages. It started in the middle ages through religious academies with their "headmasters," and entered into our thinking for the 20th century and we still have not progressed very far as a society. The biggest change over the centuries was when unions arrived in America and teachers became organized for collective bargaining. Our schoolteacher relations changed from "master-servant" to the "labor vs. management" of industrialized America. We went from the feudalism of the past to the industrialization of the 19th and 20th centuries (See, *New* Commission, 2007).

Both systems have entrenched us in the "master-servant" relationships of an era long gone that has not made our schools everything they can be. Our labor relations laws and processes reflect that relationship and have not yet allowed our school systems to grow past that archaic adversarial system into communities where **"professional thought guides us."** If we are ever to have great schools, we must change that dynamic and create **"true professional learning communities"** that are governed by mandated collegial behavior. **The sine qua non for great schools is collective collegial endeavor. The sine qua non for collegial behavior is democracy.** All the principles of American democracy must become embedded in our schools if we are ever to do all we need to do for our children.

If you think that maintaining our autocratic, adversarial labor vs. management history in education will create great schools, just look at our schools. The worst schools are governed the least democratically and have the worst leadership in place. That is precisely why they do not work well for children. That is a major reason why we still have such a wide achievement gap between the majority America and minority America.

The key to any outstanding school is outstanding teachers and support staff. We can never escape that reality. If we want our schools to be professional organizations, we need outstanding professionals in them and they must be truly empowered to be professionals. Professionals must be trusted to govern themselves. There is no other way to make our schools everything they should be. Without true professionalism in schools, our best and most outstanding teachers leave. They "vote with their feet!"

In urban America with our antiquated bureaucratic governance system, our best and brightest educators have left in large numbers. They have been for years. It is commonly referred to as the "brain drain" and it is a real and sad consequence of the institutionalized illnesses of our bureaucratic school governance systems throughout America. When good people have no say in what is going on around them and no control over the world of schools that they live in, they feel powerless and debilitated. They leave the school, the system and even the profession. **The brain drain in America's urban school systems is a symptom of the "unhealthy organizations" that bureaucracy most often produces. And our children must attend those schools.**

We must grow as an educational community and grow as a nation. Since the late 1980's, there have been many efforts to democratize schools and make them places where issues are hashed out and everyone works together in concert. The whole charter school movement came out of the realization of our leaders in the educational community of universities, colleges, government think tanks and local schools and school systems that the bureaucratic structures of our school systems were failing our children (*New* Commission, 2007). Today, our School Reform Commission in Philadelphia and other school system bodies of school directors and trustees struggle with how to set up schools that meet the needs of students, their families and the school communities we serve. They struggle with how to govern them, lead them and manage them so the end result is that our children grow in every way as individuals and achieve to high levels in a wholesome environment.

We will take a hard look at some of the issues of charter school governance later in this chapter, but we should keep in mind that they were created in most states to empower teachers and community members to start and control their own schools. In Pennsylvania, charter schools were explicitly started for that reason and the General Assembly, the legislative body of the state, mandated that they be "non-profit corporations" with "boards of trustees." The Pennsylvania *Charter School Law,* like those of most other states, mandates that the charter must state how members of the board of trustees are "appointed or elected." 24 Pa.C.S. §17-1719-A(4).

Clearly, our legislatures contemplated charter schools being democratic organizations, and one of the ethical and public policy issues we will consider is this: If boards of trustees for charter schools can be selected by some individual, or some coalition such as the coalition of founders or some other entity, or their trusteeships can be "handed down" to others of their choosing in some manner, then have we not created property rights in our public schools for individuals or groups of individuals? Then where do the fiduciary duties of the board of trustees go? Who are the beneficiaries? Do fiduciary duties go to the founder or coalition of founders or a supervening group? Or do fiduciary duties go to the children of the school, their families and the school community. **Whose school is it? Remember, it is a "public" school! What is our public policy?**

Most school systems in America are basically democratic organizations. In Pennsylvania, like the other states, the members of the "board of school directors" are by law elected by the local community. It is only in big cities that we have appointed school boards, and it is largely in urban America that schools are taken over by the state and reform commissions are appointed by governors or other governmental officials. In Philadelphia, the schools were taken over by the state pursuant to a written agreement between the governor and the mayor of Philadelphia consistent with Pennsylvania's *Education Empowerment Act* that provided for the state takeover of schools. 24 Pa.C.S. §§17-1701-B—17-1716-B. The agreement created a School Reform Comission (SRC) consisting of three members appointed by the governor and two members appointed by the mayor. Again, none are elected or chosen by the people of Philadelphia. The issue there is do we then have a school system that is governed by and for the government and politicians, or do we have a school system that is governed by and for the people?

While there are many reasons why smaller school districts throughout America have better achievement test scores, it would be very interesting to do a research study that correlates the degree of democraticity in school systems to student achievement and other indicia of successful schools. But this we know for sure, most of our blue ribbon schools can be found in school systems that have elected school boards. And we all must admit, our urban school systems with their lack of democracy in governance are largely failing our students and communities.

Certainly, school systems that have elected boards of school directors are more responsive to the voices of parents, teachers and other stakeholders. The board members know that eventually the citizenry of the local community that they are supposed to serve will get their opportunity to "vote the bums out." Yes, those school systems are smaller and the local community and the board members are more likely to know what is happening in their schools, but that is precisely why the schools in those schools systems are better. The governing boards are **"closely connected"** to the schools and know what is happening in them. The community holds the trump card and a significant portion of the community care about their schools. But most importantly—the community has the right to vote for their school board members!

Let me give you two great examples of how "community standards prevail" in democratically governed school districts. First, in Chichester, Pennsylvania, just a few years back, the superintendent of schools was put on the hot seat by the school board who hired a lawyer to investigate issues within the district. The lawyer pursued the superintendent like an attack dog and she put so much undue pressure upon the man that he committed suicide. The Chichester community was so insensed at the state of affairs that they voted out the entire board of school directors. They made a clear statement as a community, "We do not want that stuff to be happening in our community."

Another example that has to do with curricular decisions: Most of us have read about the school district in Pennsylvania where the school board wanted to instill "intelligent design" as a science to be taught along with the theory of evolution. It was clearly an effort to impose religion and the religious beliefs of a few upon the many. Not only was it ruled to be an unconstitutional effort to "establish" a religion in public schools, but the community voted out the school board members who were behind the effort. The community stood and spoke through the electoral process of democracy.

In both those school districts, democracy was the "purification process" for things they did not want to see happening in their schools and school districts. Eternal vigilance is the price of democracy. It is only through democracy that right and justice prevail. Without the schools being open to the scrutiny of the community in a transparent and public manner, we can never be sure that right prevails.

In large urban school districts, the people have no such say in what happens in their school system and they have very little if any say in what happens in their schools. They have no power to do anything. They are stuck with their schools for better or for worse. That is why the school choice movement is beginning to take hold—at least people then can "vote with their feet." I submit that the ability for the school community to demand to be given a meaningful voice in what happens in their schools is precisely why those democratically governed school districts produce more blue ribbon schools. They have more say in what happens in their schools and who becomes school leaders including the superintendent and the principal! They have a truer voice. They have more democracy.

Here is a contrasting example of what happens when there is no democracy in school governance: In Camden, New Jersey, the schools have been taken over by the state, the elected school board was removed, and a board of control is running the school district. A principal of one of its finest schools went public and said that his superior, an assistant superintendent, told him to cheat on the state test that is used to evaluate progress toward the requirements of *No Child Left Behind* for Adequate Yearly Progress as measured by standardized achievement tests. Within two months he was evaluated by the exact superior he had accused of breaching professional ethics, and he was recommended for removal from his position. The superintendent supported the removal and it went to the appointed board of oversight. They ratified the action and the governor of New Jersey declined to get involved. The principal was fired for doing the right thing for children! Where is the ethics? Where is the moral purpose?

The principal did what was the ethically right thing for children and was therefore removed from office. Yes, he does have a cause of action in a whistleblower's suit, but that is of little avail to the students and the school community. A student spoke volumes. She was crushed and said, "What they are saying to me is that they do not believe I can pass the test on my own, that they have to cheat for me to do well. What does that say about me?" What does it say about our system? Yes, the elected school board did not work miracles in Camden, but the appointed school board did worse. Why? Because of the inherent inability of the bureaucratic governance system to produce a moral result!

Because the principal did the right thing for children, he was stripped of his livelihood. Even more scandalous is the fact that they illegally took his health benefits away and he had a young daughter that had a serious stomach disorder and needed those health benefits to survive. Several months after that event, the Superintendent of Schools was accused of other breaches of ethics in office, and was removed in the face of a criminal action. What a disgrace in America!

Please always remember this: We are talking about public schools and our children are compelled to attend them or pay for a private school or be home schooled! Our schools and school systems must be communities of high ideals, competency, fairness, good faith and fair dealings. So how do we ensure that?

It is one thing to say that everyone should have a voice in what we do in schools, but it is yet another to create a school governance structure that ensures that actually does happen. If we want to set the conditions for best practices in schools, we need to set the conditions through our governance structures. Democratic leadership practices are the best leadership practices for our schools, and it logically follows that democratic governance systems are the best practices for school governance!

If we want to have great schools for our children, we must have democracy in our schools. Democracy in education is paramount!

7.1

The Essential Elements of Democracy

Our Constitution sets forth the ideals of governance we choose to live by in our country. We cannot leave those ideals at the schoolhouse steps because it is in those ideals that we find our greatness.

I have always been involved with my local school governance since I became a teacher in Philadelphia, but it was not until I witnessed the state takeover of our schools did I begin deeply contemplating the issues of school and organizational governance. The old school board was disbanded and the School Reform Commission was enacted. They went about sorting out the issues of founding and governing charter schools, independent schools, privately managed schools, and traditional schools managed by the school district. At the same time, I read a few articles written in response to the debacle of the Enron corporation that called for more democracy in the governance of corporations. I studied laws controlling corporations and schools and read numerous statutes and articles on governance of organizations, but by far my most helpful source was our history book used in Philadelphia's high schools—*The American Vision.* How profound a discovery—it was like the apple hit me in the head.

There it was right there in the chapter on our American governance system, our Constitution, its Bill of Rights and other amendments. Right there in our history book were laid out all the elements of democracy. Right there in front of me was all that is necessary to set the conditions for great things to happen within schools!

Before we look at various ways to incorporate democracy into the governance of regular school district schools, charter schools as nonprofit corporations, and most importantly, our failing urban schools, let us take a look at the principles of governance America stands for and our children have died for. And could we please remember this as we review them—our children are dying for them today as we try to instill democracy in Iraq. Yet we do not determine to wholly instill those principles in all of our schools! Where are our heads?

The three most basic elements of an effective democracy are: (1) separation of powers, (2) those governed choose their own leaders, and (3) term limits on leaders. Added to that, the other concepts that are essential to effective

democratic governance can be found in the amendments to our Constitution especially the Bill of Rights. All we need to know is right there!

We have already visited much of what must happen within schools for them to be successful. The Constitution of the United States of America provides all the answers to the governance questions for our schools. The most important ideals necessary for successful schools can all be found within it. In addition to the three most basic ideals noted above, the most important rights provided for the people in the Bill of Rights and other amendments are the right to free speech, the due process rights including the right to participate in the governance of our schools which is embedded in our Constitution and the 14th Amendment that guarantees equal protection of the laws.

We will look closely at the traditional model of governance of schools through enactment of boards of education, and the "nonprofit corporation" governance structures, but first, let us now take a look at the governance ideals represented in our Constitution and compare them with what actually happens in schools.

Separation of Powers

Separation of powers is in our Constitution because our framers recognized that absolute power corrupts absolutely, and they concluded that a "balance of power" was necessary for good governance. It is also true for schools, especially when the board of school directors or board of trustees is not "closely connected" to the schools, and therefore, cannot possibly know what is happening in them. The question for 21st century school governance really boils down to the question: **Does the leadership team sit at a round table, an elongated table, or at a table beneath the throne. It may sound facetious, but that is really the issue!**

It was because England was ruled by a Kingship, the ultimate dictatorship, and the feudalism of the eighteenth century that democracy emerged in America as a better form of governance. Our bureaucratic schools are governed by the same feudalistic practices of the eighteenth century. Look at the organizational charts of any bureaucracy. Power is delegated down from the school board, to the CEO, to regional superintendents or specific offices such as the Office for Senior High Schools, and then to the principals. Management in today's bureaucracies is of little difference than the ruling class of the nobility—the aristocracy.

The principal in bureaucratic schools has virtually unfettered, absolute power because whatever they do, whether right or wrong, is almost always supported by the bureaucrats above them. In exchange, the principal is expected to be unquestioning in his or her loyalty to his or her superiors in the chain of command. Failure to do so is "insubordination," punishable by removal from the position and eventual firing. Why are a principal's acts always supported either right or wrong, moral or immoral? Because those in power want to make it absolutely clear to the teachers and staff that they are in power! It is the power game—the, "I am the boss and you are not" syndrome. That "I am in charge" mentality is directly destructive to the collegial processes we must facilitate to create great schools! It is based on the archaic, eighteenth century notions of feudalism and the modern day phenomenon of bossism.

In Philadelphia, and elsewhere we can be sure, the joke we talk about in the trenches when leadership and principal positions and opportunities are announced and centralized selection processes prescribed is that they are looking for "yes men and women." It is said that they will never select anyone that is not a "yes" man. They will never select anyone who wants to challenge the process. But as our experts in leadership tell us, great leaders do just that—challenge the process! (Kouzes and Posner, 2003b, p. xiii). **Great leadership is not a yes game—it is a why can't we game!**

The only growth from that headmaster as a superior being mentality that our school governance structures went through was in the growth of unionism in school systems. When teachers organized, it was to demand their human rights as individuals. They were by law granted rights for collective bargaining and **"mutual support and protection."** The extensive labor contracts we see today now stand as a large part of the governance structures for schools. But again, that labor vs. management mentality most often creates nothing but **adversarial relationships** between management and subordinates. As a result our schools are often infected with union busting tactics and teacher bashing by administrators that have become institutional illnesses. Debilitated morale and negative synergy within the school community are the symptoms of that **unhealthy mentality.**

Juxtapositioned to that relationship, are the issues of parental and student rights in schools. Do they have a right to participate in the processes of schools and decision-making? Or does the school board and administration dictate all things? Certainly, the Federal statute *No Child Left Behind* and related regulations mandates parental involvement but what are the parameters? Although it is probably an "open question" under constitutional law because there are no precedents directly on point, I believe the only answer the Supreme Court could hand down is, yes, parents and students of age do have a constitutional right to participation in those processes. I call that **"participative due process"** and I believe that right is embedded in our due process provisions of the Fourth, Fifth, Sixth and Fourteenth Amendments. Schools are public bodies and every citizen certainly has the right to be heard.

Parental rights in schools do permeate the schoolhouse walls through various statutes. The most often recognized parental right is through the Federal *Individuals With Disabilities Education Act (IDEA)* that requires that parents be part of a disabled student's Individual Educational Planning Team (IEP team). There are various other Federal and individual state statutes that do give parents various "statutory rights" but not too many explicitly state parents be given the right to participate in the governance of their schools. Various state "sunshine acts" do require school boards to have open meetings and allow community members a right to speak at those meetings. Yet we applaud the abstract concept of "shared decision-making" and "shared leadership." To truly give parents a real and **"legitimate voice"** in what happens in their schools, we need to have **"shared governance."**

A modern issue is whether the community at large has a right to participate in the governance of our schools. In most local school districts in America they do participate in governance because they get to vote for school board members. But does their right to participate stop there? A major theme of the last Principals' Academy I attended was "community engagement." What is the process? Where are the parameters?

These are just some of the issues and rights that need to be balanced in our schools. **Our founding fathers recognized the need for there to be a "balance of power" in order to "balance the equities" through governance.**

The **"balance of powers"** our forefathers created is the legislative branch, the executive branch and the judicial branch. When I first answered the questions of the "Grand Hyperbole of School Governance," I created a constitutional design for a charter school I wanted to found. After contemplating all the issues for months, I felt that the "constitutional design" was so much superior to the "corporate design" for school governance because of the balance of power issues of governance. There are ways to "reconcile" the two governance models and the issues of balance of powers. Many of America's greatest organizations are created by constitutions including the teacher's and administrator's unions!

The school governance constitutional design I first created included a board of trustees, a school council and a chief executive officer. The board of trustees stood as the judicial branch that watched over the processes of the school and had the power and authority to determine whether things were happening as they should and also the power and authority to step in and correct any improprieties. The school council stood as the legislative branch that created the educational plan, set policies, listened to the people, and had **"legitimate powers"** within the organizational structure of the school. The CEO, who was really the "lead teacher" was the executive branch with the duty and responsibility to run the school in accordance to the governance plan and wishes of the school community.

There was a "supremacy clause" just like in our Constitution to mandate that supervening governance bodies, their policies and mandates, statutes and regulations were followed. Centralized initiatives in curriculum and instruction could still be implemented via that mechanism.

Yes, the school community chose the CEO/Principal and there were term limits just like in our Constitution of the United States of America. In just about every situation I reviewed where school councils were enacted, and the school community was allowed to choose the principal of their school, it was the school council that did the choosing. The democracy was in the fact that the individual school council members were elected democratically or selected by local union representatives who were elected, and in turn, chose the representatives of the teachers and staff for the school council.

In my first constitution for a school I developed a way for the CEO/Principal, preferably and hereinafter called the lead teacher, to be directly elected by the staff and parents of the school just like the president, governor and mayor is directly elected by the people. That is the most democratic way to do it. I based it on the same election process we put in practice in Philadelphia for local school communities to vote on whether to establish a school council. Each "family" who had a student enrolled in the school had one vote and each staff member had one vote. If both the families and the staff voted in favor of establishing a school council, it did so. In my original constitution, in respect to voting for the lead teacher, there was a tiebreaking procedure.

We actually did use that process in voting for a school council at Furness High School in Philadelphia. It worked fine. The problem that ensued is that, subsequently, the state took over the school district, Paul Vallas, was hired as the CEO, the recently imposed principal of Furness unilaterally disbanded the school council, and the top down style that was imposed upon the school district by Paul Vallas's "Chicago regime" made it clear where the new power structures of the school district lied. It was definitely not with the people of Philadelphia or the school community of Furness High School. Our school has been going down hill ever since.

Later in this chapter, we will take a deeper look at school councils, their make up, and what we need to do to make them work for children. The SRC governing Philadelphia's public schools in their Declaration of Beliefs has stated that their goal is to establish school councils in every school. The issue that needs to be resolved is what enforceable "legitimate powers" does a school council have within the organizational governance structure of our schools?

My experience in several schools and study of governance lead me to believe there has to be a separation of powers for schools to become great schools. That is one of the elements for setting the conditions for great things to happen in schools and debating out all the issues that ultimately do arise in schools.

Choosing Our Own Leaders

There is nothing more basic to democracy than the notion that the populace chooses its own leaders. That is the ultimate accountability. For schools to become great schools, the entire school community must be involved in the process of choosing its leaders. That is the only way to establish **"leadership credibility."** Without credibility, the leader is powerless to lead. At the heart of effective leadership is credibility! We can not escape that reality.

Think back to Chapter 5, "Leadership for the 21st Century." Remember Kouzes and Posner's unequivocal statement made after over twenty years of studying effective and ineffective leadership—**"The foundation of leadership is *credibility*."** It is also true that **"the foundation of an effective leadership selection process is *credibility!*"** Those two concepts are inseparable.

Unless the followership sees the principal selection process as ultimately credible, the leader will have difficulty establishing the requisite credibility to lead the community effectively. **The greatest gift we can give a new leader for a school is the gift that they were chosen through a credible process that was an extremely "inclusive process" with maximum "transparency."** It must be open, honest, fair and inclusive. Everyone in the school community must be involved in the process. If the followership does choose its own leader, it will go beyond themselves to help that leader be effective. That is just human nature and it is supported by the psychological phenomenon of cognitive dissonance: "If we chose the principal, how can we say he or she is not good? That makes us not good so let's help him or her be a good principal."

When a principal or any other school leader such as a CEO is imposed upon a school community, they have a steep mountain to climb before they are accepted as the leader. Remember Kouzes and Posner's statement from their study of leadership: "It seems there are a number of tests a leader must go through before the followership grants them the title of *leader*" (1986). **That is why impositional leadership is so bad.** It is not only a terrible way to "match" a leader's style with the school community, it puts the leader at a disadvantage in establishing trust. Remember trust and respect must be earned!

Whenever I have seen a principal sent to a school to "turn it around, it has always meant "straighten out" those teachers. I have never seen that work in my experience, and when we get to the chapter on toxic school cultures, we will see that is precisely the attitude that creates a toxic school culture!

Again, let me repeat this question: What would you say if our President was chosen by our Supreme Court, and in turn he chose the governors of our states, and in turn they chose the mayors of our cities and towns, and in turn they chose the members of the legislatures. We would say "that is insane." We would say that is totalitarian. We would say, "Where are we? In Russia?" Well, that is precisely what we do in school system bureaucracies. And we wonder why so many of our schools do not work for children?

Schools are communities just like our cities and towns. They need to govern themselves, and lead themselves if we are ever to set the conditions for great schools. **It is, and always must be, the collective school community that is accountable for the educational product of schools!** They must do that within the **"supremacy clause"** of whatever founding body supervises the establishment of schools and all the supervening laws, regulations and initiatives that derive from those supervening governmental bodies. That is how our blue ribbon schools and school districts do it in the vast majority of our municipalities in America. They take the mandates of the legislatures and state departments of education, add what the local community wants, and then implement it all through their own individually substantiated manner. Why can't we do it in our big cities? We will answer that question when we get to Chapter 9, "The Psychological Perspective." It is all about power and ego—two of the most corrupting forces known to man! We need honesty in this conversation.

That is why the autocratic attitudes found in the leaders of our big city bureaucracies, and even in many of our small municipalities, are so destructive of the organization and debilitative to those working in our schools and so frustrating to the parents who want their schools to excel for their children. There is a definite lack of credibility and fairness in how we choose our leaders and impose them and other aspects of schooling upon the schools. It is like, what would happen if Washington D.C. ran our local communities? It would not work would it? Then why would we think it works for schools?

In Philadelphia, like other school bureaucracies, there are no discernible rules and regulations for how we choose our principals and other school leaders. The sad reality is that we all are slapped in the face with the hard reality of our times—"They do whatever they want." That is the refrain of the choir in the trenches. The process for choosing principals in Philadelphia changes by the week. There is no consistency, there is no logic, there is no *credibility.*

The joke in the trenches is, "Whose friend or relative are they putting in today?" That is a sad statement. Some people have to go through long principal training programs. Some people are chosen unilaterally by regional superintendents or such. Some people are "put in" because they happen to be in the right place at the right time. Some people are put in place simply because they were the only assistant principal when the principal was removed or left abruptly. What would we say if our president, governors and mayors were "put in" in that manner? It would be a call to arms. Where is the call to arms for our children and their parents in schools?

Prior to the state takeover of Philadelphia's schools, there was a process for the selection of principals by the local school community. It was called the **"site selection process."** That is basically the process that is used in most blue ribbon school districts in America. A team of teachers, support staff, parents, community leaders, administrators, and in high schools, a student, selects the principal and the assistant principals. That is how many principals are chosen in America. If done in a credible manner, it can often work effectively, but if a mistake is made, there must be a process for correction.

In the Haverford Township School District in Pennsylvania, a school district that contains blue ribbon schools, they have even a more inclusive way of choosing their principals. Before the school board makes a final decision, they first, in an open manner, invite input from the parents, community at large and faculty of the schools. The School Board then "votes" on the basis of that input. It is a completely **"informed decision."** They vote on what they see as the best interests of the school community which really does have the best interests of their children at heart. If the community does not like what the school board does, they "vote the bums out."

Yes, Philadelphia is broken down into regions and the regional superintendents want to choose their principals. And the school communities want to choose their principals. In turn, the school principals want to choose their own teachers. The reality of the matter is that there must be a **"symbiotic relationship."** Both teachers and principals need to be chosen for schools in a collective and community based manner. That is the only way to support and maintain **"collegiality."** Remember, we are all in this together.

Kouzes and Posner accurately point out that **"leadership can not be exercised from a distance." Neither can effective governance be exercised from a distance. We are hooked to that reality.** That is why charter schools are being created—to make governance of schools local. Charter schools, if instituted and governed properly, are the realization of the concept of **"school based management"** that has been with us for many years now.

A caveat that everyone should keep in mind when we select by representative committee is the issue of **"stacking."** Because of the games people play, especially people in power, there are often attempts to "stack" the committee with like minded people. I have seen situations where temporary "Acting Principals" and other administrators have actually gotten away with choosing the selection committee members and thereby controlling the whole selection process. That is similar to how the president of the United States tries to stack the Supreme Court with either liberals or conservatives. Stacking is not a democratic ideal. It is unethical in most situations and creates serious credibility issues.

To make a selection committee democratic, it must be truly representative. Our president was originally elected through representatives, because our form of government is a "representative democracy." However, our nation determined that did not work well enough so we went to a direct election system only blemished by our electoral college system. When the selection committee is elected democratically or selected by a democratically elected body such as a parent organization or elected union body, only then is the process seen as credible.

What is really demeaning and disheartening in bureaucratic situations is when "paternalism" sets in. The initial process in Philadelphia for site selection of principals and assistant principals was that the selection committee chose three final candidates and listed them as numbers 1, 2 and 3. The central administration then determined if the choices were acceptable to them! How demeaning to the professionals that man our schools and actually hold our schoolhouses together. I assure you our central administrators are no more qualified to choose the principals than the teachers. They are great people, believe me they are, but they are no more qualified to "vote" than anyone else in our school communities. For them to think that they are is pure egotism. There is no place in a collegial organization for paternalism. What I realize every day when I observe teachers in our schools is that most of them are at least as smart as me!

It is again, just the power game. **If the professionals in schools cannot be trusted to be professionals, there is no hope for our schools. Professionals can choose their own leaders—so can parents—so can community representatives. They all must have power in the process or they can never have a "true voice."** If we do truly set up credible systems for schools to choose their own leaders properly, I would argue our schools will improve dramatically. **Leadership matters—and so does leadership credibility!**

A caveat for choosing representative committees to choose the principal is that, once selected as a committee member, the representative usually votes their own inclinations. They do not think, "How should I vote given the makeup of those I represent?" They think, "Who do **I like?**" I'll vote for that person." Anyone who has substantial experience in interviewing before a selection committee for a job, realizes that selection committee members come with their own biases and inclinations. That is readily apparent and brutally clear in the face of the interview process.

The issue really is who is empowered to "vote" for the principal within the organizational power structure. We can never escape that question when we speak of governance of any organization. Someone or some collective body in any organizational structure must be empowered to "vote" for the principal leader. Someone must elect the principal leader! It is usually the school board, trustees, or school reform commission members. In Philadelphia, the CEO is elected by the members of the School Reform Commission. Five people have the organizational power to vote. Then the CEO has the singular power to "vote" for the principals of schools. They can delegate that vote to someone. It could be the Chief Academic Officer, a regional superintendent, or another type of bureaucrat. The terms "selection" and "appointment" are just other names for "vote." The power to unilaterally appoint a leader is really the power to vote being placed in one person. In autocracies, the vote goes to the king or his nobility. **In American democracy every member of the organization gets to vote! Every member of the community gets one vote. Everyone is equal—each citizen gets one vote. What a novel thought for school governance!**

Who gets to vote for our school leaders is a primary issue for school governance. We can never escape the importance of that issue. In your answer to the "Grand Hypothetical of School Governance" who got to vote for the leader of the school?

In the corporate world there are a variety of types of stock. Stock in corporations are the ownership rights in the corpus of the corporation. Essentially, there are two types of stock: "voting" stock and "non-voting" stock. There are major corporate issues there, but the right to vote is a major issue in any type of organization whether public or private. **Who holds the power and "right to vote" is a major issue in every organization. I would argue it is the most important issue we need to decide upon in our grand discussion of school governance!**

One reason I believe so much in the need for democracy in education is that my experience has shown me so many times that every other way of choosing our leaders is just so ineffective and devoid of merit. The most ineffective way I have experienced, and sadly it is the way many bureaucratic school systems choose their principals, is through a testing procedure. In Philadelphia, the City Charter requires all civil service positions to be tested positions. The process that has always been in place, sometimes for actual placement of principals and often for screening prospective principals, is a handwritten essay examination where they give one or two essay questions and score the answers. Principals are then chosen and assigned based on the score on a subjective test!

First, the scorers are almost never trained in any credible manner. Second, nobody takes the time to read the answers carefully. Third, if your handwriting is poor, nobody will pay attention to what you write. Fourth, there is always a "model answer" that the scorers are given as the right answer. That model answer is often an arguably wrong answer and is always just someone's opinion. What it always boils down to is a game of "who can match the model answer!" Imagine that. The leaders of one of our most important organizations are chosen based on a game of who guesses the right answer! Again, what would you say if we chose our president, and our governors and our mayors in that manner?

What amazes me is that we still use such questionable testing practices in our educational organizations, when as educators, we use the concepts of "validity" and "reliability" every day when we test our students on achievement tests and informal tests! There is just no way of creating a formal handwritten test for our leaders that has any indicia of validity and reliability whatsoever! It is like giving a written test to decide who makes the baseball team! **Leadership is not a science it is an "ability." It can only be tested in the field under actual playing conditions.**

Our prospective school leaders can only be effectively tested through democracy. When I was chosen by the site selection team at Furness, they first telephoned teachers they knew from other schools where I had worked. It is only after they got opinions about my true character from people who had seen me perform in the field, that they chose to vote for me!

A far superior way to "rate" prospective principals would be to visit the schools they work at and ask the teachers, support staff, parents, and in high schools, students their opinions. With what we know about psychology today, that could be done in a very organized manner. Every organization or person that has studied leadership has their own leadership assessment tool. A more valid assessment tool would include indicia of "Leadership in the Eye of the Followers!"

That leads us to another "who gets to vote issue." The arcane practice of principals being chosen "for" schools by central administrators who have never even set foot into the school they are choosing the principal for! How could they possibly make an **"informed decision"** on what type of leadership the school needs? That happens time and time again in America's schools. I can well argue on the basis of legal precedent that the leadership of a school district who has the responsibility of choosing a principal for a school has a **"legal duty"** to consult with and get input from a school community before they make any decision as to who they are going to select and appoint as a principal of any public school in America. The legal principal of **"informed consent"** is well settled in our law. If decision-makers choose to choose principals for schools and CEO's at any level, they have an affirmative duty to use **"due care"** in choosing the principal or CEO. Due care responsibilities would factually manifest themselves in requiring that the decision-makers actively and professionally seek out information about the school and its community that would enable the decision-makers to make an **"informed decision."**

I submit that failure to do so is negligence under our law. Negligence is lack of due care. It is the lack of reasonable effort that an ordinarily prudent person would use under similar circumstances. All people under our American jurisprudence system have a legal duty to use the level of due care consistent with the level of care a reasonable person would use under similar circumstances. That is known as the **"reasonable person standard"** and failure to do so makes us legally liable for damages under our laws of negligence. In school settings, we are all professional employees under our state statutes. Therefore, we have a higher level of due care. It is not just "the reasonable person standard" we must use; it is the **"reasonable professional standard"** we are legally obligated to use.

The problem for the schoolhouse community is what is the remedy under the law for breach of that professional responsibility? Can we sue our school leaders for damages? Can we sue our school leaders for breach of their fiduciary duties of loyalty, care and good faith? If you or I drive our cars with a lack of due care and we hit a person and cause damages, that person has a legal cause of action against us. They can sue us for money damages. Is there such a practical legal remedy for breach of the duty of care and loyalty in public school settings? Not really.

That is why we need democracy. **That is why it is imperative to have democracy in the governance of schools. It is the purification process for wrongs in schools! The only viable remedy we have for breach of professional responsibility to our schoolchildren, their parents and the entire school community is to "vote the bums out!" That is accountability!**

This is the scenario I am speaking about that just happened less than two months previous to my writing of this chapter. The central administration announced a position for several "turn around principals." What they planned to do is send them to Virginia for a college program that purports to be able to teach principals how to turn schools around. They imposed the principals upon the school communities without including them in the selection process at all. They interviewed for that position and used questions designed to determine if the candidates had the school district's qualities of leadership that I described in Chapter 5. The interviewers had never even visited those high schools and never did a professional analysis of the needs of the school community. One administrator was in charge of the Head Start program for pre-kindergartners and the other was a former principal of an academically selective school. Then we went to another two interviewers. One was a professor from Drexel University and the other was the new Regional Superintendent who had run an elementary school that did raise test scores.

Not one of those principal selectors had any experience or expertise on turning a high school around. Not one of them had taken the time to visit the schools and speak with anyone in the school community. Yet they are the only ones who were going to "vote" for the principal leader of that community! Now ladies and gentlemen of the jury, I submit to you that is negligence. It is breach of the duty of care I spoke about in chapter 2. I guarantee you those schools are not getting turned around any time soon. Check out their standardized test sores in two years. The proof is in the pudding!

Why should they get to vote for the leader of those school communities? They do not belong to those school communities. They get to choose the principals because of bureaucratic elitism and administrative arrogance.

I am sorry folks, but democracy is just a better way of choosing our leaders.

Again, it comes down to the analogy I spoke of at the beginning of this section: Does the leadership team sit at a round table, an elongated table, or at a table beneath the throne? It may sound facetious, but that is really the issue! And the answer in America can only be that we are equals. **We do believe in equality, don't we? If we do not, then there is little hope for our children.**

A "Why Can't We?" Question

One of the inspirational moments that led me to write this book happened shortly after the takeover of Philadelphia's schools. James Nevels, the School Reform Commission Chair who was appointed by the Governor and Paul Vallas, the new CEO invited us to a "Principals' Night Out" at the newly built National Constitution Center across from Independence Hall in Philadelphia. The Constitution Center entertained us with a spectacular program complete with voices of the past of our nation's founders and greatest leaders. It was awesome to see and certainly was inspirational.

Afterwards both Jim Nevels and Paul Vallas made great speeches about the benefits of our great American **"participative democracy"** and all it has done for Americans. Of course, they spoke about equality and the need for our schools to provide equal opportunity for all if we are to meet our American ideals. At that moment in time, Tomas Hanna, a strong willed autocrat who was in charge of the new principal selection process, sat next to me, but symbolically, on the other side of the aisle. Yes, we are friends, and yes at that time we had had a disagreement. I believed in democracy and he was at that time acting in autocracy.

My question for all three is this: **Why can't we govern our schools and school system on the same principals embedded in our Constitution?** Food for thought! Remember Kouzes and Posner's conclusions on leadership. Our leaders are judged by their actions not what they say. Paul Vallas has a reputation for going around saying how parents need to be part of our schools, but when it comes right down to it, our parents are more often than not excluded from the governance of our schools.

But here is another "Why can't we?" question I wish to ask, and it is this: It is the modern trend for school districts and their teacher selection teams to ask prospective teachers to give them a "demonstration lesson" when they are interviewing for a job. The rationale is that it is an actual view of how they would teach and make the selection process more valid.

Well, here is a scenario of a process that would give us a similar "demonstration lesson" of how a prospective principal would fare in a real life situation that is comparable to what he or she would actually do as leader of the school. It would also be the most democratic way of choosing our principals. It would actually be the highest level of democratic practice in keeping with our Constitution. It is not only possible to do it this way, but it is far superior to any other process for choosing our leaders, and is superior to the selection committee. It is the same process we use for choosing our presidents, governors and mayors of our cities and towns—**direct election of the principal or lead teacher of a school by the members of the school community.**

It can very well be done using the same process that has already proven successful in our schools in Philadelphia for voting on whether to have a school council or not! So do not sit and think it can never work, because it can. Each school community member who is employed at the school would get one vote. And each "family" who has a student or students enrolled in the school would get one vote. To make it equal and fair each group, staff and families, would vote separately like our House of Representatives and Senate does. If there is agreement, which I believe would most often be the case, then that person would be the principal leader for a specific term in office. If there is not a consensus, all you need is a run-off election and a tiebreaker scheme.

Before the election, every candidate would be afforded the opportunity to present his or her case to the school community in an assembly in the auditorium. They would have one hour to speak to the faculty, parents and any community member who wishes to attend. The candidates would entertain questions in an open format, and the school community could judge for themselves and decide who should be their leader. Or is that too American?

That is certainly a more open, honest and ultimately fair and *credible* process than the selection committee approach or any other approach I have alluded to herein. It eliminates all the games people play in selection committee dynamics and certainly gives everyone input into the process. All the applicants would have to be certified by the state the same way we do it now, and local school districts could even have a testing procedure and create a **"pool of eligibles"** that would qualify the applicants. In Philadelphia and other school systems, a pool of eligibles has often been used in the past.

In the process of principal selection, there has always been the question of whether to choose someone from within the school such as a vice principal or go outside and bring someone in to run the school. The best way to decide that question is ask the school community—only they can answer that. Trust the school community. They are great people everywhere. As was stated by the great CEO of the computer chip-maker Monolithic memories, Irvin Federman, "Trust is a risk game—the leader must ante up first" (quoted in Kouzes and Posner, 1986, p. 56). So Supreme Leaders of the land of equality—ante up!

It is time we started thinking outside the box. Look at the data. What we are doing now is not working well for our children in bureaucratic school systems. If we want to create schools that serve our children, their parents and the total society, and "set the conditions for greatness," we need to change the way we are governing our schools—it is a "Why can't we game!"

Why can't the school communities of our schools choose the people they want to have as their leaders? Why can't they have the principal they want? Why not?

Term Limits and Renewal

"We need renewal! Renewal for our schools! They need a renewed vigor! They need new life, new ideas, and new leadership! We need change! What we are doing is not working! Our teachers and staff are tired and in need of inspiration. Everyone seems to just be doing the same old things. We need reform!" That is a constant call from both inside and outside of our schools, especially when our schools seem to lose their collective enthusiasm, their morale and even hope. Renewal and change are two of the driving forces behind the whole school reform movement. When we speak of democracy we must recognize that term limits are in our constitutions for a reason. **The beauty of term limits for leaders is that it gives us automatic renewal!**

The third essential element of democracy is the time limit on term in office for our leaders. It is how we ensure we get and keep our outstanding leaders. It is how we ensure our school communities renew their vigor and life every so often. It is part of how we set the conditions for ensuring constant positive synergy and change with the times and new ideas in education. Term limits for our school leaders are as necessary to good school governance as they are for our states, cities and towns, because they too, are ultimately communities.

Schools are communities and their demographics of student and parent populations do represent the demographics of the local community as it pertains to that school. It is the **"community standards"** that must always prevail in a democratic society. The hopes and aspirations of the students and parents must be the guiding forces for our schools. Yes, they do need to be inspired to dream, to hope, to work hard for achievement, and that is a mission for leadership, but if we are to find and keep that great leader for that community, we need term limits. As was said before, the mission of school communities is a collective mission. Leadership matters and it is a collective mission to always improve leadership. Leadership always must change if we are to have a student, parent and school community based focus. Otherwise, we are always sadly stuck to the community serving the leader and not the leader serving the community.

If a leader is not outstanding, at the end of his or her term, all we need to do is choose someone else. If the new leader is outstanding, we keep him or her. If not, we select someone new again. In that manner there is a constant seeking out for the best leaders. In most school districts in America, principals and other school leaders are given term contracts and are reevaluated at the end of their term, but in our urban areas meshed in bureaucracy, principals are often principals for life. And as Haberman points out, urban school districts are stuck with many **"administrative non leaders"** (Haberman, 1999). There are many schools in America that are stuck with ineffective leaders because of the lack of mandatory term limits.

Let us take a look at how it works in Philadelphia, again, our seat of democracy. Principals in Philadelphia are governed by the state statute that created the Commonwealth Association of School Administrators, a collective bargaining association. Under that law and related court and administrative law decisions, once a principal is "appointed" by the school board, he or she is a principal for life. The principal can only be fired or demoted if violative of a very few atrocious acts, insubordination, job abandonment, or if they are proven incompetent with documented evidence. In reality it boils down to a principal is appointed for life unless proven to be incompetent or guilty of an egregious act. They can be removed from any particular school because of "managerial prerogative" but they still must be paid their full salary. What happens in Philadelphia and other bureaucracies in America is a principal who is removed is sent to an administrative office, but at the first opportunity, the district sends them right back into another principalship at another school because they cannot justify paying the salaries of principals who are not doing principals' work. They impose that principal upon another school community. And what do you think is the result?

Look at that scenario. The standard for keeping principals for life is "slightly above incompetent." And what makes matters even worse is the fact that unless a supervisor takes the time and makes an effort to document the incompetence pursuant to union due process procedures, even incompetent principals get to keep their jobs. It is Haberman who points out that "principals are almost never removed unless the building is out of control" (1999). Look at the standard. Principals in bureaucracies never lose their jobs because they are "ineffective." They only lose their jobs if they totally lose control, the building is in chaos, and usually only when the lunacy hits the newspapers!

Think of the reality of the present state of affairs in Philadelphia. A principal is appointed for life or until he or she retires! Not even our state Supreme Court justices have that kind of job security. No other leaders of communities are given life terms! So why should we do that for principal leaders of schools in America?

Term limits prevent ineffective leadership from continually burdening our schools, and if coupled with a democratic practice for choosing the leaders, our best leaders will emerge and be kept in place. Also requiring recognition is the fact that one's ability to lead is greater when he or she first begins to lead. The renewal factor benefits a new leader, but once in office, the leadership chemistry peaks and then starts to decline. **The rise and fall of a leader's inspirational effectiveness inevitably occurs.** A term limit gives the leader and the community an easy way out. All leaders see and feel their effectiveness dwindle and that is an inescapable phenomenon.

Term limits and the ability to have real input into the leadership selection process for schools will tend to keep our professionals in our schools. Good teachers who see ineffective leadership at the helm of their school and have no ability to control their own destiny, lose hope and enthusiasm. They often leave the school and school system entirely. The brain drain is real and so is what Ted Sizer writes about in *Horace's Hope* (1996). **Professional educators of great ilk like Horace need to have a real sense of control over their life in schools. That is a basic human need we can never escape and is a prerequisite for great things to happen in schools.**

The dilemma for school governance and principals' unions is where do they go from here? What subsequently happens to a principal who is at the end of the principalship term? Should they go back to teach? Back to a vice principal position? Do they move upward in the bureaucracy? Do they move out of the system or do they get to go into another principal's position elsewhere within the district. The issue is the process and it can be worked out if reasonable people put their minds together. There are many of us who would probably gladly go back into teaching if the situation were right and we got to keep our salary level!

Again, the bottom line is does the principal serve the community or does the community serve the principal? Principal centered leadership is always poor leadership. Community centered leadership is always good leadership. Leadership for the 21st century is about the community—governance for the 21st century is about the community, too. When we have term limits for our leaders and democratic practices for choosing our leaders, we have true community centered governance.

Our standard for our principals should be "the outstanding leader standard" and the only way to attain that standard and ensure that standard is maintained is to mandate term limits for our leaders. Our students, their parents, our school communities and the community at large deserve great leadership in our schools. The main inhibitor of our schools becoming great schools is ineffective leadership and many of our urban schools are plagued by ineffective leadership. Term limits are necessary for good governance of our schools. They are necessary elements of our democratic governance ideals Americans stand for. We need to put term limits and all democratic principals into our governance practices of our schools. Our children deserve effective school leaders and the standard for school leaders should be **"outstanding leadership." Only democracy can ensure that.**

The Bill of Rights and the Amendments

The Bill of Rights and the other Amendments to The Constitution of the United States of America were enacted to ensure that democracy works effectively, to recognize and effectuate individual rights, and to protect the people from our government. Those ideals represented in the Amendments to our Constitution are equally as important to good school governance as they are to the governance of our nation. If we are to truly have great schools that meet the needs of our students, their parents, our communities and our nation, we must govern our schools according to the very same principals.

It is of utmost importance for the creation of outstanding and effective schools that we bring our Constitution and American democratic ideals into the schools through the open door of democracy and not block them at the schoolhouse steps. Yes, effective schools for children depend on the democratic ideals being alive and well in the fiber of everything we do in schools. Schools just can not function well without democratic ideals being at the foundation of life in schools. Think back to the studies of our experts on leadership and look at what they advocate as good leadership practices. **Isn't it amazing? All of what we have learned about good leadership is embodied in the ideals of our Constitution and the ideals of America. They are necessary elements of good schools.**

They are also mandatory elements of our schools. The Bill of Rights and all the Amendments do apply to our schools. They do apply to the governance of our schools. They are not optional. They are mandatory! All of the rights explicit and implicit in our Constitution apply to the schools. The rights of all American citizens apply to everything that happens within the schoolhouse walls and to everyone and every body that governs them.

And yes, sadly, our children, their parents, our school workers, the local communities, and our total society need to be protected from the excesses of the government of our schools. What I have often seen done to children by administrators in the name of education is plainly Faustian. The administrators may be well meaning, but the propriety of many things I have seen happen in schools to both children and adults are at best clearly questionable. In the face of the high stakes testing and what I have witnessed done to children, it is increasingly clear that we need to reaffirm our belief in the ideals of the Bill of Rights and other relevant Amendments. It is vastly more important that we teach and live by the ideals enunciated in our Constitution than live by the ridiculousness of the ideas of high stakes testing and the power structures of archaic bureaucracies.

When we get to the institutional illnesses inherent in our bureaucratic governance systems, it will become brutally clear that our ideals must prevail and be incorporated in the governance of our schools. The very reason institutionalized illnesses exist in our school systems is that our ideals of our Constitution are not instituted in our schools and school systems. We can never set the conditions for great schools to emerge until we set the conditions for democratic ideals to guide everything we do in schools. That can only happen through our governance structures that we enact.

May we at this point, review the Bill of Rights and the Amendments that are most important to the governance of our schools and school systems?

The First Amendment is the first amendment because without it we can have no democracy. The right of free speech is paramount to a free society. It is paramount to outstanding governance of our nation and it is paramount to outstanding governance of our schools. Freedom of speech and freedom of the press is how the great ideas of man arise and become incorporated into what we do as a society and is how the great ideas of education emerge. It is also how we debate ideas and draw conclusions as to what actually are the "best practices" in education.

Yes, the best practices of education are highly debatable. "Best" is an opinion. It is not a fact. And yes, parents and citizens in America have a right to speak their peace and have their ideas legitimately heard by the governing body of schools. In Chapter 5, "Leadership for the 21st Century," we visited the concept of the "open climate" for debate and resolution of issues as a necessary element for outstanding schools and it is a necessary element of good school governance. It needs to be protected and it **is** protected by the First Amendment to our Constitution.

It must be protected zealously both from the inside and outside of our schools for the benefit of all individuals within our America. I can not count all the times I have witnessed the basic rights of students and adults violated within our schools. It is only through the freedom of speech and the freedom of the press that the wrongs can be righted and great schools for everyone can emerge. What is truly sad is how many times I have seen the right of free speech in schools destroyed by the retaliatory measures of those in power, especially principals. Remember, we study history and governments so we can make our world better. The history of mankind is replete with examples of totalitarian leaders crushing freedom of speech. To crush freedom of speech is to crush thought itself. Nowhere is it more important to protect free speech than in our public schools. Those wrongs can only occur in the absence of democracy.

Let me give an example of how basic rights of speech are denied in schools. A teacher speaks up and writes a letter to the school board that students who do not read well are not receiving the appropriate remedial help to enable the student to develop the necessary reading skills to enable the student to function effectively in society. The principal becomes angry that the teacher has gone "over his head." The principal then observes the teacher's class and writes an unsatisfactory observation along with a disciplinary memo threatening the teacher with an unsatisfactory rating. Or, at the end of the year, the principal gives the teacher the worst teaching roster in the school and makes life miserable for that teacher. Or, if the teacher holds a leadership position within the school, the principal cuts the program to eliminate the teacher's position. Or, at the end of the year the teacher's position is cut from the school and the teacher is effectively "exiled by the king." These are just a few of the practices in schools that occur every day! Retaliation against people who speak their mind is an institutionalized illness inherent in all bureaucracies.

What is the remedy for such retaliation to deprive teachers of their speech rights? There is no effective remedy in our schools. Grievance procedures fall short because they depend on specific contract language and a viable remedy. Complaints to higher ups usually fall on deaf ears. The only remedy is democracy. The elements of democracy that would remedy that are the school community chooses its own leaders and term limits. If a school leader's tenure is characterized by such actions, the remedy is to vote the bum out! That is another reason why democracy is imperative to the well functioning of our schools! It is the only effective remedy to the ills of our schools.

Look at what happened in Camden, New Jersey. When the principal exercised his right to free speech and went public about being told to cheat on the state achievement tests, he had his job and livelihood taken away by his superiors. That is retaliation my friend. It is despotism and has no place in our schools. That ridiculousness would never happen if the school community had the right to choose its own leaders. Without that element of democracy being alive and well, there can never be free speech in schools. The students' best interests can never be debated out and effectuated. How sad.

The other element of the First Amendment is also an issue within schools but is too monumental an issue to deal with here. The establishment clause and the free exercise clause and the balance of those ideals within schools have seen an appreciable amount of litigation over the years. Certainly, students do have the right to exercise their religious thought and practices within schools, and public schools cannot establish religious practices within schools. But how those two ideals are worked out within schools is largely dependent on the exercise of free speech and debate.

Also essential to effective school governance are the due process rights embedded in the Fourth, Fifth, Sixth and Fourteenth Amendments to our Constitution. While most Americans are somewhat familiar with how due process rights affect us in criminal and disciplinary procedures for both students and adults within schools, not many of us are aware of the due process rights to participate in the governance and decision-making processes of schools. It can be well argued that the **"procedural due process"** rights that ensure our right to participate in the educational decision-making processes of our public schools are even more important than our **"substantive due process rights"** because they are preventive in nature. How does it go? "An ounce of prevention is worth a pound of cure?"

Closely connected to the right of free speech is the **"right to be heard."** The right to be heard on matters of public concern is why school board meetings are public. Everyone has the procedural due process right to be heard before laws and regulations are enacted by public bodies. It is part of the "rule-making" procedure. It is constitutionally based and applies to the states through the Fourteenth Amendment. I call that **"participative due process." It is the right of the people to be part of the decision-making processes of public schools.** It is a necessary element of good decision-making. It makes decisions informed decisions and not arbitrary.

The right to be heard is no different than the **"voice giving"** for everyone in the school community. It is especially important for parents because it is their only avenue to the exercise of their speech rights. But to make the giving of voice meaningful, there must be true cognizance paid to the voice of constituents by the decision-makers who comprise the decision-making body. How do we effectively ensure their good faith? Well, the answer is again in democracy. The decision-making body must first be comprised of elected officials, and then we must watch them and vote according to what we see. That is the only way to ensure the good faith, loyalty and care of our boards of directors and trustees. "The price of democracy is eternal vigilance."

Now let us take a hard look at the Fourteenth Amendment and the Equal Protection clause. It is the equal protection clause that states that the states may not deny any citizen the **"equal protection of the laws."** It was originally enacted to protect the rights of the freed slaves and has been used to win court cases guaranteeing the individual rights of citizens. When students are compelled to attend schools and employees agree to be employed by public schools, they do not give up their rights when they cross the schoolhouse door. They have a right to equal protection of the laws.

Coupled with the Fourteenth Amendment is the Fifteenth Amendment. The Fifteenth Amendment guarantees the right to vote for everyone in the United States. It was enacted because African Americans were often denied the basic right to vote. Now look at this reality: According to the National School Boards Association, 96% of school boards in America are elected. It is in the large urban cities that we find most of our appointed school boards, and our large cities is where we have a large percentage of our minority populations. Do you think there might be a connection there?

While I do not wish to make racism the issue of this work on school governance, it is an inescapable issue of school governance. In Pennsylvania, the school takeover movement began while Governor Ridge was in office. Philadelphia was then run by superintendent David Hornbeck who fought for more money for the schoolchildren of Philadelphia. He said he needed more money to run the schools effectively and stated that the reason Philadelphia was shortchanged in educational funds received from the state was because of institutionalized racism. In effect he was calling Governor Ridge a racist. Not long thereafter, David Hornbeck resigned stating that he believed Philadelphia would never be given the funds needed to run our schools effectively as long as he was in office. **The whole state takeover movement of Philadelphia's public schools can be traced back to David Hornbeck implying Governor Ridge's school funding procedure was racist in nature (Gill et al, 2007)!**

The final Bill of Rights issue we need to address is the right to a fair and impartial hearing in disciplinary and criminal proceedings within school districts. They are called "procedural due process" rights and they are guaranteed to all Americans pursuant to the Fourth, Fifth, Sixth and Fourteenth Amendments. In school districts, students are removed from schools regularly and often placed in disciplinary schools comprised of many of our criminally inclined youth. Assignment to such schools is often a make or break issue for many of the students. There are often good kids who end up forced to attend those schools. In large school districts, it is usually the school district and often individual principals that stand as "accuser, judge and jury" for such cases. There are a multitude of issues therein that are just too complex to be dealt with here. **But to be brief, when one single individual in a governance system is granted the power to stand as the accuser, judge and jury, it is "constitutionally repugnant."** Those hard issues can not be ignored in the realm of school governance and I can not tell you how often I have seen basic human rights denied students and their parents in schools and school districts.

There are also due process issues for employees within school districts and we will address them in the chapter addressing employee discipline within democratic school structures. But here, it would be appropriate to just recognize that in our public school systems, employees are often victim to inproprieties of a system that relies on individual supervisors, often principals of schools, who stand as "the accuser, judge and jury." That is a prescription for ridiculousness.

Yes, there are a multitude of multifaceted issues that rise within schools and school districts. Many of them deal with basic human rights and the statutory right to a **"free and appropriate public education"** that can be found in the *Individuals With Disabilitieis Education Act, No Child Left Behind,* and relevant state statutes and constitutions. If we are to have great schools for children, we need to deal with all of those issues in a proactive and open manner. While there may be remedies for some issues via judicial processes, many of the issues cannot be practically and effectively resolved via the law suit or administrative complaint. They can only be pragmatically addressed through the democratic governance process.

Yes, democracy is imperative.

7.2

School Councils & Why They Don't Work

School Councils have not worked well because they have no true and legitimate power within the governance structures of schools. They are powerless and ultimately ineffective when the participants realize the central administration and the principal do whatever they want anyway. That is a shame because they have so much potential in the legislative process.

School councils were initiated in many school districts throughout America to allow the local school community meaningful input into the decision-making and governance processes of schools. School councils have not worked very well in most schools because they usually have no legitimate power in the governance structures of schools. The principals and central administrators do whatever they want anyway. They have all the power.

School Councils were originally created to give voice to the local school community and its stakeholders in the decision-making processes of schools. The genesis of such initiatives came out of the work of Ted Sizer and the Coalition of Essential Schools and psychologist James Comer who promoted **"school planning teams"** to engage and include parents and teachers in the decision-making process of schooling. Sizer and his Coalition of Essential Schools movement promotes democracy in education and it is one of the Coalition's ten primary principles. Comer saw the poor interrelationships among stakeholders and individuals within schools as the primary inhibitor of good school dynamics and believed inclusive school planning teams are necessary for effective school dynamics (1984, 1986, and 1996). Both authors believe such legitimate democratic practices yield **"true student centered instruction"** and support that yields a more responsive and better education for our children.

There are a variety of specific structures for the composition of school councils, but the concept of the school council is always basically the same: to give voice to parents, teachers, the community at large and, in high schools, students. It was to give stakeholders a **"legitimate voice"** in the decision-making process of schools and thereby make their schools better schools that are more responsive to the students and community of that particular school. Chicago was one of the leading school districts in that area and they, as did most cities that tried school councils, had mixed results. In Philadelphia, there was a similar movement that began in the late 1980's, grew through the 1990's when the Pew Charitable Trusts put up a large amount of money to promote "governance councils" and "school councils" were promoted by the subsequent Superintendent of Schools, David Hornbeck. Since the school district was taken over by the state, the School Reform Commission has stated in their beliefs and principles that they want every school to have a school council, but they have hired Paul Vallas as the CEO and he has set in motion the most autocratic, top down and exclusive administrative governance system I have ever seen in my thirty-two years in the system.

Putting idealistic concepts into practice is easier said than done. The reason school councils have not worked well in schools as governance bodies is because they have no **"legitimate power"** within the organizational governance structures of schools and school districts. To give school councils **"actual power"** that is enforceable under the law or policies and practices of a school district, the power must be granted in the organizational documents that create the school entity. Without such power the group almost always just becomes a mere advisory council. If the council members see that their efforts are ignored by the principal or central administration, they become debilitated and the council falls apart. When people see their good faith efforts go unrewarded and made into a mockery, they normally become disenchanted and their efforts discontinue. That is a **"recurring theme"** in school council dynamics.

Here is a true to life example that recently happened in Philadelphia. Prior to the school takeover, all high school administrators were chosen by site based selection committees consisting of the local school council or teams of teachers, parents, support staff, community members and students. The principal and assistant principals were chosen by the site selection teams and promptly appointed by the school board. Subsequently, the schools were taken over and principals were centrally appointed through processes that seemed to change by the week and whims of the autocratic governance mentality put into place by the CEO, Paul Vallas. A new principal was sent to that school without even one iota of inclusion of the school community. The new principal created issues within the school community that was a great school community accustomed to a high level of cohesiveness. When they complained about the principal and the principal realized the assistant principal that had been chosen by the school community was the favored administrator of the school community. She unilaterally cut his position at the school! There was no input from the school community allowed at all.

The central administration supported that action. The act of the school community choosing its own leader was totally disregarded and rendered meaningless. When the issue was raised to the School Reform Commission, the Commission remained silent and allowed that to happen. **So what do their words mean about**

every school having a school council? I guess they mean nothing. And what does that say about the credibility of the leadership? What did happen was that Paul Vallas, the CEO, responded with a letter stating, "The building principal must make informed and sound educational decisions for his or her school. If we at the central office expect high school principals to perform at the highest levels while servicing our children, it is important that we allow them to make the decisions they feel necessary to deliver positive results." How disingenuous, everyone at that school knew that the decision was "not a sound educational decision." It was a "Machiavellian" decision made for self serving reasons not in the best interests of children.

That statement made by Paul Vallas that the principal must make decisions "for the school" is not only demeaning to everyone in that school community, but a smack in the face to them. Members of the school community are not children that need decisions made "for" them. They are professionals, parents and concerned citizens of America. It is time we come out of the eighteenth century. It makes a mockery of the school community and a mockery of the words that stand above the School Reform Commission in their meeting room that "every school should have a school council." For what reason? So they can be ignored at will? Principals in schools stand in a position of a type of trustee. What is the remedy for self-dealing by school administrators that is in violation of their **"fiduciary duty of good faith?"** The answer is not in a civil action. It is in democracy. It is giving actual and legitimate power to school councils and/or the school community.

Blind support of principals' acts, whether right or wrong, moral or immoral, is an institutional illness of bureaucracies reminiscent of feudalistic times and totalitarian regimes. There is no place for it in America—it is not part of the **"American Vision."** When CEO's such as Paul Vallas go around saying that they want parent and school community participation in schools, and then their actions actually exclude parents and school community members from the decision-making processes of schools, they **lose their credibility** and their ability to lead. People just laugh at them.

To make those words in support of school councils credible, school councils must be granted actual and legitimate powers within schools. Look back to Chapter 5 and review Kouzes and Posner's words about credibility being the foundation of leadership and leaders need to "do what they say." **Credibility is not only the foundation of leadership, it is also the foundation of school governance structures. Without credibility in what we do, we are lost.**

Successful principals and school leaders do not make decisions "for" schools. They make decisions "with" the school community in a collegial manner. Leadership for the twenty-first century can be no other way. What I realize every day in my leadership practice as a school administrator, is that the people I lead are just as smart as me, and in many instances, they are a lot smarter than me. For us to cling to the archaic notion that principals or CEO's are "supreme beings" able to make decisions for us is preposterous. There is no principal or CEO or administrator in America that is smarter or more able to make good decisions for children than those people that make up his or her school community. That notion is absurd. It is the twenty-first century.

Decisions for schools need to be made collectively and collegially in a democratic manner. That is what the notion of school councils is all about. The task of school councils is to build consensus. The task of the leader is to mold discussion and dialogue into plans of action. The effective leader for the twenty-first century is a consensus builder. Consensus building is an art, but it is not really a difficult art. The essential concept is that everyone must be heard and listened to in a respectful and legitimate manner. All ideas must be discussed and the discussion must be led toward the development of a cohesive plan of action that the community can call its own.

Yes there are times when the issue is just too hotly contested to be molded into consensus. That is when rules of order and the vote of the council must be incorporated. That is why we have rules of order and empowerment of councils. It is all about teacher, parent and community empowerment.

But to have true power and voice there must be a mechanism to enforce the decisions of school councils. The central administration or the supervening governance body, the school board or school commission, must empower the councils legitimately. They must create credible appeal processes for situations in controversy. Those appeal processes must be genuine review and not "principal support and rubber stamp processes." It must be a good faith mechanism.

What happens all too often is that a school council meets, creates an action plan to get the input of all stakeholders, gets the input, and creates a plan based on the input, and then the principal does what he or she wants anyway. That is debilitating. The words of one excellent teacher, Joe DiRaddo, echo in my mind: "But who makes the final decision? Then why should I waste my time?"

Many principals and administrators do make good use of "advisory councils." They are the ones that have the wisdom to listen to them and put into practice what they advise. **Advisory councils have "persuasive authority" but not "mandatory authority."** Wise leaders listen to them and give meaning to their voice by following their advice. Good leaders are good followers.

The bottom line is that if we are to have school councils, we must give them credence. Their decisions must be given **"full force and credit."** The best way to do that is to give them legitimate power through the governance structures of our school organizations. That can only be done trough the governance documents of an organization such as its constitution or the "charter" for schools, or enactments of legislators or policy resolutions of school boards that grant or mandate enforcement powers and procedures.

Yes, democracy is imperative.

The Potential of School Councils
&
How to Make Them Work

School councils have great potential for improving the governance of schools. If created and empowered effectively, they offer stakeholders an opportunity for meaningful voice and input into the decision-making processes of schools and fulfill the democratic principle of participative due process—the right of the people to participate in the governance of their school communities. Similar to the legislative branch of our constitutional governance system, they can be structured to provide the "balance of power" that the framers of our Constitution determined was essential for effective democratic governance. The concept of balance of power is a pillar of American democracy and is an ideal that has "set the conditions" for the greatness of America to emerge. Perhaps if we governed our schools similarly, we would set the conditions for greatness in schools to emerge.

In a constitutional model of school governance, the school council would be the legislative branch and the principal or lead teacher would be the executive branch. The school board or board of trustees would be the judicial branch with the responsibility to supervise the appropriate functioning and interaction between the school council and the principal. The school council is the legislative branch that creates the educational plan and sets school based policies after appropriate inclusive leadership processes. The principal's responsibility would be primarily to "execute" the educational plan and policies of the school and provide leadership in the decision-making processes similar to the manner in which the president of the United States provides leadership for our governmental process. The school board or board of trustees would also have to remedy disputes between the two branches or create a system to resolve disputes similar to our judicial system.

This constitutional model of school governance has the potential to provide a viable and powerful mechanism for teacher and parent empowerment that would create the "sense of ownership" that is essential for outstanding organizational dynamics. If we are to effectuate the level of organizational synergy that makes our best schools exciting places to live and learn, we must create the sense that it is "our school" and it is everyone's responsibility to make it all it can be. The constitutional model offers many possibilities for effective school governance because they can be instituted in a variety of ways.

The way to make school councils work is to give them "full force and effect" through the governance document that creates the organization such as a constitution, charter, or articles of incorporation. It can also be effectuated by school boards or boards of trustees creating policies that mandate their establishment and provide mechanisms for enforcement. For our schools to be effective schools for the twenty-first century, we can no longer allow principals to maintain the mentality that "I will make the final decision." It is time we grew past that paternalistic attitude. It has proven to be so destructive of what we know about good leadership and good governance.

A school council can take many forms of membership. Optimally, there should be a workable balance between parents, teachers, community members, administrators and sometimes students. Ideally, they should be comprised of elected members, but there are some instances when there would be appointed members. One way that school council officers have been appointed is the elected officials of a union building committee select members of the school council. The president of a parent association is usually automatically a council officer and others can also be elected. A school council should be limited in number because groups become less effective if they are too large. A fair approximation of a workable group is to have between 10-15 members.

Of course, an effective leader is essential to that group and that leader must be elected to maintain credibility. The council leader is often elected by the members of the council but could be elected directly by the members of the total school community.

The principal, as the executive officer of the executive branch, would then have to be selected or elected. In many bureaucracies the principal is appointed from above, but a more democratic way is for the principal to be selected by the school community itself. That can be done through the usual site based selection process where a selection committee is formed, or the school council itself can choose the principal. In the first constitution I wrote for a democratic school, I developed a viable way for the principal to be directly elected by the school community members. That is arguably the more democratic way to choose our executive leader. If the principal is selected by the school council or a selection committee, it is important that their membership is chosen democratically. Never forget the importance of "credibility" in the process. Our studies show it is of the utmost importance.

However chosen, it is important that the principal or lead teacher understand his role in this rubric. He or she must be an effective executor of the wishes of the community, its policies and ultimately its educational plan. The principal runs the daily operations of the school and makes appropriate decisions with the input of his or her leadership team. The school council must understand that it does not run the daily operations of the school. Its function is to legislate policies and create the educational plan in a collegial manner. Roles and responsibilities must be defined through discussion, debate and consensus building. There must be rules of order that enable a vote in the event consensus is not established. Remember, it is the "process" that makes democracy, democracy.

The school board or board of trustees must oversee the process and resolve disputes. In the first constitution I wrote for a school, I designed the board of trustees to be similar to the Supreme Court of the United States. It even consisted of nine members. The difference was that I had three parent trustees elected by the parents, three teacher trustees elected by the teachers, and three community members. One community member was elected by the parents, one was elected by the teachers and one was elected by the school reform commission. That is just one way of constructing the board.

Once this constitutional structure becomes operational, it offers great hope for a responsive governance system that will enable the requisite democratic processes to take place that will result in decisions being made truly for the best interests of the students. For that to happen effectively, there must be open discussion and debate that is molded into action plans that can be embraced by the community as a whole. Remember, effective schools are about the collective vision, the common mission, and collective endeavor. That requires a sense of ownership in "what we do."

That sense of ownership that makes good schools great is developed through the process of democracy.

School Council Model of School Governance
AKA The "Constitutional Model"

Judicial Branch—Board of Trustees

- Oversees the operations of the school
- Assures the school functions as envisioned in the organizational document
- Assures the appropriate interplay between the school council and the principal or lead teacher
- Assures participative due process
- Passes resolutions necessary to the operation of the school
- Resolves disputes between branches of governance and individuals or groups within the school community
- Makes final determination of disciplinary actions
- Members are elected democratically or appointed by a body that is elected democratically
- Term limits and reelection or reselection

Executive Branch
Principal, Lead Teacher or CEO

- Executes the mandates and policies of the board of trustees, supervening governmental body, and education laws
- Runs the daily operations of the school
- Does all executive acts necessary to fulfill the collective vision and mission of the school
- Presents recommendations to the school council for the educational plan
- Implements the final educational plan and school based policies
- Presents a recommended school budget to the school council for approval
- Supervises staff and executes student and employee discipline procedures
- Is elected by the school council, board of trustees or directly elected by the school community

Legislative Branch—School Council

- Develops the educational plan & local school policies
- Assesses, evaluates and revises the educational plan
- Implements participative due process procedures for involving all stakeholders in the decision-making process of the school and assures parents, teachers, staff, students and the community-at-large has an opportunity to be heard
- Participates in the budget-making process and passes the final approval of the budget after holding public hearings where all stakeholders have an opportunity to be heard
- Is comprised of teachers, parents, students (in high schools) staff members, and community representatives
- Representatives are elected directly or appointed by an elected body, or a combination of both

School Community

Teachers   Parents   Students   Support Staff   Community-at-Large

- Elects the board of trustees, principal & school council or has meaningful input into their selection through an open, transparent process; or elects those who are empowered to vote for officers and officials; and/or has meaningful input into who is on the "election" committee and who is chosen as the principal.

Note: It is important to note that under the "Constitutional Model" the principal, lead teacher, or CEO does not stand in a superior hierarchical position to the school council. They are equals. School councils that have been placed in a lower organizational position do not work because it creates a paternalistic relationship and renders the school council as a mere advisory group. There are many variations of this basic format that can be created. The powers of each branch must be formulated in the charter or constitution of the school, or in the mandates of law or the supervening school board. The school council has sometimes been placed in a superior position to the principal, but that organizational design changes the balance of power to a corporate design and the council becomes another form of board of trustees.

7.3

The Traditional Model

The traditional model of school governance is based on democracy. The registered voters of our local communities normally elect the board of directors for their school district. It is only in urban America that the right to vote has been taken away from the people. Why is that?

The traditional model of school governance is based on the corporate design. Generally speaking, school districts throughout America are vested with powers granted to them by the legislatures of the states through legislative acts commonly known as statutes or codes—usually called "school codes." School districts are created as "bodies corporate" and are governed by a board of directors. The board of directors are either appointed or elected for a specific term in office. According to the National School Boards Association, 96% of school boards in the United States are elected (2004).

The corporate design is a fairly basic concept. A corporation is a legal entity comprised of stockholders. A "stock" is an ownership right. A corporation may have one share of stock or thousands of shares of stock. Those stockholders are commonly known as shareholders. Shareholders elect the board of directors to manage the corporation. In turn, the board of directors select officers of the corporation who are empowered to run the corporation. Corporate practice in America is a complicated morass of laws, regulations and legal precedents and there are different types of stocks, voting and non voting, and different types of voting schemes such as cumulative voting. In the case of school districts with democratically elected school boards, voting rights are based on the normal democratic practice of one person, one vote.

The stockholders of school districts are the residents within a school district still known as citizens. In normal practice throughout America where school boards are elected, any person of voting age who lives within the boundaries of a school district and is registered to vote may vote for his or her school board directors. Therefore, the basic governance structure of school districts under the corporate design is this:

(1) The *residents* elect the individual directors to the board of school directors;

(2) The *board of school directors* manage the business of the school district and select the officers who run the school district; and

(3) *Officers* do what they are told to do by the board of directors (Adapted from Conard, Knauss & Siegel, 1977, p. 731).

In some school districts, usually large urban school districts, the members of the school board are appointed by the mayor or some form of city council. In Philadelphia, Pennsylvania, under the school takeover law, the schools are governed by the School Reform Commission whose members are appointed by the governor and mayor—three members are appointed by the governor and two are appointed by the mayor. The issue is whether school board members should be elected or appointed and which way is best will always be an issue of debate. But even when appointed, appointments are made by an individual or a small group of individuals who are "legislatively empowered to vote"—an appointment is still a type of "vote." The only difference is that that the people have been left out of the voting process.

The issue is always one for democracy. The fact that 96% of our school board members in the Untied States are elected speaks volumes about America's values and belief in democracy as our common notion of good governance practices. Even where school board members are appointed, they are appointed by mayors or city councils of some sort who are elected by the people. There lies the argument that appointed school boards are part and parcel of democracy. But still we must always be cognizant of the fact that the majority of appointed school boards are found in our cities where such appointments are often subject to mechanisms of power in big city politics.

The question that must be asked when school board members are appointed is to whom does the school board member owe his or her duty of loyalty, care and good faith? A school board member is a type of trustee. It is a **"public trust." It is not a politicians' trust.** Look back to Chapter 2 where we discussed the issues of fiduciary duties and then look back to "The Grand Hypothetical of School Governance." Ask yourself the question: to whom does the board of school directors owe their fiduciary duties? I would argue that it is a balancing act between the local community, the students, their parents and the school community. **The standard of care is good faith and the task of the board is to "balance the equities."**

Once in office, school boards are constitutionally and legislatively required to function in a democratic manner. They must hold open meetings and they must create policies and practices through "resolutions" in an open process. This open process is a legal due process requirement. **The foundation for the due process requirements that bind school boards to open meetings with specific processes for policymaking, rule making and procedure making is in the Amendments to the *Constitution of the United States of America*, subsequent common law precedents created by courts of appropriate jurisdiction, and "sunshine acts"**

enacted by state legislatures. See, for example, *Sunshine Act,* 65 Pa.C.S. §701, et seq. School boards or school commissions are bound by law to operate in an open manner that gives everyone an opportunity to comment and advocate for whatever issues are properly placed before the board.

The bottom line is that school boards and school commissions are empowered to "manage the school district." They normally do so by appointing a superintendent of schools or chief executive officer (CEO). The modern trend in large school districts is to appoint a CEO who in turn appoints a chief academic officer (CAO). While the CEO is responsible for managing all the affairs of the organization, he or she usually delegates the academic functions of management to the CAO so the CEO can focus on the other issues of management and leaves the academic stuff to the CAO. For our purposes here, we will call this head honcho the superintendent of schools because a rose by any other name is still a rose.

Under the corporate design, the superintendent manages the school system and individual schools and offices under the direction of the school board. There are some management issues such as final budget approval that can not be completely delegated to the superintendent under various state laws, but in practice, the superintendent is usually given wide latitude in how he or she goes about running the school district. How much the school board actively participates in the management of the school district is specific to each individual school board.

How democratically or autocratically a school system and its individual schools are thereafter governed is largely determined by the dynamics of those two structures—the school board and the office of the superintendent of schools. In small school districts where school boards are **"closely connected"** to the schools, the school board can take on a more active role in what goes on in schools. In large school districts, the democratic practices of school boards fall to the practical necessity of **"delegation of authority"** which is really the **"delegation of powers"** within the organization.

The question for the governance of individual schools then becomes: **Does democracy in schools end at the superintendent's office or does it filter down through the individual schools themselves?** It could be well argued that the larger the school district, the more autocratic the governance practices become. This phenomenon can be traced to the delegation of powers throughout the system and the workings of the executive branch of this governance structure. In large school systems, we not only have many administrative offices but we also have regional superintendents. That is where bureaucracy rears its ugly head.

However the supervening administrative functions are delineated, it still comes down to the individual schools and how they are governed. In the traditional model, the principal runs the schools. They have whatever power they are allowed by the school board and supervening power structures. In practice, the superintendent of schools usually sets the managerial tone of the school district. It is his or her leadership style that always seems to permeate the system.

In large urban school districts and even many smaller districts, the principal has been given substantial power and wide latitude to be the decision-making authority. The degree to which he or she shares his or her power is largely a matter of the individual leadership style and leadership belief. The human dilemma is that we are normally selfish when it comes to giving up our power.

We have already visited many of the issues surrounding this tradition of giving principals absolute power. Shared leadership is a concept that developed in response to the negative effects of giving a single individual unilateral authority to make the final decision on all issues within schools. In the traditional model, any shared leadership is at the graces and wisdom of the principal because there is no mandated shared governance in the power structures of schools.

Whether the principal leads and manages in an autocratic or democratic manner under the traditional model is up to the principal unless directed to operate in a certain manner by his or her superiors in the line of authority. The principal can almost always make the final decision regardless of what anyone else thinks. The traditional model becomes ultimately **"paternalistic"** as if the principal were a superior being and that mentality is demeaning to everyone else in the school community. The powers of a leadership team, parent committee or school council can only be advisory in nature. **In reality, the final decisions under the traditional model almost always become based on the "self interests of the principal" unless the principal has the wisdom to operate in a true inclusive manner and give true cognizance to the will of the group.**

Schools and principals have always operated with a leadership team. It was formerly referred to as the principal's cabinet and usually consisted of the vice principals, department heads, coordinators of specific programs and other teacher leaders that are particular to any given school. The concept of the leadership team has evolved in recent years to be as inclusive as possible even including the custodial staff leader, and there have been progressive school leaders that have invited anyone to be on the leadership team who wants to be involved.

The issue always boils down to whether the principal becomes a mere delegator of administrative tasks or actually includes them in leadership and the decision-making process. This goes back to the credibility issues discussed in Chapter 5.

The main question for democracy under the traditional model is do we vote for a dictator or a democratically inclined leader and who gets to vote? The school board has the final voting power unless delegated in some manner. The voting power can be delegated to the superintendent or individuals within the system or they can be delegated to a group or committee. They could, under a progressive school board, be delegated to the entire school community under an electorate system. That is how our towns and cities choose their executive leaders—we elect them.

When I was contemplating the issues of school governance and the issue of selecting or electing the principal, I asked a teacher about the issue of whether teachers would elect a dictator for their principal. I asked that specific teacher that question because she had worked under the famous "dictator" principal of the School District of Philadelphia, Lou D'Antonio. He ran Bartram High School with an iron fist and teachers never left the school. They felt safe and secure under his leadership. The hallways and classrooms were free of disruption because Lou would not tolerate any. I asked the teacher if the principal of Bartram were elected by the teachers, would they have voted for Lou D'Antonio. Her answer was an unqualified, "Yes!"

That is another reason why the best way to match a principal's leadership style with the needs of the school community is through a democratic process. The school community knows what it needs. Outsiders can never truly understand the school community. You must live in that school community eight to twelve hours every working day to understand it and its leadership needs. Yes, a school community will vote for a directive leader if it perceives that the leader is or will run the school effectively. Only those who are led can see and judge the effectiveness of the leader.

Trust the local school community. It is the risk we must take. Choose our leaders democratically. It is the American Vision and the American way.

7.4

The Governance of Charter Schools

Charter Schools were designed to empower teachers and school communities to create new professional opportunities, be responsible for the learning program, and govern themselves independently of school district bureaucracies. The concept of "ownership" of "what we do" is integral to that philosophy.

Nowhere is it more important to ask the question **"Whose School Is It?"** than in the realm of charter schools! Charter schools are being created all across America to fill a wide variety of needs and educational philosophies of the American populace. They are schools that are founded by individuals or groups of individuals who wish to establish and operate schools based on a particular philosophy or theme. Like all schools, they need to be governed and the essential question is still—**Whose school is it?**

The charter school movement arose from the belief that schools that were operated independently of local school systems and were relieved of many of the requirements and regulations imposed upon regular public schools would do a more effective job of meeting educational needs of children and provide parents with a choice of schools for their children to attend. Charter schools are public schools. The movement started as a realization that many of our school systems, especially our large urban school systems were not doing the job of adequately educating all of our children to high levels of achievement.

It can be argued that they are the epitome of "school based management" that was a movement in education during the 1990's. The school based management movement was an effort to govern schools at the local level. The results varied but the death knell of that movement lies in the fact that the power within public systems has always been centrally located and centrally controlled. The charter school movement was created to make those schools truly independent of the centralized power structures of school districts that were viewed as preventing outstanding schools from emerging.

Charter school laws throughout America are basically similar in the legal provisions they establish. For us to understand the legal nature, purposes and ideals of charter schools it would be of benefit to visit a representative charter school law governing the establishment of charter schools. Since I am familiar with the Pennsylvania charter school law and Philadelphia stands as one of the nation's leaders in the establishment of charter schools, I have chosen the Pennsylvania charter school law as a representative sample. After all, Philadelphia is the seat of the institution of democracy for our nation. It should serve as an example of democracy in education for our country as well. Shouldn't it?

The Pennsylvania charter school law states the general purposes of the establishment of charter schools in its section on legislative intent. The purposes stated are generally reflective of the purposes of the charter school movement in America. *24 PS 17—1702—A: Legislative Intent* states:

> It is the intent of the general Assembly, in enacting this article, to provide opportunities for teachers, parents, pupils and community members to establish and maintain schools that operate independently from the existing school district structure as a method to accomplish all of the following:
>
> 1) Improve pupil learning.
> 2) Increase learning opportunities for all pupils.
> 3) Encourage the use of different and innovative teaching methods.
> 4) Create new professional opportunities for teachers, including the opportunity to be responsible for the learning program at the school site.
> 5) Provide parents and pupils expanded choices in types of educational opportunities that are available within the public school system.
> 6) Hold the schools established under this act accountable for meeting measurable academic standards and provide the school with a method to establish accountability systems.

The Act goes on to state that charter schools "may be established by an individual, one or more teachers who will teach at the charter school, parents or guardians of students who will attend the charter school, any nonsectarian college, university or museum located in the Commonwealth; any nonsectarian corporation not for profit...any corporation association or partnership, or any combination thereof." 24 Pa.C.S. §1717-A(a).

"A charter school may be established by creating a new school or converting an existing public school or a portion of an existing public school." 24 Pa. C.S. §1717-A(a). The conversion of an existing public school to a charter school may be initiated by any individual or entity authorized to establish a charter school." 24 Pa.C.S. §1717 –A(b). In order to convert an existing public school into a charter school, more than 50% of the teachers at the school must sign a petition in support of the conversion to a charter school, and more than 50% of the parents or guardians of the pupils attending the school must also sign a petition in support of the charter school conversion. 24 Pa. C.S. §1717-A(i) & (ii). The Pennsylvania "conversion clause" states that any individual or entity authorized to start a charter school under the law can "initiate" the conversion of a regular public school into a charter school.

The ideals stated in those sections are basically the ideals of the charter school movement. It seems clear that the legislative intent is that charter schools would be governed by the local school community. For those ideals to actually become reality, we must set the conditions in the governance structure of charter schools. The purpose of charter school governance is to enable and ensure that those practices actually do occur in schools for the benefit and best interests of the children who attend those public schools. So let us look at the governance provisions established by our charter school laws, the issues they attempt to resolve and the issues they ultimately create.

But first, let us keep in mind the essential realities of effective schools. No matter how our charter schools are ultimately governed, we are still hooked to the fact that effective schools are effective school communities. We can never escape the realities we discussed in Chapter 5 about what good leadership is and we must recognize that effective school governance creates the framework and procedural structures for great school communities to emerge. It is still about the community of schools, collegiality, the common purpose, the collective mission and the collective vision. It is about raising issues, debating them out and agreeing on a course of action to meet the educational needs of our children. Leadership will always be about creating excitement and energy in what we do. If our charter schools do not do that, they have failed, and so have we.

Charter schools are created as corporate entities. They are nonprofit corporations and the legal language of charter schools is that a charter school is a **"body corporate"** under the corporation laws of each state. See, for example, 24 Pa.C.S. §1717–A(a). Corporate law is mostly within the jurisdiction of individual states but there are some federal laws that do apply to non profit corporations within states pursuant to the supremacy clause of the Constitution.

As nonprofit corporations, charter schools are bound by the same corporate structure we spoke of in the preceding section. They must have boards of trustees or directors who are entrusted with the duty and power to manage the charter schools. In Pennsylvania and most states, the charter school statute mandates that charter schools have a board of trustees who are empowered to manage each school. The fact that the statute creates "trustees" rather than "directors" is significant because it can be legally argued that trusteeships require a higher standard of care, good faith and loyalty because it recognizes that schools are a "public trust."

The basic structure of charter schools is virtually the same as the structure of local school districts. The essential difference is that a charter school has no "residents"—or do they? Someone or some group of people must be empowered to vote for the board of trustees. Students enrolled in a school are a type of resident and so are their parents. The teachers and professional employees are also a type of resident. They are all certainly stakeholders. Are the stakeholders of a school any different from the residents of a school district or the stockholders of a corporation?

No matter how we view it, the corporate structure is still:

(1) The *stakeholders* (stockholders or residents) elect or some individual or some body with the power to appoint the trustees elects or selects the individual *trustees* to the board of trustees;

(2) The *board of trustees* manages the business of the school and selects the officers who run the school; and

(3) *Officers* do what they are told to do by the board of trustees (Adapted from Conard, Knauss & Siegel, 1977, p. 731).

The issue of how the board of trustees is elected or selected is the major issue of charter school governance because it is the board of trustees who hold the power to manage the school and oversee and control the management of the school by its officers. It can be well argued that the real power to control charter schools lies in who gets to elect or appoint the board of trustees. **If an individual or group of individuals controls the power of appointment of trustees, they really control the management of the school.**

The essential question for boards of trustees is to whom do they owe their fiduciary duties? Think again back to Chapter 2 where we discussed the fiduciary duties of trustees and the statement of our leading expert on corporate fiduciary duties of trustees. He stated, **"The first question that must be answered when we represent boards of trustees is 'whose organization is it' because it answers the question to whom does the board of trustees owe its fiduciary duty of care, loyalty and good faith."** The essential question then and always is whose school is it? Is it the founder's school or the coalition of founder's school? Is it the teachers' school? Is it the parents' school? Is it all of those stakeholders' school? Where does the public at large stand in relation to charter schools? **Whose school is it?**

I do not think we will get any arguments that the essential purpose of schools is to benefit the students who attend those schools. They are the beneficiaries of the trusts of schools. The founder is not the beneficiary of the trust of schools. The government is not the beneficiary of schools. The employers of Americans are not the beneficiaries of the trust of schools. Yes, all those elements of America do benefit from well educated students, but the primary beneficiaries of schools are the students.

Charter schools as public schools will always have the legal duty to act in the best interests of its students. So how do we ensure that charter schools are indeed governed for the best interests of the students and not for the best interests of the founder or coalition of founders? Remember, self-dealing is a breach of fiduciary duty and is actionable at law. So again, how do we set the conditions for the best interests of our students to emerge as the guiding principle for what happens in charter schools?

Think back to the "Grand Hypothetical of School Governance". What were your answers? Now, think about those questions within the confines of charter schools as corporate entities with boards of trustees and their purposes as stated by the legislatures of our states. They are the issues of school governance.

What and where are the rights of parents whose children attend those charter schools to "participate in the governance of charter schools." Do the sunshine laws apply to charter schools? Do parents have participative due process rights in the governance of their schools? I believe so—constitutionally, statutorily and as a basic human right of mankind. In Pennsylvania, the charter school law specifically states that the board of trustees comply with the *"Sunshine Act."* 24 Pa.C.S §17-1716-A(c). How do charter schools resolve the issues of curriculum, pedagogy, special education, discipline, expulsions, and budgetary expenditures, etc? What is their "right to be heard" in a meaningful way and have their concerns legitimately and fairly addressed?

The Sunshine Act of Pennsylvania certainly provides those statutory rights and so do the sunshine laws of most other states, too. For procedural due process to occur, school board actions and policies must be enacted through "resolutions" adopted at public meetings. Citizens must be given "notice" that the actions are pending and the opportunity to be heard on those matters before a resolution is passed. Additionally, anyone may speak on any matter pertaining to the schools governed by the board. See, *Sunshine Act,* 65 Pa.C.S. §701, et seq.

How about the teachers at a charter school? What are their rights to participate in the governance of the school? Do they have legally enforceable participatory due process rights in the governance of charter schools? **One of the stated purposes of charter schools as cited above is to: "Create new professional opportunities for teachers, including the opportunity to be responsible for the learning program at the school site." For that to actually happen, they must have the "power to control the learning program" of the school. The only way that can happen is if they have legitimate power within the governance structure of the school. It can happen no other way. It can be no other way.** Clearly, there is legislative intent supporting the philosophy that schools should be governed and controlled by the school community.

The Pennsylvania statute requires that the charter for all charter schools contain a provision determining: **"How the board of trustees is appointed or elected."** 24 Pa.C.S. §17-1719-A(4). The public policy and legal issue of whether the board of trustees is elected or selected is the primary and essential question for the proper governance of our public charter schools in America. If we allow a founder or group of individuals the power to "select" the board of trustees and allow them the power to pass down "trusteeships" to those they personally choose, have we not then granted property rights to them? Have we not then granted property rights in our public schools to what are actually individual citizens?

Look at that scenario closely. Under those circumstances the rights of trustees are handed down to others similarly to the distributions of a "Will" that creates a testamentary trust. The provisions of a testamentary trust are enforceable at law and are not normally changeable by the trustees. The provisions of a will are distributable because they are property rights. What happens if, because of changes of circumstances, a group of individuals wants to change the theme or philosophy of the school? Is the charter created by the coalition of founders determinant? Or are the wishes of the populace of the school the determinant factor? **What would you say if our local city or town councils had the right to appoint succeeding council representatives? Who would they then be representing? You would say that is crazy! So why would we allow that to happen in our public schools?**

Under the charter school law of Pennsylvania, the trustees are "public officials" and are bound by the "Public Officials Law." 24 Pa.C.S. § 17-1715-A(11). Their fiduciary duties definitely lie to the students in a school and under the "corporate community" legal doctrine that was discussed in Chapter 2, to the entire "school community." How do we ensure that they are true to their duties? The answer to that question is either (1) through the legal system, or (2) through a democratic system of school governance. The most pragmatic way and arguably the only viable way is through establishing a truly democratic governance structure for charter schools. **That is again, why in America—there is the imperative for democracy in all of our public schools.**

Under the democratic imperative for our charter schools, there is always the basic question of who gets to vote for the boards of trustees of charter schools? The question is always bicameral. Either the populace of the school elects the board of trustees or the board of trustees is appointed by an individual or group of individuals who are granted the power to appoint through a legitimate organizational document. The constitutional question pursuant to the Fourteenth Amendment is that in all areas of American jurisprudence where governmental officials are appointed, those who have the power of appointment are either directly elected by the people or are appointed by someone who is elected by the people. That legality is controlled by the democracy of our Constitution. If we, as a public policy, allow our public school boards of trustees to be appointed by individuals who are not elected by the people, or appointed by officials who are not elected by the people, or not elected by the stakeholders enrolled or employed at the school, it is constitutionally repugnant and violative of everything America stands for in its principals and values of governance!

It is because of that legal analysis, the constitutional questions it raises and the analysis of the "Grand Hypothetical of School Governance" that it is imperative that the boards of trustees of charter schools be elected by the stakeholders of a charter school's school community. If the board of trustees is to be "selected" in some manner, there must be a specific rationale and process delineated in the charter itself or the laws governing charter schools that meets Constitutional muster. Charter schools are American public schools and they must meet all Constitutional protections afforded the American people. Remember, we are speaking about our children here!

In Philadelphia itself, there is considerable question as to whether many of the charter schools are valid legal entities. From my readings of the actual charters of the charter schools in Philadelphia, they are very unclear as to how the actual trustees are "elected or appointed" as required by the Pennsylvania charter school law. That is problematic from a legal and ethical standpoint and the whole charter school system can be brought to question through our court system. The practice of the School Reform Commission of "declaring" some public schools charter schools without more is also constitutionally and statutorily questionable. In Philadelphia, individual charter schools and the whole charter school system as implemented is ripe for legal challenges. All that is needed is the right issue and controversy to emerge.

There is always the constitutional issue of whether a law is constitutional "on its face" or "as applied." The question of whether a law is written consistently with our Constitution is a question for all laws. If a law is written consistently with our Constitution it is said to be constitutional "on its face." How a law is "applied" is another constitutional issue. If a law is being applied in a manner that is not consistent with our Constitution it is said to be unconstitutional "as applied." Charter school laws are normally constitutional as written but in actual practice they may be operated unconstitutionally. The school boards and legislatures overseeing all charter schools in America should take notice and review their charter school documents, practices and procedures to ensure constitutionality and high ethical standards. Our children deserve the best practices.

There are two caveats that must always be considered when we view the ethics and constitutionality of charter school governance and operations. First, is what I call the **"Enron disease caveat."** Enron was the giant corporation whose corporate executives mismanaged the corporation, hid it from the employees and stockholders, and ruined the retirement accounts of thousands of Americans. Enron became infected with the disease of immorality because its board of trustees was chosen and put in place by the CEO, and in return, the board of trustees gave the CEO everything he wanted including a multimillion dollar salary while he was running the corporation into the ground. All of the executives were living high while the proverbial Rome was burning. Some of the perpetrators of the fraudulent practices have already been sent to jail. Any scenario where the CEO or any individual who is being paid with charter school money has the power to select and appoint trustees, is essentially an unethical situation that is ripe for impropriety. That can just not be allowed to happen in American public schools.

Second, is the **"landlord caveat."** By law, charter schools must be nonprofit organizations and no individual is supposed to profit from the charter school except as a salaried employee. The scheme to get around that provision that is happening in some situations is this: Most charter schools must rent facilities. The best way to profit from charter schools is through a rental contract. The charter school operator either owns the rental facility or rents the facility and then sublets the facility to the charter schools. The landlord is the one who thereby profits from the charter school and the whole scheme is to profit from the setup. Thereby a private individual exploits the situation into a profit making scheme for himself. Smart huh? School boards must be vigilant on behalf of our children and our communities. That is another weight in the scales of justice tipping toward democracy as imperative for our charter schools.

If charter schools are to become democratically governed organizations, we must answer the question of who votes for the leaders and how do we vote. Possible voting scenarios were discussed earlier in this chapter, but it is necessary to focus on some issues here. A possible scenario that has successfully worked in the case of voting for school councils is the "one family one vote" process. When a family enrolls a student in a charter school, the family then becomes eligible to vote for the leaders of the school—the board of trustees. A progressively governed charter school may also want to extend voting rights to vote directly for the principal of the school. My first democratically governed charter school constitution did exactly that.

The issue then becomes, how about the teachers and other staff members? Do they get to vote? They are stakeholders and the democratic answer would be yes! How about the larger community? They have a stake, too. The easy answer and the most simple answer under a total school community approach is that the parents could vote for one third of the board of trustees, the teachers and staff could vote for one third of the board of trustees, and the at-large community could vote for, or the mayor or school board could appoint, one third of the board of trustees. That would give us a balance.

Those scenarios are questions that can be answered in several different structures and they all can be debated to fruition. **But the issue of who gets to vote for our leaders will never go away.**

The issue of how long should the term of office be for the trustees of charter schools is also always an open question. Those issues were discussed previously in this chapter, but it should be remembered here that in a democratic society there needs to be some term limit and it may be good to have the terms of trustees run in a "staggered" manner in order to get some type of continuity. They are considerations for school governance and they need to be addressed in the charter school charters themselves.

If charter schools are to become effective schools for our children, they need to be governed and led in a democratic way that ensures all that needs to be done for children are done for children. In the world of education there are just too many issues, too many factors, too many situations, too many individuals to do it any other way. **The imperative for democracy is just too strong—it is "The American Vision."**

7.5

Independent Schools—A Superior Model

The model most likely to produce collective endeavor that meets the "best interests of the students" standard and yield the requisite synergy and responsibility of the local school community for educational outcomes is this simple independent school model. Think about it!

A viable form of school governance that offers great possibilities for outstanding governance of schools as communities is the concept of the "independent school" as laid out by the Pennsylvania General Assembly. An independent school is a type of hybrid between a charter school and a regular high school and may be a much better form of school governance. It certainly offers more flexibility and a better opportunity for the local school community to govern the school. What astounds me is that the School Reform Commission in Philadelphia with its mission of reforming public schools and creating a variety of options and choices of schools has not yet instituted that model. I guess sometimes it takes a while for the apple to hit the right people on the head.

Under Section 5-502.1 of the Pennsylvania Public School Code, **Establishment of Independent Schools,** a school district may, upon the approval of the board of school directors, designate any school of the school district as an independent school. 24 Pa.C.S. §5-502.1 et seq. There must be an agreement between the school board and the governing body of the independent school. The Act provides that: **"The governing body of the independent school including its composition, membership and selection process, shall be established by the board of school directors. The governing body shall include representatives of parents and teachers."** 24 Pa.C.S. §5-502.1(a). **Teacher representatives must be "selected by a vote" of teachers employed at the school. And the governing body of the school has the authority to decide all matters related to the operation of the school pursuant to the agreement established under subsection (b) of the Act.**

Under subsection (b) the agreement must, inter alia, do the following:
1) Describe the governance structure of the school.
2) Prescribe the educational goals and mission, and the curriculum to be offered.
3) Describe the academic, fiscal and other goals and objectives for which the independent school will be held accountable and the evaluation criteria

and procedures that will be employed to determine if the school is meeting its terms and objectives.

4) Grant the independent school allocation of, and control over, its funding and budget. The independent school's funding shall be determined by the agreement.

5) Grant the independent school control over its educational program and curriculum.

6) Prescribe the authority to select both professional and support personnel and establish working conditions.

7) Define the terms by which the agreement may be terminated, modified or renewed.

8) An independent school must be for a term of at least three years but no longer than five years unless renewed.

9) Employees of an independent school shall be "employees of the school district."

The independent school model described above may very well be a superior model for effective school governance for several reasons, but these are the most salient:

First, the independent school model is a superior school governance design because it places the responsibility for the governance and well functioning of the school squarely on the school community where it belongs. The best answer to the question whose school is it is that it is the school community's school! Sorry but that's the truth. Think about it. For all the reasons laid out in this book, practical reality, leadership realities, fiduciary duties of trustees, constitutional, pedagogical, psychological, educational, curricular, ethical and others, it is a superior model.

The reality is that instructional decisions for the best interests of children can never be made adequately without knowing the children you are making those decisions for. They can never be made from afar. Great governance like great leadership can never be exercised from a distance. It just does not work that way. You just can not make educational decisions correctly from afar. One size for all students has never worked in the past, is not working now in cities like Philadelphia and New York, and will never work in the future. It does not work anywhere. There are just too many individual realities of students from so many differing walks of life. There are too many differential needs and too many variables.

What I have seen imposed upon schools and students within them because of macro-political ridiculousness, especially under *No Child Left Behind,* is quite frankly a disgrace to our profession as educators and our great mission of outstanding equal education for all. **The best interests of students, while spoken about often, are almost never the basis of fundamental decisions for children.**

They are almost always made for the self interest of macro-political players. That is the sad reality of today's world of education and it is time for change.

The teachers are the professionals we must rely upon and the parents are the caregivers and the ones responsible for seeing their children are served appropriately. My experience in over thirty-two years of working in schools is that teachers are the professionals with the most knowledge about good educational practices. If we can not trust them, there is no hope for great schools. They can very well collectively govern themselves, choose their own leaders, decide upon and implement outstanding educational programs and determine the best curriculum and instructional practices for children within appropriate parameters. Remember, "Trust is a risk game. The leader must ante up first." Trust the teachers and parents—they are good people.

The independent school model is the best model I have discovered with the best chance to "set the conditions for outstanding schools to emerge." For great schools to emerge, professionals must be allowed to run their own schools within the confines of professional standards and codes of ethics. The parents must be involved and have say in what happens in schools. Both groups must have legitimate power within the governance structures of schools for great governance, great leadership and great schools to emerge. And if parents abdicate their responsibilities, then the teachers must act **"in loco parentis"** for the best interests of the children they serve. They do that every day, every year, every decade in schools and they will continue to do that as long as schools exist.

And yes, the larger school community can be made part of the process—**"the participative due process"** of schools. The whole nation and all of the local communities will benefit from allowing school communities to become great school communities. The bottom line is increased student achievement both cognitively and affectively—that serves everyone.

Second, the independent school model eliminates the issue alluded to in the previous section on charter schools where a coalition of founders may run a school for their best interests alone. It eliminates the issue of whether granting the coalition of founders control of schools creates ownership rights in public schools. **It eliminates any question of whose school is it?**

Let us be clear on this ultimate reality: It is the quality of teachers in a school that is the main determinant of whether a school is a great school or less than adequate school. We can never get around that fact. We are always hooked to the reality that great teachers make schools great. As an attorney, I can not in good faith say to any teacher, and I personally know hundreds of great teachers, "Come with me and we will start a charter school and do great things for children." I can not in good faith say that to any teacher in America. Why? Because in moving to charter schools, they would be giving up their personal security. They would be taking a risk that could jeopardize their personal job security that they now have as regular school district employees with the protections of their union and collective bargaining rights.

One of the best provisions of the independent school model is that it requires the school to use regular school district employees. The Pennsylvania Act states, "Employees assigned to an independent school shall be employees of the school district." 24 Pa.C.S. §5-502.1(c). In most instances in America that means that the school's employees must be members of the American Federation of Teachers or the National Education Association. That gives them job security, and as we will see in the chapter on "the psychological perspective," security is a basic need of human beings without which they can not perform at their highest capacity.

With the independent school model any great educational leader can say to his or best colleagues, "Let's go start this kind of school and we will do great things for children without risking our personal welfare." **Now that is a great idea! Why can't we do that?** That would enable great teachers to get together and do great things for children.

Third, the independent school model enables there to be flexibility in creating a board of trustees or school council that serves the needs of the school community and has the legitimate power necessary to run the schools from a school-as-community model. The makeup of a board of trustees may take on a variety of forms and so can a school council. In my original response to the "Grand Hypothetical of School Governance" I created a board of trustees made up of three teachers elected by the staff of the school; three parents elected by the parents; two community members, one elected by the parents and one elected by the staff, and one school board appointee elected by the school board. The board of trustees were responsible for overseeing the management of the school by a CEO like the Supreme Court oversees the governance of our country and states. The CEO was directly elected by the parents and school staff in a balanced voting format. That is just "one way of doing it." There are many others.

The independent school model as described here is very similar to the governance model described in "Hilltop Babe Ruth" and similar to the model advocated by the *New* Commission on the Skills of the American Workforce (2007). The work of the new Commission is detailed in Chapter 7.6, but it should be noted here that they recommend that schools of the future be "limited liability companies (LLC's) owned and operated by the teachers." The flaw in that model is that it eliminates the parents and community from having any legitimate power. The teachers, as stockholders, control the governance of the school. Any input from parents would only be advisory in nature and the opportunity for voice giving would be granted at the wisdom and grace of the teachers.

The independent school model is superior to the "school-as-teacher controlled LLC" model because it has the additional benefit of keeping public schools public. It eliminates the privatization of our public schools for private benefit, and thereby keeps the public interest and the public trust at the forefront. In essence, a school controlled by teachers as stockholders in an LLC would be "the teacher's school." The Independent School model would be everybody's school similar to the model represented by "Hilltop Babe Ruth."

The issue is that for great schools to emerge, we must find a way to get schools to function in a truly collegial manner with a common vision and collective mission. All of our studies on great schools and great school leadership point in that direction. The independent school model affords us the best chance of accomplishing school-as-community governance that is responsive to the needs of the children and the individual school community that serves them. "Why can't we" in America, create some independent schools under this model? Our children deserve the best practices.

7.6

Pirate Democracy
&
The Privately Managed Schools

"To ensure democracy aboard pirate ships, the entire crew was governed by a strict set of rules and regulations ensuring that disputes were justly settled, booty was equally shared, and the injured were fairly compensated. The ship's "articles"—or code of conduct—were conceived and constructed by the pirates themselves and spelled out the rights, duties and powers of a ship's officers and crew. They were written out, signed and sworn to over a bible or boarding ax by all aboard. This democratic system aboard ship placed authority in the collective hands of the pirate crew."

The issue could not be said more poignantly than in those words about pirate democracy by Pat Croce in *Pirate Soul* (2006). His words capture the essence of the issues of governance in the face of the movement in America to have some of our schools managed by privately organized companies. Some of them are "for-profit" companies and some of them are supposedly "nonprofit." The questions always remain: Who is profiting from our public schools and how are they profiting? What do they provide in return for the money they collect? To be specific: **What is the quid pro quo?**

Again, we can never escape the essential question of this book: **Whose school is it and who should have the authority to govern our schools?** If we are to allow our public schools to be managed by contractors, then what are the parameters of their relationship to our governmental bodies and our citizenry. Where do they, and where should they, stand in the rubric of the governance of our schools? All across America we are seeing private management organizations gaining contracts to manage public schools. Whether these relationships benefit our schoolchildren or ultimately become another ineffective drain of our resources that should be given directly to our schoolchildren is an open question. **So is their constitutionality an open question.**

The nation's largest experiment with privately managed schools was embarked upon by the School Reform Commission in Philadelphia. Six private managers were awarded contracts to manage 45 schools. In a similar vein, The *New* Commission on the Skills of the American Workforce, after its comprehensive studies of the leading schools world-wide, recommended in its report, *Tough Choices or Tough Times,* that "one way" to create high performance schools is to create schools that are "operated by independent contractors, many of them limited liability corporations owned and operated by teachers" (Executive Summary, at p. 15). Such scenarios raise many legal and ethical issues that we must resolve as a society.

The primary question they raise is where do the parents and the children who attend those schools stand? What are their participative due process rights to participate in the governance and decision-making of their schools? How about the teachers who are employed at those schools? Do they have a right to participate in the governance of their schools? How do we balance the equities in constitutionally consistent ways? Are we allowing privatization of public education to enter through the back doors of our schoolhouses? What is our public policy? Where do we stand?

The Pennsylvania Supreme Court has already ruled that private management organizations can not be granted charters to operate charter schools, but they can be contracted with to provide services to charter schools. *West Chester Area School District v. Collegium Charter School,* 812 A.2d 1172 (Pa. 2002). The New Commission suggested that one of the possible new models would change the role of school boards so that their "primary role would be to write performance contracts with the operators of those schools, monitor their operations, cancel or decide not to renew the contracts of those providers, and find others that could do better" (*New* Commission, 2007). The question always arises as to what are appropriate services that can legally, ethically, and pragmatically be contracted to private managers in a public school setting?

The *New* Commission was comprised of some of our country's most outstanding leaders in education and public policy development. They contemplated schools being run in alternative ways. A more complete description of the make up of the commission, its mission, and a discussion of their findings and recommendations can be found in Chapter 9, "The Unions & Their Potential Greatness." But for our purposes here, it must be remembered that contracting for privately managed schools is only one way of "contracting" with schools and organizations for school management. There are other models discussed throughout this book and we are looking for the model that best "sets the conditions for great schools to emerge."

The *New* Commission also proposes that local school boards would also be responsible for gathering a large range of data, forwarding them to the state and sharing them with the public and with parents of the children in those schools. But before we look at the data on privately managed schools, let us consider and keep in mind the research based realities of creating great schools.

No matter what form of management is imposed upon a school, the quality of education the students receive is still determined by how well that group of people perform as a school community. Democratic leadership is still required and those governed need to be included in the governance of their schools including the choosing of its leaders for the requisite organizational synergy to emerge.

If privately managed corporations are given the task of running our schools or even owning our schools as professional limited liability corporations as the *New* Commission suggests, we still have the same issues of organizational governance. We still have the same issues all over again. Who has the power to choose the board of trustees and who has the power to choose the CEO? What is the legitimate power of the stockholders if our schools become LLC's, and what is the legitimate power of the stakeholders in a public school setting? We still have the issue of whose school is it? Because it is in that answer we find the answer to the question: To whom does the board of trustees owe their fiduciary duties? In the case of privately managed schools, to whom do they owe their fiduciary duties? Do they owe them to the stockholders of the management corporation or do they owe them to the students who attend those schools, their parents, the school community and the at large community? What is the answer?

Once we allow schools to be privately managed, we still have the same issues as stated in the "Pirate Democracy" lead to this chapter. We still need the "articles"— or code of conduct that spells out the rights, duties and powers of the organization's officers and crew. How is the "booty shared?" In for-profit corporations like Edison Schools, they still have all the issues of corporate governance. In nonprofit corporations we still have that same problem. The people who run and own the stock in nonprofit corporations still must divide up the profit among themselves. Because you see, in nonprofit corporations the people who run the corporation do "profit from the corporation" by drawing salaries. Yes the employees and officers of nonprofit corporations are the ones who profit. The term "nonprofit" may be one of our greatest legal fictions in America. Just look at the salaries of those who run our leading nonprofit corporations.

This is not to say, of course, that charter schools are not legitimate nonprofit corporations, or that independent schools are not legitimate nonprofit corporations. Certainly, if the design proposed by the *New* Commission is embraced where the teachers are the stockholders of a school organization there are ways to set up a legitimate governance structure. And certainly, the governance model represented by "Hilltop Babe Ruth" can be constructed to be a legitimate nonprofit corporation. It is just to say that without the total domain of democracy controlling the governance of our schools, we better keep our collective eyes open. Our children depend on it.

Now let us take a look at the data of one of our nation's largest experiments with schools run by privately controlled "educational management organizations" (EMO's)—the "Philadelphia experiment." The Rand Corporation in conjunction with a Philadelphia based organization, Research for Action, performed an independent study of the results of the performance of privately managed public schools in Philadelphia. The SRC spends approximately $18 million per year extra to pay for the contracted management services. The question really is, is it worth it?

When the state of Pennsylvania took over the public schools of Philadelphia, there was strong political pressure to privatize the management of Philadelphia's public schools because of a history of low achievement and financial distress (Gill, Zimmer, Christman & Blanc, 2007). In fact, then Pennsylvania Governor Tom Ridge hired Edison Schools, the nation's largest for-profit EMO, to review district operations and make recommendations for improvements and reorganizations. Naturally, they recommended that they themselves be given the schools to manage. Charles Zogby, Governor Ridge's secretary of education reflects that they believed the private sector could do a better job and they needed outside expertise (Gill et al, 2007). As a result of this "agenda to privatize the public schools," the newly formed School Reform Commission implemented what is known as **Philadelphia's "diverse provider" model.**

This diverse provider model is of national importance because it is the first large scale effort to outsource to private contractors the "core functions" of public schools—the design and delivery of educational programs. The scale of the private management is larger than in any other district in America. It involved 45 schools. The Rand study describes the issues and implementation of the model but its conclusions are based on standardized test scores in reading and math alone (Gill et al, 2007). Policymakers should read that study carefully because it offers a window into what could happen in other low achieving schools around the country because state takeover, restructuring and private management are three of the interventions prescribed by the federal *No Child Left Behind* Act (NCLB).

First, let me raise the caveat of the **"scope and breath"** of the management relationship to the schools and the school district that the EMO's have been afforded. In the face of the issues that were raised by the public concerning the private management of public schools, the School Reform Commission created a term known as **"thin management."** Exactly what that means is unclear, but in effect it means that they only have limited control over what happens in their schools. They are still controlled by many of the mandates of the central bureaucracy including the centrally mandated core curriculum and pacing schedule for instruction. They do have the freedom to initiate programs, provide professional development, control pedagogy and scheduling, and purchase books and other instructional resources.

How they manage and lead their schools is up to them. They are still hooked to the realities of school governance, leadership and organizational dynamics. Schools are communities; they need to be governed and led; the best leadership and governance is still democratic in nature; how the leaders are chosen is still of utmost importance; the fact is still there that a leader must either be chosen by the community or imposed upon the community; and every member of the school community needs to have a legitimate voice in what goes on there if the requisite synergy is to build for the schools to become great schools. They are still hooked to those realities.

According to the Rand study, the fact is that the schools run by EMO's did not perform as well as the schools managed by the regular structures of the Philadelphia School District as measured by standardized test scores. That is the bottom line. They have had five years to change the performance of their schools and they failed to raise test scores as much as the other schools in Philadelphia. They did raise test scores some, but not nearly enough for anyone to say the experiment was a success. In their defense they were given some of the lowest performing schools in the city. But the expectation and their promises were that under their management, those schools would improve. They did not.

There are some who argue that they need more time and that there are some benefits because of the private managers. But the reality is as one parent said in response to the Rand findings, **"Anyone who is standing up and defending these private contracts can't be doing it for educational reasons. It's been five years, and they're not really defensible anymore. My daughter and her school are suffering for it"** (Snyder, 2007). The conclusion of the Rand researchers is that the EMO's did not perform as well as the regular school district schools and there is no evidence or reason to believe that they are going to produce positive results in the future (Gill et al, 2007).

It is true as the CEO, Paul Vallas said, that you cannot look at the results monolithically. We do need to look at the results on a case by case individual school basis. But that is a main theme of this book: You can not make effective decisions about schools from afar. Only those people who are closely connected to the schools can possibly know the truth about the effectiveness of management and the leadership. We can never make blanket conclusions about anything in education yet alone the efficacy of school communities.

But the truth is that nationally, hired firms for the management of schools has had little effect. Such experiments have been tried in many of our major cities, including, Baltimore, Dallas, and Hartford. Most of those cities have ended those contracts because the EMO's have failed to produce (Woodall, 2007). The question is why?

The answer to the why have the EMO's failed to perform question is simple: They do not know anything anyone else does not know! They know nothing more about pedagogy than the rest of us. They know nothing more about leadership than the rest of us. They know nothing more about good management than the rest of us. They are largely made up of people who have made no significant contribution to the world of education and many of the people connected to those organizations were less than accomplished school leaders to begin with. They have no special expertise whatsoever. If they know anything the rest of us do not know, they have a moral duty to the schoolchildren of America to write a book about it and let us all in on it. But the fact of the matter is they can't write a book about it because they have nothing more to offer us than what we have already done in America's schools. That is the inescapable bottom line.

Superimposed upon that reality is the reality of what normally happens when management organizations are imposed upon school communities. Most of the best and brightest within the community flee. The Rand study cites the fact that in the schools that private management organizations were given to manage, popular principals left and teacher transfers proliferated. The analogy is clear: It was no different than what happens when a country is taken over by another country through war—the people flee. **The result of the Philadelphia experiment highlights the fact that leadership in a democratic society can never be properly imposed upon a school community. It does not work in Philadelphia and will not work anywhere in America.**

Another case in point is what happened in Chester, Pennsylvania. When the state took over the schools, the appointed school board hired Edison Schools to manage Chester High School. Edison hired the principal and the school district hired the teachers and the superintendent. The experiment was an utter failure that resulted in the school district being placed in receivership (See, *Commonwealth of Pennsylvania, Department of Education v. Chester-Upland School District Board of Control,* 2006). The Court in its Findings of Fact described a comedy of errors and conflicts as a result of the imposed management upon the school community.

When the state of Pennsylvania took over Philadelphia's public schools, they mandated the privatization of our schools. The legislature even appropriated millions of dollars for that experiment that was earmarked for the private managers. The republican governor imposed the republican agenda upon our schoolchildren. The School Reform Commission reformed our schools largely based on that mandate. It was hard to determine then just who were the clients of our school system. **It appeared then, and still often does appear, that the clients are the EMO's and their businessmen not the schoolchildren of Philadelphia. May I remind us that our fiduciary duties are owed to our schoolchildren!**

This is the fact of the matter: The School Reform Commission called for proposals from private management organizations immediately upon the takeover. The EMO's were invited to present their offerings publicly in several settings. They did have awesome power point presentations for the public to see. The presentations were impressive visually. The problem was that they offered nothing new in education. All of the proposals that any of the EMO's made for improving education had already been tried in Philadlphia's schools. They offered nothing new whatsoever. And the fact still remains they have nothing new to offer.

The truth is and the truth always will be that there is nothing new in education except technology. Those of us who have been in education for years have heard that statement over and over and realize it is true. The same old issues and concepts just keep reappearing in education. They are the same now as they were when I entered education 35 years ago. They will still be here a hundred years from now. They will still be the same issues all across America and the world. They are not going away. **The process of governance and leadership of our schools is what is important and that is a democratic process. It is the "process" of democracy that is imperative.**

The fact is that private educational management organizations are formed to make money off of our schoolchildren. We can not escape that reality. If anyone argues that point they are naïve. If they can offer us a service that is worthwhile, then we can contract for that particular service. But we must guard against the exploitation of our schoolchildren by entrepreneurs that want to profit from our public schools. **Governance can never be contracted away in a democratic society.**

Yes, privately managed schools are still hooked to all the issues of school governance and leadership that are raised in this book. Moreover, they must face two issues of governance: (1) the governance of their own corporation as an entity, and (2) the governance of the public school they are hired to manage. The bottom line is that they have been around for over 15 years now and they have not produced the revolutionary results they have advertised—and they never will.

The Philadelphia experiment is a case in point of private educational management organizations being appointed as managers of public schools. The results were clearly ineffective when we look at their performance within the rubric of achievement test scores of their students. The conclusion of the researchers in the Rand study is simple: ***"In sum, with four years of data, we find little evidence in terms of academic outcomes that would support the additional resources for private managers"*** (Gill et al, 2007, at p.41).

The EMO's can argue that they were never given complete control of those schools and were not allowed to hire and use their own teachers. But if they were allowed complete control of public schools, the schools would no longer be public schools. It is also true, that if schools were organized as LLC's with teachers and others as stockholders as the New Commission suggests, they would no longer be public schools—they would be private schools. What we would have then is a voucher system for private schools that entered through the back door of the schoolhouse! Is that what we want?

You see, the issue never goes away: **"Whose school is it?"**

Let me conclude with this question: How many of you when you answered the questions raised by "The Grand Hypothetical of School Governance" chose a governance structure for our schools that called for a for-profit corporation to be imposed upon a school and dictate what is going to happen? **Is that how we effectuate the best interests of our students?**

7.7

The Takeovers of Our Schools

The further we get away from democracy in education the worse our schools become. It is time to right the course of our ship. Our children's lives depend on it!

"You are just in the wrong place at the wrong time! You have done nothing wrong."

That was the message Deidre Farmbry, the Superintendent of Schools, repeated over and over again to the school community members of the School District of Philadelphia as they lost their jobs to the corporate raiders that descended upon Philadelphia. What a Faustian experience it was. If I had not seen it with my own eyes, I would not have believed such things happened in America. But they do.

I will never forget the day the school district was officially taken over by the state of Pennsylvania. I went to the school district headquarters to visit the superintendent's office. What I heard still echoes through my mind. There were a few school board members and higher level school district officials huddling in the next room in desperation that the enemy was coming. It was as if their fortunes were about to be raided and their homes pillaged. Fear permeated the air. What a telling memory.

Deidre Farmbry was the sitting superintendent of schools who stood tall as the turmoil ensued and havoc was all around us. Dedicated educators in the central administration were losing their jobs left and right as the new School Reform Commission (SRC) was instituted. Her leadership amongst the lunacy was outstanding as she constantly reminded us all to, **"Focus on the students."** She urged us to remember that it was they who were important and not get caught up in the whirlwind of the takeover. She held meetings all over the district and explained the realities to everyone and urged us all to consider ourselves as free agents.

She earned my utmost admiration and respect for what she did. She knew she was expected to hold the district together for several months and then she would be replaced when they "put their own man in." She handled the situation with the utmost class and dignity. It was amazing. Here was an African American woman who grew up in Philadelphia, went through the Philadelphia school system, taught in Philadelphia and emerged as the superintendent of schools who was forced out without any input from the people of Philadelphia or Philadelphia's school communities.

Yes, she was replaced by a politician from Chicago. Look at the picture. Here was a woman who dedicated her life to the schoolchildren of Philadelphia being replaced by a man from a different city who was dedicated to nothing but his political fortunes. He was billed as a budget man. Well, five years later we are at the same place we were then—over $150 million short and we are in another budget crisis. What is worse is that the man is not even an educator. His first act of leadership was to create fear within the school system and brag that he was "jettisoning people." He removed people for the "shock effect." So much for the mentality of the man. We knew he knew little about instruction, but what amazes me more is how little he knows about leadership and school governance. He took us backwards fifteen years in the arena of school governance and leadership.

Philadelphia was once one of our nation's leaders in inclusive, democratic practices in the governance of our schools. We were leaders in the development of small learning communities and schools within schools where teachers were empowered to do what is best for children. Principals had to go through a "site selection process" and be chosen by a committee of local school community members before they could be appointed as principals. Paul Vallas took us back into the feudalistic system of the past with his archaic military mentality where they do whatever they want whenever they want. Even that old style military mentality is being abandoned in America's armed forces. The SRC let him do it. They made the mistake of allowing him to be a loose cannon. He has since lost his credibility, and as Kouzes and Posner state: "Credibility is the foundation of leadership. Once a leader loses it, he can never gain it back.

But before we delve into the Philadelphia story and lay bare the real reasons for the takeover of Philadelphia's schools, we all should visit the school district down the river from Philadelphia. The Chester-Upland School District in Pennsylvania stands as a prime example of what we can never allow to happen to our school districts in America. It stands as a prime example of what we can never allow to happen to our school communities and ultimately the schoolchildren of America. It stands as a prime example of why we need to stick to democracy as the governance system for our schools.

In the case of Chester-Upland, the Pennsylvania state Department of Education recently sued to place the school district in receivership. *Commonwealth of Pennsylvania, Department of Education v. Chester-Upland School District Board of Control*, __ A.2d __, No. 496 M.D. 2005, (Pa.Cmwlth. October 16, 2006). The democratically elected school board was removed pursuant to state action in 1994 because the school district was in **"financial distress."** Since then, there have been three different appointed boards of control and the situation in Chester-Upland has become progressively worse as the system moved further and further away from democracy. There was another Special Board of Control (SBOC) appointed in 2002 pursuant to yet another school takeover law. The results are shocking to anyone who cares about children and their schools.

The Commonwealth Court in its "Memorandum Opinion and Order" found that the Special Board of Control (SBOC) has mismanaged the school district and "has not been sufficiently attentive to the needs of children." *Chester-Upland* (Pa. Cmwlth. 2006, at 1). The Court placed the school district in receivership pendente lite and named the Secretary of Education as Receiver. **The Court stated unequivocally and very poignantly: "Courts do not have the expertise nor training to direct the day-to-day operations of school districts. Of course, neither do politicians such as the presently appointed Chairman of the SBOC."** *Chester-Upland* (Pa.Cmwlth. 2006, at 46) But what is even more poignant is the statement in the Amicus Curiae brief in the interest of the Chester-Upland Community Parents and Students on the Move: **"The accumulated impact of these educational failures creates conditions that are almost literally killing the children of Chester-Upland."** (Brief For Chester-Upland Community Parents on the Move, Amicus Curiae, In Support of Petitioner at 9, *Chester-Upland (Pa.Cmwlth. 2006).*

The parents and students of Chester-Upland asked the Court to order several provisions mandating the inclusion of the Chester-Upland community, parents and students in the process of governance of their schools. But most importantly, they ask the Court to order the Receiver to: **"Develop and implement a process for gradually returning control of district schools to a locally elected school board."** It is their contention that, "Parent involvement and community participation are key factors in the process of successfully managing local schools and improving educational conditions and outcomes." *Amicus Curiae,* Chester Upland Community Parents at 13. They argue that the school district has been run by partisan outsiders who do not live in the school district, are affiliated with the opposing political party to the majority of those in Chester-Upland, and are distrusted by the Chester-Upland community. The situation is untenable and the result is irreparable harm to their children and community.

The Commonwealth Court of Pennsylvania held hearings and the Court's "Findings of Fact" tell the story. It is important to note as we go through the facts is that the whole thing started because the Chester-Upland School District was and still is financially distressed. Financial distress appears to be the common denominator for school districts that are taken over by the state. Financial distress for school districts always starts with economic distress for communities and it always comes down to economics and the way we finance our public schools.

The Chester-Upland School District was controlled by a democratically elected school board until 1994 when it was declared a financially distressed school district by the state Secretary of Education. A special board of control was put in place and ran the district from 1994 to 2000. In 2000, the state enacted a new Education Empowerment Act and the district was certified as an Educational Empowerment District because of a history of low test scores. An Empowerment Board of Control was appointed by the Secretary of Education to replace the SBOC. In 2002, the General Assembly amended the state statutes, then Governor Mark Schweiker signed them into law, and then Secretary of Education Charles Zogby appointed Michael Gillin, the Register of Wills of Delaware County, to another newly enacted SBOC. The Court of Common Pleas of Delaware County, the county where Chester-Upland is situated, appointed two other members of the SBOC. There were only three members of the SBOC and they voted to appoint Michael Gillin as the chair of the SBOC.

One of the first things Michael Gillin did was to negotiate himself a five year consulting contract with the Department of Education that netted him $50,000.00 per year for five years. Mind you, this is the Register of Wills of Delaware County. The only qualifications he has to run a school district is that he is politically connected to the Republican party of Delaware County, Pennsylvania. The tale of complete mismanagement and incompetence of the school district ensued.

At the time the latest SBOC took control of the district, Edison Schools, the nation's leading private manager of schools, ran eight of the nine schools. Edison employed the principals and the district employed the teachers. The Court documents the fact that there was tension between Edison, the district administration, the teachers and the community. The Court also documented serious deficiencies in the charter schools of Chester. The bottom line is that the district is a mess and so are its schools. Chester High School is riddled with oversized classes and the school has been out of control. Edison Schools has since abandoned the school district and its schoolchildren.

In September, 2004, a financial consultant was hired by the SBOC at the insistence of the Department of Education. The consultant testified that the district was a "disaster." He testified, "Every single aspect of everything that we looked at was either not being done, being done improperly or being done incorrectly." The Court also accepted the consultant's conclusion that the individuals managing the district "didn't know what the heck they were doing." He had not seen a situation in so much financial chaos at any other school district with which he had been involved. *Chester-Upland* (Pa.Cmwlth. 2006, at 21). The consultant further testified that the state of affairs was particularly unacceptable since the district had in its possession, but did not use, an excellent software information management system for which it had paid hundreds of thousands of dollars. Additionally, the IRS was threatening to impose "immense" fines because the district did not file payroll reports for two quarters.

The financial consultant also refused to work on the budget for the year 2005 because it was "fake" and he refused to put his name on it. His opinion was that the budget was "fictional" and testified, "I would think Ernest Hemingway wrote it." Even though the SBOC knew that the budget was fictional and incompetently drawn up, the SBOC approved the budget and sent it to the Department of Education. The situation was a travesty.

Now add this to the rubric: The largest charter school in the district, Chester Community Charter School is managed by Charter School Management, Inc. (CSM). CSM's CEO is Vahan Guregian. Mr. Guregian's wife, Danielle Gureghian, was listed on the letterhead of Mr. Gillin's law firm as being of counsel for Mr. Gillin's law firm. Mr. Gillin also rented office space to CCCS! CCCS was also allowed to illegally expand its enrollment by Mr. Gillin's SBOC. What a travesty of self-dealing, a clear breach of fiduciary duty. My grandmother would put it as "being in cahoots!" It appears Mr. Gillin and his friends conspired to scam the schoolchildren of Chester Upland. That is the bottom line.

The view of the community is represented in the Amicus Curiae brief of the Chester-Upland Community Parents and Students on the Move written by the lawyers for the Pennsylvania Education Law Center. They assert that the parents and community of Chester-Upland have been illegally frozen out of the governance process for their public schools. They cite numerous violations of state and federal statutes that require parent and community input into governance and decision-making including the Sunshine Act and Right to Know Act. They accuse the politically appointed Board of Control of disregard for these basic legal requirements and near contempt for the role of parents and community. They argue that "without vigorous involvement by parents and community leaders in local school reform and governance" there is "little hope for improving our public schools."

The people of Chester-Upland only want to have a voice in the governance of their schools and control over what happens to their children. That is not only a statutory right, but it is also a Constitutional right. **What has happened in Chester-Upland is a prime example of what happens when politicians run public schools. It is a sad example of what happens when democracy is taken out of the governance of our public schools. It can not be allowed to happen in our America.**

The people of Chester-Upland asked the Court to require the receiver to create structures for open and effective governance of their schools. They ask that there be a new multi-member decision-making body put in force and a district-wide advisory board to provide input and support. They asked for diverse working groups to be established to address key educational issues. And finally, as mentioned previously, they ask for a return to their democratically elected school board.

What the parents, students and community ask for is simply all the elements of effective school governance and leadership that all of our research shows is necessary for outstanding schools to exist. All of those research based elements of effective education are well documented throughout this book. That is really not too much for them to ask—and demand.

So let us go back up the Delaware river to Philadelphia where the schools were also taken over by the state of Pennsylvania about the same time and take a look at the Philadelphia story. We discussed in the previous chapter the Rand Corporation and Research for Action third party research study entitled *"State Takeover, School Restructuring, Private Management, and Student Achievement in Philadelphia* (Gill, 2007) and that study is cited here as the authority for most of the facts that I relate in this section. But again as we look at the facts we must be cognizant of the ever present two themes: It all comes down to financial distress and the power politics of politicians that know very little about education and pedagogy and want to impose their political agendas upon school communities.

The state of Pennsylvania took over Philadelphia's schools in the face of a budget crisis that had been festering for years because state funding had declined and the school district did not have enough money to run its schools. Then Superintendent of Schools, David Hornbeck, had called the state's funding policies racist, infuriating the Republican Governor Ridge and many others in power. There was special legislation directed at Philadelphia to forcibly take over the schools because of financial and academic distress. David Hormbeck resigned because he felt Philadelphia would never get enough money for its schools as long as he stayed in office. Shortly thereafter, Philadelphia Mayor John Street signed an agreement with the new Republican Governor Mark Schweiker for the takeover of Philadelphia's schools.

Charles Zogby, Governor Ridge's former secretary of education explained the state's perspective that they believed the private sector could do a better job of turning the school district around. He cited continuing low standardized test scores and asserted their belief that they needed outside expertise. The nine member board of education that had always been an appointed school board with the mayor having the sole power of appointment was replaced by the School Reform Commission (SRC). Three members were appointed by the governor and two were appointed by the mayor. The appointees were reflective of the thinking of the time—three members were private sector corporate executives, Jim Nevels, Daniel Whalen, and Martin Bednarik; one member was the president of Philadelphia University, James Galagher; and one member was Sandra Dungee Glenn who has a history of public service and advocacy in the political arena.

The SRC was granted unprecedented powers to reform and restructure the school system. They had sole power and authority to determine which charter schools were allowed to operate, hire private management companies to run schools, and to impose their restructuring initiatives upon school communities. There was a strong political movement to privatize the schools that met with an uproar from student and community groups. As a compromise they created the "diverse provider" model that was discussed in the previous chapter. They also created the concept of "thin management" where they justified the imposition of private educational management organizations (EMO's) upon school communities. They hired Paul Vallas from Chicago to be the CEO of Philadelphia. He had recently been fired from his post as CEO of Chicago's school system and had lost an election for Governor of Illinois.

The period that ensued was highly tumultuous. Paul Vallas brought with him his team from Chicago to run the school district. They made sweeping changes with little input from the community. In the trenches, the teachers and administrators referred to Paul Vallas and his friends from Chicago as the "Chicago regime." They went about changing everything that had been done before simply because it was there before. They had no idea what was working and what was not working. All they wanted to do was change everything. Paul Vallas created an atmosphere that everything that was there before was bad and everything he wanted to do was good. It was like *Animal Farm* came alive.

Paul Vallas created an atmosphere of hysteria and top down management that we had never seen before. Dedicated Philadelphia educators were routinely walked out of their offices by school police officers as if they were common criminals. The teams he created to "walk through" schools and judge what was happening had an attitude that was despotic in nature and reminiscent of the Salem witch-hunts. Principals were removed for "shock effect." School communities were excluded from participation in the governance of their schools like I had never seen before. Where he got the idea that is good school leadership and governance, I do not know. That style is not encouraged by any legitimate authority on school governance.

The sad part is that mentality permeated the entire school district. Many of our finest and most able educators left the system and there is still a lack of outstanding leaders in our district to this day. Thankfully, the atmosphere has settled down some and the school district is moving back toward professional and collegial practices. Almost all of the people he brought with him from Chicago have since left Philaldelphia and capable school leaders are beginning to emerge again.

Yes, under the leadership of Jim Nevels, the Chair of the SRC and the other SRC members, there have been some significant improvements in many aspects of Philaldephia's schools. There are also many failures. And yes, in all fairness to Paul Vallas, he had a hand in those improvements. An evaluation of all the improvements and failures is not possible here, but the creation of the High School of the Future, the Constitution School, and the Franklin Inststitute School are examples of improvements. The fate of many of our comprehensive high schools that remain riddled with violence and low test scores are examples of failures. The best evaluation of the results of the takeover can be found in the Rand report and I urge everyone to read that report.

The most significant improvement is the fact that the state assessments for NCLB show improved scores in math and reading although a majority of Philaldephia's students still perform significantly lower than the students across the state and do not attain proficiency at the high school level. There is much hoopla about the rise in test scores. **But let me put a caveat in the spin concerning those scores: many insiders believe the rise in test scores are attributable to the fact that we spend so much time "teaching to the test" and do not reflect real academic gains.** The bottom line is, of course, high school test scores, and they have not significantly improved over the five years of the takeover. It is the high school test scores that are least effected by teaching to the test. You see, test preparation only takes us so far. Once we do the "A" job on test preparation, then we are left with true academic ability and the need to develop true gain in reading and math ability. **What real gains we have made, and we have made some real gains, can be directly attributed to the dedication and hard work of the teachers in the trenches and the local administrators.**

The "diverse provider" model that the SRC has implemented was discussed in the previous chapter. Let it suffice here that there are only three models that were implemented: (1) charter schools run by the founders or coalition of founders, (2) privately managed schools where private managers were imposed upon the schools, and (3) regular schools managed by Paul Vallas and his subordinates. There are no "independent schools" where teachers and parents sit on the board of trustees. That model was fully discussed in chapter 6.7. And there are no schools based on the model suggested by the *New* Commission where the teachers at a school are the stockholders and in control of what happens. The teachers in Philadelphia have not been asked or provided the opportunity to propose alternative schools either. They are ideas for consideration.

While the SRC has unprecedented powers to reform and restructure schools, the commissioners are in the learning process also. So are we all. They must remember that they are the safe-keepers of the democracy within Philadelphia's school governance systems. They state in their beliefs that all schools should have school councils. They would be well to effectuate those beliefs. But as of now they are merely words on the wall of the auditorium in which they conduct their business. Very few schools actually do have school councils, and where they do, they have no legitimate power and authority—everything is still dictated by Paul Vallas and his crew of autocrats. **We must all remember that for our schools to be great schools, they must be the people's schools—not the politicians' schools!**

Because of the standardized testing mandates and its focus on "Adequate Yearly Progress" of *No Child Left Behind,* we in education have focused so much on the single factor of gain in standardized test scores to evaluate our schools that we have lost sight of so many of the factors that make our schools great or not so great. Standardized test scores are just "one element" of good schools. If that is all we can see about our schools, we have already lost the battle for great schools. There is so much more. Whether the schools meet the needs of their students who attend them and the communities that the schools serve is the bottom line. That can only be evaluated through the tests of the process of democracy.

Yes, we can look at all kinds of statistics such as promotion and graduation rates, report card grades, acceptances into colleges and universities, drop-out rates, etc., etc. But the people of the school community are the ones who really know how successful the school really is. There are miracles happening in every school in America. What is success in schools that help children in poverty can be so much different than what is success for our affluent schools. Schools can only be assessed and evaluated compared to itself and others similarly situated.

Yes, the test scores of Philadelphia's schools have gone up somewhat, but not at the high school level. Yet, at the very same time as these words are being laid upon the paper, there is a crisis in Philadelphia's schools that is dominating the news in Philadelphia. It is the crisis of school violence that continues to plague our comprehensive high schools. That crisis only illuminates what we have neglected in Philadelphia in our tunnel vision of high stakes testing. What we have lost focus of is the fact that we must build school communities to have great schools and the only way to build great school communities is to govern them democratically.

What we see happening in Philadelphia is the breakdown in the community of our schools. We have seen the breakdown of the community within our school district. That has happened because we have had imposed upon us an autoctratic governance structure that has virtually eliminated indicia of democracy in the practice of school governance. Our leaders, from the School Reform Commission to the principals and management organizations have been imposed upon school communities without democratic input from those communities. The result is a continuing breakdown of our school system.

What needs to change in Philadelphia and in many school districts in America is the culture of our governance system. It is the culture of our school administrations that must change if we are to have great schools. **That is the reform we really need. We need to return to democracy to save our schools.** In the later chapters on the psychological perspective and the institutional illnesses inherent in bureaucracy, we will view the human realities that make it imperative that we return to democracy as the governing principals that must guide our schools. They are the principals that make America—America.

In the era of high stakes testing, we have lost our course and focus on what is important in America. We must renew our focus on the principles embedded in our Constitution and the ideals we stand for in America. We spend too much of our time studying standardized tests and how to artificially make those scores rise, and not enough time on the ideals of America. We should spend far more time studying those American ideals and how to make them come alive in America's schools.

As we look at school takeovers and the issue of whether school boards in America should be elected or appointed, may I point out one more thought. There is a better way to help out our struggling school districts than states taking them over outright and eliminating democracy in their governance. The better way is to create a partnership with those school districts. It would be much better for state governments to require struggling school districts to use the assistance of state appointed experts to help them through their financial struggles and their management struggles than to take them over outright as if it were a hostile takeover. You just can not effectively take self governance out of local school communities.

There is no law in America that forbids school boards from reflecting a balance of elected and appointed members. There is no law in America that forbids school boards from reflecting a balance of state, city and elected representatives. School boards can reflect all kinds of new approaches to democracy and balance of power. For instance a nine member school board could consist of three members being appointed by the state governor, three members appointed by the elected mayor of a city and three members elected by the people. There are a host of possibilities that could be conceived by visionary leaders, but always remember, it is the collective vision that counts.

In my view, democracy dictates that our leaders be elected—it is the least bad way. Without democracy our schools have already lost our battle for great schools. Yes, democracy is imperative for the governance of America's schools.

8

"Torch"
Rebellion &
Toxic School Cultures

The phenomenon of toxicity in school cultures is a result of terrible leadership and management. It is an institutional illness caused by the principal of the particular school and the autocracy from above. Stop blaming the teachers!

"**T**his was a wonderful place to work until you came here!**"** Those were the resounding words of a highly respected physical education teacher at University City High School in Philadelphia, as he pointed at the principal. They were made directly to the principal as she stood on the stage of the auditorium right beside the president of the school board. It was rebellion at "Uni." The school had descended down the vicious cycle of toxicity. It was caused by the principal and everyone knew it.

You can not possibly understand what it is like to work in an atmosphere of toxicity unless you have lived there in that schoolhouse. Believe me, you can not. It is Faustian and it is debilitating. At the time, I was ashamed of my school community and myself, too, because I was a primary school leader there who had failed to stop the storm. I even had a difficult time talking about it to people outside our school because it was so shocking. It was a year later that I finally got words of solace from a professor at graduate school who later became the president of the principals' union in Philadelphia, George DiPilato. He said, "I know exactly what you are talking about. I worked in a situation like that before and I know how debilitating it can be. **The school district created it and it is the school district that has the responsibility to stop it.**"

University City High School was always a crazy school but it was always a wonderful school, too. As I look back on my twenty years there through the lens of my later experience in urban schools, I see so clearly what a wonderful place it was and what wonderful things we did for children there, 90% of whom came from families living in poverty. It had and still has a school culture and ethos all its own and no outsider who has not worked there can ever know it. That is why outsiders can never adequately choose its leader. **Only the school community understands itself and only the school community can decide upon its leader.**

135

And it is only the school community that can determine when a change of leadership is due. That is why there is an imperative for democracy in our schools. With democracy and its term limits, leaders are always chosen anew and there is seldom a need for rebellion or removal from office by a superior in the bureaucracy. That is the beauty of democracy—it allows our communities to renew themselves and reassert the reason for their being.

Yes, University City was a wonderful place to work for eighteen years under the leadership of Dr. Davis B. Martin. He was the epitome of the leader characterized by Kouzes and Posner as discussed in chapter 5. He was the father figure of many and the patriarch of the school community. The closeness of the faculty was phenomenal in the context of controversy that always was part of the school. The school had been born out of the civil rights movement and those issues were the issues of our school. It became part of its ethos, its collective mentality. As I look back on his leadership of the school and think of all the issues that need to be balanced in our schools, the respect I have for the man grows and grows. He handled serious situation after serious situation, change after change, mandate after mandate, controversy after controversy, all the while maintaining his pleasantness, humor and positivity at all times. He had **"people wisdom"** and that is the most important trait of a successful democratic leader.

When he retired, "they" sent us a principal with an autocratic attitude that she was going to heroically straighten out the teachers and the school. Her confrontational style, poor interpersonal skills and negative attitude toward the teachers immediately caused the school to descend into toxicity. It is as simple as that. All the negativity that Powers and Powers found in their studies of autocratic leadership began to ensue. Hard feelings and discord permeated the school and the leader began to use coercion and power plays to manage the school. Student discipline broke down and gangs of students roamed the halls. Violence and disrespect among the students festered throughout the building. The school became out of control. It became a vicious downward cycle into chaos that would not stop until the principal was finally removed.

How can such a wonderful school with a wonderful community atmosphere turn into such a terrible place to live and work? It is a recurring phenomenon and it happens every year in schools in America. Thankfully, it only happens in a small percentage of our schools. The sad thing is it happens so often in our urban schools where we are desperate for good schools to help poverty stricken children rise above their plight. If anyone thinks toxic school cultures do not affect the children, they are living in denial. It is no different than a child living in a home where the parents are constantly fighting. It becomes psychologically debilitating to the children.

Powers and Powers described the phenomenon in their classic study that we discussed in chapter five (1983). Let me reiterate their important points here: **They** concluded from their research that an autocratic leader's behavior will only be accepted "as a necessary burden" if that leader is seen as "especially competent." If not, "his or her tenure in office will be marked at least by hard feelings and discord and at the most by hatred and fear that can paralyze the operation he is supposed to make more efficient by his management." (at p. 26)

Again, this quotation is especially poignant about autocratic leadership and right on point when we look at the phenomenon of toxic school cultures:

> When heroic leadership is the dominant mode, a number of undesir-able and dysfunctional consequences are produced. Heroic leaders must maintain control over others since to lose that power entails a loss of ability to give orders that will be obeyed. Coercion, threats and power plays are common and they often engender feelings of resentment and acts of confrontation. As one respondent in our study of administrative style and student performance stated. "The top-down style of manage-ment alienates us. There is a real 'us {Administration}—they {teachers}' mentality. We are not working together to benefit students. We are locked in an adversarial relationship." Another respondent wrote, "Ignoring and not listening to teachers' ideas and concerns...does not allow for creative and innovative teaching, thus students do not get the benefit of a happy rejuvenated teacher—one who is constantly learning and improving." Another teacher said that the authoritarian leadership in her school "{gives us} a depressing feeling of hopelessness and neglect."

The autocratic, authoritarian, "King on the Throne" leadership mentality is really not leadership at all. It is poor management and leads to negative synergy and a definite and debilitating down-spiral of interpersonal relationships within a school or any organization for that matter. It is so prevalent in bureaucratic school systems it is "an institutional illness that is part of the mentality of unhealthy organizations." The collective ethos caused by that mentality ultimately leads to a destructive atmosphere and school climate. Again, what do you think is the effect on children who must attend a school like that and live there for much of their day?

Yes, toxic school cultures are caused by the mismanagement of schools, not by the teachers. There have been calls from leaders outside the schools for "reconstitu-tion" of schools. What is normally meant by those who call for reconstitution of schools is that the staff of those schools be removed and a new staff assigned there. That is not the answer. The answer is in choosing effective leadership for the schools and that can only be done through collaboration with the school community in choosing its own leaders. You see, that is how wholesome school communities work. That is how competency in management and leadership works.

University City was a great school community before the change in leadership. It descended into toxicity because of the negative attitude of the principal who was imposed upon the school. Immediately upon her removal after a year and a half of abysmal leadership, the school was "turned around" by the succeeding principal and the very same school with the very same teachers and support staff became the leaders of the "small learning community movement" in Philadelphia. The total atmosphere of the school changed. It went from a school where a group of parent and community activists actually "took over a teacher's classroom" as the teacher tried to teach her class to a school where the school board president of Trenton, New Jersey, visited and described the school as the only urban high school he had ever seen with such a positive atmosphere. He immediately offered the school's principal, Dr. James Lytle, the Superintendency of the School District of Trenton, New Jersey—and he accepted.

How was the school transformed? Let us take a look and see—and get a lesson from the Torch!

Torch

"Torch" is the nickname of Dr. James Lytle of the University of Pennsylvania. In 1995, he was as a central office administrator in the School District of Philadelphia. He got his nickname because of his flaming red hair and his redish skin tone. He was a tall and thin caucasian with a very soft and mild manner. He was a nurturing, caring individual more like a teddy bear than the stereotypical image of the myth of the urban principal who "runs his school" as the strong man in charge. His story of how he turned into the leading instructional leader in Philadelphia and turned University City High School into a model of urban school renewal is a classic for all times.

In 1995, David Hornbeck was brought to Philadelphia from Kentucky to run the School District. As a man of his times, he came to Philadelphia with an agenda of reconstitution of our schools and the district itself. In another example of the ridiculousness of corporate elitist thought, he told the entire administrative staff of the school district that he wanted them to resign and "reapply" for their jobs. This was supposed to be a symbolic act of their allegiance to him and their desire to be on his team. Not wanting to lose their jobs, everyone did exactly that—except Torch.

No, Torch said, "That's ridiculous. I'm not doing that." As a reward for his rebelliousness, he was assigned to a closet in the administration building. He reported to that closet every day for several weeks and did nothing in that closet but sit. His punishment for his civil disobedience. Henry David Thoreau where were you?

That was happening about the same time that he decided that they needed to remove the principal of University City High School. The management, in typical bureaucratic fashion, did not remove her because of her year and a half of negative leadership in the school. No, they only removed her when they found that the token money was funny! By that time the school was totally out of control and a splendid mess.

Yep, rather than keep punishing Torch with solitary confinement, David Hornbeck sent him to U-City High. When Torch came to University City, we were laughing and joking that Mr. Hornbeck probably sent him there to "The Killing Fields" to be eaten alive by the toxic school community there. Here was this flaming red haired, bearded, nerd of a man walking into "the most troubled school in Philadelphia." Many people laughed in anticipation of his torture.

Ironically, Torch knew the school community well and had insight into its nature. He also had a keen understanding of teacher empowerment and the philosophy of small learning community school restructuring. So what do you think happened? He turned the school into a model of urban school reform and completely turned the school around. He left the school three years later standing as a hero with a reputation of being a great instructional leader.

What he did was empower teachers and the school community to do what they thought would work. **Torch used a "teacher empowerment model" to transform the school into a model of urban school renewal.** He taught the teachers what the small learning community movement was about and empowered them to create "SLC's" to their own choosing. He used a democratic, laissez-faire leadership style to facilitate the process and enabled teachers to strive toward self-actualization in their desire to do good for children! He thereby created excitement and synergy that I had never seen before in our school or school district and have never seen again since our school district was taken over by the state and Paul Vallas was hired as our CEO. Paul Vallas killed that type of synergy with his autocratic style he brought with him from Chicago and imposed his "Chicago regime" upon Philadelphia.

Torch's first act as the new principal was to announce on the loud speaker that he was having a **"leadership team"** meeting after school in a large room in the basement. **Everyone in the school was invited to be on the leadership team! He also announced that the first meeting would focus on the school budget that just arrived from downtown.** What a change in leadership style. It went from completely autocratic where the principal did the budget in secrecy, to a completely open climate with full transparency. Just that alone created amazing excitement and synergy.

What happened is that there were about seventy-five staff members there that afternoon. Torch went over the budget allocations on the blackboard and interpreted them for the staff. The next day fifty staff members showed up and the process continued. The next day thirty showed up and the next day about fifteen showed up. Those fifteen were the ones that actually did the decision-making and performed the leadership. All the others did whatever was asked of them in small group meetings and kept their eyes on things. It was amazing to see all the new initiatives that they created and the fun they had doing their jobs.

That kind of synergy can never be imposed upon a school. It must be caused to rise from the community and become part of its ethos. It must be seeded, fed and nourished.

Torch led the restructuring of the total school into small learning communities by empowering teachers to form their own SLC's with the themes and purposes they thought would best motivate and support students to achieve. New courses were designed to meet specific needs and the core curriculum was adjusted accordingly. Some new curricula were necessarily created to meet specific course requirements. Project based instruction and student-as-worker instructional techniques flourished.

The school was brought under control by placing the disruptive students in one SLC called "Opportunities." Students who were transferred to the school through disciplinary proceedings had to go through the "Vestibule program" before being assigned to an SLC. Before that happened they had to show their responsibility by attending school every day for two weeks. Very few students ever made it through that program. Each SLC was given a "cluster of rooms" where all the students had to stay. Each SLC was separately housed and were in fact separate schools.

All of a sudden the school was under control. Some SLC's moved to intensive (block) scheduling and others followed the next year. The atmosphere and tone of the school changed to be softer and more caring. The difference between night and day, hope and despair. The whole tone of the school changed from toxic to nurturing. Yes, there was still strong debate between and among teachers, but it was debate about what methodology and structures should be put in place. It really doesn't matter who won the arguments. **What matters is that the small groups of empowered teachers believed in what they were doing. There can be no great teaching unless the teachers believe in what they are doing. That is the essence of great teaching not the imposed strategies of the hierarchy.**

The point is that it was the community that turned itself around by being empowered to control its own destiny. All that was needed was a leader who had the foresight to see the school as a community—a community of offerers and a community of learners. What happened is that the school was empowered to be a true professional learning community. The school was a model of urban reform and it was one of the leading schools in Philadelphia and America in the small learning community movement. It was a shining example of urban school renewal.

The sad thing is that once Torch left, the school went right back into another cycle of toxicity because another dictatorial principal was imposed upon the school community. Again, the principal had the mentality that she was going to straighten out the teachers through dominance. The school went from good to troubled to great to troubled in synchronicity with the quality of the leader. The staff was essentially the same during all those periods. There were times of excitement and times of turmoil. There were times of great positive synergy and times of negative synergy. There were times when the school was a healthy organization and times when the organization was unhealthy to say the least. It all depended on the leader.

The only difference in the school community was that brought on by the leadership. **Yes, leadership matters!**

What are the secrets to turning schools around.? Actually, there are no secrets. It takes the kind of leadership Kouzes and Posner describe as cited in Chapter 5. It takes empowerment of teachers and the school community. It takes a school community working together for a common vision and collective mission that emerges from and is decided upon by that school community. The school community knows what it needs to do. It takes competent management and inspirational leadership. It takes renewal. It takes professionalism. It takes creativity. It takes central administration support in terms of freedom and resources to do what is necessary. It takes self-actualization of individuals and the collective ethos of the school community. It takes doing creative things for children in terms of courses, programs and small learning communities. They must be true professional learning communities.

But most of all, WE NEED DEMOCRACY IN EDUCATION to turn schools around. Yes it is only through democracy in education that we can change schools from unhealthy organizations caught in the negative cycle of toxicity into healthy organizations that work as a community. All issues need to be resolved through the processes of democratic governance and leadership so that the best interests of students emerges and becomes the guiding principle. It takes everyone being involved including teachers, parents, students, and the larger school community. It takes us all.

There are colleges that purport to be able to teach administrators how to turn schools around and offer graduate school programs for that purpose. How successful those programs are is yet to be seen and gauged, but of this I am sure—no program to turn schools around will succeed without containing the elements listed below. To turn schools around you must do at least all of these things:

- Control the students: There must be rules established, clear and consistent consequences, and progressive discipline culminating in suspension and exclusion from school for the perpetrators of violence and extreme disobedience. There must be a comprehensive rewards system for teaching students appropriate behaviors. There must be enough enforcers who are competent, physically big and in possession of good interpersonal skills.

- Empower teachers and the entire school community for students, staff and parents.
- Involve the total school community in choosing its leader.
- Collegially establish and implement core curricula and differentiated curricula specifically tailored to the students in the school and their needs in a truly student centered way.
- Create support systems and services for students, staff and parents.
- Enable the local school community by the central administration providing adequate resources and support services.
- Be innovative but keep the traditional stuff that has always worked before.
- Large schools seem to be better off with small learning communities so adults get to know the students and build positive relationships. Small schools are ultimately better.
- Create a warm, caring, nurturing and trusting environment.
- Remember it is not rocket science—it is common sense.
- Trust the teachers. They are great people—really they are!

Yes, the phenomenon of toxic school cultures is a real phenomenon in some of America's schools. It is a breakdown of the organizational dynamics between and among people within the school community. Because of the stresses and pressures of the situation and the negative human dynamics that ensue, the ethos of the school becomes unhealthy. Organizationally, it is very similar to an individual person's psychological breakdown of his or her ego when the stresses and pressures of life become overbearing and the psyche suffers cognitive overload. The collective psyche of the school is no different. The ethos of the school becomes unhealthy and the result is an unhealthy school climate. When an unhealthy school climate exists, it is not a good place for children to be.

The cure for organizational toxicity in schools is "democracy in education." Remember the Torch!

9

The Psychological Perspective

Almost every educator in America has taken several courses in the science of psychology and our collective knowledge of psychology is so vast. So why do we so often leave that knowledge on the schoolhouse steps when we cross the threshold of our schools?

Schools are bastions of psychology. Everything we do in schools is subject to the realities of human psychology. We are all human beings and we are all psychological beings. We can never escape that fact. If we are to create great schools and set the conditions for the school communities within them to flourish in what we do for children, we must understand psychology as it works in schools to the best of our collective ability. We must also put our knowledge into action as we educate and develop our children, enact school governance provisions and lead our school communities. It is no small task.

How basic human psychology plays out in schools is by far too complex a subject to be dealt with in depth in one book let alone one chapter of one book. But it is essential to understand some basic psychological theories that obviously are at work in schools and are critical elements in the interplay of human dynamics of schools. We will briefly visit just a few of them here. The educational community of America should expand its study of school psychology within the schoolhouse walls and use our knowledge of psychology more effectively to improve and reform our schools.

Every psychologist I have witnessed who has ever done a professional development program on anything that has to do with the psychology of group dynamics has espoused the benefits of inclusive, collegial democratic leadership for the group as a whole. **What we know about group and individual psychology points with a large finger to the democratic imperative for our schools!** We all have a basic human need to be included in our social community. We are social beings as a result of our psychological makeup and our evolution. It is also clear that when people are included in the decision-making of their community, they feel more connected to their community. They have more of a sense of control over their existence and they have a sense of common purpose. Commonality inspires a synergy that makes the organization superior to its parts and a leader is always the catalyst for an inspired or disinspired synergy.

We often speak about the positive psychology of group and organizational dynamics but in our desire to always be positive we also often avoid discussions of the realities of human nature. In the trenches of our schools, we speak poignantly and honestly of the corrupting forces of mankind being behind the motivation of so many people's actions especially those who seek power. **Part and parcel of the democratic imperative for our schools is that democracy prevents the negative and corrupting forces of man and woman from dominating the dynamics of leadership and governance.** We do need honesty in this discussion.

It is because of those negative realities that our "sunshine laws" are enacted for public bodies. Never forget that our public schools are public agencies. Sunshine laws bring participative due process rights to life by requiring that governing bodies of public agencies have open meetings and provide the public with an opportunity to comment on issues before the board. Sunshine laws are essential elements of governance and they should be applied to every individual school in America, not just the school boards of America, if we are to set the conditions for great schools to emerge and be sustained.

The corrupting forces of mankind can all be traced to four main categories —power, ego, money and sex. The great philosopher Friedrich Nietsche, would argue that all things boil down to the need of nature and consequently man to seek power. However, we only visit those issues here because we need to use our knowledge of those issues to develop better ways of leading and governing our schools. The point here is that we need to acknowledge those forces so we can create governance structures that protect everyone from their abuses. Abuse of power is a recurring theme everywhere in America.

So let us first visit the basic needs of every human being in our schools and progress toward understanding that every psychology that manifests itself within our schools ultimately plays a role in the development of the **"ethos of our schools."** The ethos of a school is the collective ego of its community. It is normally a healthy collectivism, but as we saw in our chapter on toxic school cultures, it can manifest itself into a negative collective psychology that causes schools and even school systems to turn into **"unhealthy organizations."** We must understand basic human psychology so we can use our knowledge to develop a positive ethos within every school so the culture and community of our schools can flourish.

The Furry Monkey

There is a classic psychological study about a wire monkey and a furry monkey and the sibling monkeys. I had asked our Psychology teacher at Furness High School for the citation to that study because I wanted to review it for this book. When he handed me a three-by-five card with the citation scribed on it, he said,

"It's about basic human needs." I replied, "No, it is about leadership." I asserted it is about leadership because leadership is about basic human needs. The best of our leaders have learned that to be a great leader the leader must nurture the basic human needs of those he leads.

Remember Chapter 5 and Kouzes and Posner's authoritative studies on what type of people are viewed by followers as being the best leaders? (See, Kouzes and Posner, 2003). Well, the furry monkey experiment explains why. Leaders fulfill basic human needs of their followers. Every group needs a leader and every follower needs a furry monkey to nurture them. That is just the way it is and before we get to a higher level of leadership, we must first begin with the basic needs of man and woman.

In the furry monkey experiment, researchers created two monkeys. One monkey was made of wire and one monkey was made of wood and warm cloth that resembled the fur of a monkey to provide a simulation of a real mother monkey. Two groups of sibling monkeys were fed milk from the monkeys. Group A fed from the wire monkey and group B were fed from the furry monkey. Researchers noticed that when the monkeys finished feeding, they all went to the furry monkey. Researchers then stopped feeding the monkeys in group B from the furry monkey and made them feed from the wire monkey. When they finished feeding, all the monkeys left the wire monkey and went to the furry monkey and spent most of their time with the furry monkey (Harlow, 1949, 1958, 1959).

The only explanation for that phenomenon is that the fur of the monkey provided fulfillment of basic needs of the sibling monkeys. Even the monkeys who were first fed from the wire monkey left the wire monkey after feeding and went to the furry monkey. That is an example of the power of basic human needs and the need for a sense of security. Like the monkeys we are all mammals and our basic needs are primal to our psychological and emotional health and well being.

Fulfillment of basic human needs is a prerequisite to successful schools and effective leadership. Children cannot learn well without their basic needs being met in schools, nor can their teachers and support staff perform at their highest potential until basic human needs are first met. All children and all adults need to feel safe, secure, loved, cared about, and well fed. They need to be treated with warmth, kindness, consideration and care. Respect for everyone's dignity and humanity is just so important in the schoolhouse. That is why a nurturing and caring school climate is essential for great schools to develop. We quite simply cannot achieve and perform to our highest levels without it.

For us to excel at schooling we must first provide a safe, orderly, caring and nurturing school environment for all of our children. Teachers and educators have been saying that for years and years. We need to learn it.

Self-Esteem & Self-Actualization Theories—
The Mockingbird Effect

Closely related to the basic human needs is the need for self fulfillment and self- actualization. The renowned psychologists Abraham Maslow and Carl Rogers are the best known proponents of self-esteem and self growth theories. Their studies elucidate the human drive and psychological need of everyone to fulfill their potentialities to achieve a healthy sense of self worth. As we fulfill our successively higher needs, we reach our self-actualization potential, are able to excel in our endeavor, and are able to achieve a sense of self acceptance and satisfaction. It is all linked to our human need for self fulfillment. We all have that need.

I poignantly call the need for self-esteem, love and belonging **"The Mockingbird Effect"** alluding to the great American novel by Harper Lee, *To Kill a Mockingbird*. That novel is taught in just about every school district in America. One of the main purposes of literature and the teaching of literature in our schools is that it shows us life and teaches us about its truth and realities so that we can improve the nature of our existence. If we, in schools, teach about these ideas, then why do we not use and effectuate what we teach and learn when we institute school governance and leadership?

Much of what we need to know about leadership and governance is in *To Kill a Mockingbird*. It is about a small town and the community of that town. Many of the issues of mankind and our community are raised in that novel and brought to life through the characters from misconceptions about others, to racism and prejudice, to understanding of each other, to the community of man, etc. One of the most important generalizations we can take from the reading of *"Mockingbird"* and one of the generalizations we should keep with us at all times as we speak of schools is this: **"Every mockingbird needs to sing, be heard, be understood, be accepted and be cared about. If we fail to recognize the song and contribution of everyone in schools, they and their songs and hope begin to die out like the light of day—that is the mockingbird effect!**

Abraham Maslow first proposed his "hierarchy of needs" theory in 1943 in a paper entitled "A Theory of Human Motivation" and subsequently developed and extended his theory over the years. He studied exemplary people such as Albert Einstein, Jane Addams, Eleanor Roosevelt, and Frederick Douglas to develop his ideas. His theory is represented in figure 8.1 as a pyramid demonstrating the building blocks of self-actualization and outstanding achievement. At the top of his pyramid are the highest levels of actualization including morality, creativity, spontaneity, acceptance, problem solving and overcoming prejudice. All of those needs, and many others, are elements of personal growth and high performance.

Figure 9.1 Maslow's hieracrchy of needs

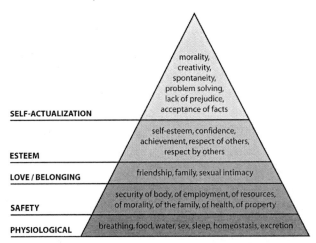

Carl Rogers offers a humanistic theory of personality based on the concept of self and self-actualization as basic to human motivation. He believed that everyone has a "self-actualizing tendency" that aims to develop all capacities in ways that maintain or enhance the person and move him or her toward autonomy (Rogers, 1959). **There appears to be a "biological pressure to fulfill the genetic blueprint" and each person thus has a fundamental mandate to fulfill his or her potential (Maddi, 1996).** The "self" is a central construct of his theory. The concept of self and one's self image develops through interactions with others and reconciliation between the feedback one receives from others and one's self perception. **Rogers theorizes that everyone needs "unconditional positive regard."** The healthy person receives positive regard from others and builds positive self-regard. "The ideal human condition is embodied in the 'fully functioning person' who is open to experience, able to live existentially, is trusting in his or her organism, expresses feelings freely, acts independently, is creative and lives a richer life; the good life" (Rogers, 1961). It is a process rather than a state of being. Rogers gives us a lifetime of study in support of the simple and undeniable concept that everyone needs some sense of self fulfillment to be a healthy well functioning human being.

Man's and Woman's never ending **"search for self"** is always alive and active in schools. So what use can we make of our knowledge about self-actualization needs and other basic human needs to develop great schools for our children? We can use that knowledge to develop excitement and synergy for what we do in schools. We can recognize that every individual from our students to our teachers to our support staff need their basic human needs acknowledged and fulfilled. We can recognize that good leadership and good governance of our schools is

dependent upon paying homage to the psychological needs of everyone. Torch used that knowledge to turn University City High School around through empowering teachers to design programs for children that fulfilled their own self-actualizing needs. **That is why teacher empowerment and ownership is so important. You can not have self-actualization without teacher empowerment. You can not have outstanding achievement without empowering teachers, parents and the entire school community. That is why top down management is always doomed to failure. The answer is in basic human psychology.**
We all need to achieve—each of us.

Proximity & Ethical Decision-Making

There is a classic study of obedience to demands of authority by the psychologist, Stanley Milgram, which highlights the necessity that ethical decisions for children and individuals in schools be made at the local school level rather than from a bureaucratic distance (1963, 1974). While the studies of obedience were focused on our human response to commands of authority figures, a highly significant result of those studies shows us that ethical decisions are more likely to be made appropriately if we actually see first hand the results of our actions. It is another weight on the scale of justice supporting the democratic imperative for individual schools and the elimination of decisions for schools being made by bureaucrats who have no first hand knowledge of what is happening in schools.

People agreed to participate in what they believed was a learning experiment where they were assigned the role of teacher and directed by an authority figure to give electrical shocks to the learner when he made mistakes. They were told the experiment was to test the effect of punishment on learning. The learner was given a list of words to remember and each time they made a mistake, the teacher was told to shock the learner. The more mistakes, the stronger the shock that was commanded. The teachers were first located in an adjacent room. They almost always complied and continued to comply even when they were told to increase the magnitude of the shock and heard the learner screaming from the other room! What is important to us here is that when the teacher was in the same room as the learner and could actually see the learner as he screamed, obedience to the command of the authority figure dropped off sharply.

That study caused an uproar on the ethics of such studies. It also teaches us an important lesson on ethics in decision-making. Ethical decision-making can not be done from afar. We must see first hand the consequences of our actions. If we are situated far away from the subjects of our decisions, we can never make good decisions. Educators who work in schools see the issues and possible solutions intimately and clearly. Educators who stand outside of schools can never see the issues and possible resolutions clearly. That is why decisions on pedagogy and instructional design must be made by the professionals who see and know the students. That is why we must set the conditions for schools to resolve their issues within their own school community in an open, honest and democratic manner. Leadership and governance can not be exercised from afar.

A prime example of the seriousness of this **"proximity effect"** is what has been happening in South Philadelphia High School in Philadelphia. The school has been out of control now for several years ever since the state took over Philadelphia's schools and the School Reform Commission hired the guy from Chicago to run our schools, Paul Vallas. Discipline has been dysfunctional and large numbers of students roam the hallways causing disorder and violence. An administrator who heroically tries to deal with the unruly students has been beaten up twice by students. All this happens while central administrators play their political power games and fail to do anything realistic to solve the problems. The Chief Academic Officer just keeps repeating his ridiculous mantra, "No excuses." There is focused attention on the school only when the mess comes out in the newspapers. Appropriate resources are never invested in the school. Why does this happen? Because those in power do not see the violence and disorder first hand! It is the **"out of sight—out of mind"** syndrome. If they were forced to work there every day and see what is going on, they would do something about it—if they had the power and authority to do so.

I wonder how many schools in America are just like South Philly High? There are many—too many.

Behaviorism and Cognitive Psychology

At the turn of the nineteenth century psychodynamic psychology represented by Sigmund Freud's theory of the interaction between the conscious and unconscious aspects of the mind was a controversial area of psychology (Morris, 2005). Freud believed human behavior was largely driven by unconscious desires for such things as power and sex represented by his concept of the "id" and the interplay of the conscious mind, the "ego." The interplay of those aspects of the mind are mediated by the "superego" which is the conscience of our minds. Subsequent to that era grew the theories known as behaviorism. The best known behaviorists are John B. Watson and B.F. Skinner.

Behaviorism is largely centered on the notion of rewards and punishments. Behaviorism plays a large role in educational psychology because it emphasizes learning as an outcome of rewards and punishments. Operant conditioning is B.F. Skinner's view that behavior is an outcome of reinforcement that occurs as a consequence of behavioristic acts. Behavior that is rewarded continues and behavior that is punished or continually goes unrewarded discontinues. Our behavior is dependent on the interplay of positive and negative reinforcements. **What is important for schooling is that "positive reinforcement teaches behavior" and "negative consequences extinguishes behavior."** Rewards and punishment should be immediate to be most effective but long term goals are rewards that affect us substantially (Skinner, 1938, 1948, 1989). We are motivated by and react to both extrinsic and intrinsic rewards. Praise by a respected leader or teacher is often powerful but it must be *authentic* (Kouzes & Posner, 2003; Whitaker, 2003).

Cognitive psychology is the study of our mental processes in the broadest sense. Cognitive psychologists believe behavior should be studied scientifically and with the modern ability for brain imaging, it has expanded to the field of neuroscience (Morris, 2005). Cognitive psychology has given us new insights into the study of thinking, feeling, learning, remembering, making decisions, judgments, emotions and rationality. The more we study psychology, the more we see the complexity of human motivation and behavior.

Cognitive Dissonance Theory

One of the more significant theories that emerged from the study of attitudes and attitude change is the work of Leon Festinger that resulted in his theory of cognitive dissonance (1957). It is especially important to understand in the context of leadership because it is integral to the **"process of change." If we are to change schools, school systems and the behavior of those who work in schools and lead school communities, we must understand the psychology of change.** One of those processes that effects change is the phenomenon of cognitive dissonance.

Cognitive dissonance occurs when a person attempts to assimilate or is presented with an idea, proposition or belief that is contradictory to a belief or cognitive construct the person already holds. The dissonance creates unpleasant cognitive tension and the tension motivates the individual to try to resolve the dissonance in some way. In the positive sense, the tension reduction can lead to new and better beliefs and courses of action. In the negative sense, the tension creates defense mechanisms to kick in such as anger, hostility and denial. The reality is that we all seek input and feedback that is consistent with our already held attitudes and beliefs. We psychologically strive for **"cognitive consistency"** as we assimilate and accommodate new ideas into our already existing cognitive constructs.

Cognitive dissonance is important to understand as we look to change the way schools and organizations are governed and led because schools and many organizations have historically been governed on authoritarian principles. If we are to change our schools into **"true professional learning communities"** where collegiality and participative processes reign, we need to change the established attitudes and beliefs of the past. We can no longer cling to the ways of the past. **Cognitive dissonance is why many people will scoff at the idea that schools should be governed democratically! That reaction will not be rationally based. It will be emotionally based. It will be based on the way things always have been and the preconceptions and egocentricity of those in power, not on the rational thought processes of the way things should be.**

Ego defense mechanisms are autonomously invoked by our minds when there is anxiety created by conflict of ideas presented to us. It is part of the normal psychological processes of our psyche but can sometimes become abnormal. Psychologists disagree whether ego defense mechanisms are always unconscious or are used consciously. Defense mechanisms allow us to maintain our self image that we are good and we are right in our thinking and actions. They provide us with a means of coping with stress that might otherwise be unbearable. (See, Morris & Maisto, 2005, pp. 418-423). Defense mechanisms include: denial, repression, projection, identification, regression, intellectualization, reaction formation, displacement and sublimation.

If we are to lead change, we must deal with change of attitudes and beliefs and that is no small mountain to climb.

The Process of Persuasion

A leader's task as a change agent is often dependent on his ability to persuade his or her followers. The power of persuasion is integral to leadership and an understanding of some basic concepts of the psychology of persuasion is essential to the development of leadership capacity. Haberman speaks of persuasive power as the most important power of outstanding school leaders (2005). Persuasion is sometimes very difficult especially when an individual or group has strongly held beliefs and attitudes.

For persuasion to be successful, the persuadee must first pay attention to the message; then the message must be comprehended: and finally, the message must be accepted as convincing (Perloff, 2003). Kouzes and Posner (2003) unequivocally state that credibility is the foundation of leadership and it is also the foundation of persuasion. Credibility of both the message and the person who is the proponent of the message is highly important (Cooper & Croyle, 1984; Petty & Cacioppo, 1981, 1986a). But when the message is about an important issue, it is the message that plays the greater role. We frequently tune out messages that contradict our own point of view, and the more effective we are at generating counter arguments, the less likely we will be persuaded. (Jacks and Cameron, 2003). Attitudes and beliefs are difficult to change if the audience has a firm commitment to their present attitudes.

First impressions are very powerful. In the field of law, advocates cling to **"the theory of primacy and recency."** That theory predicts that judges and juries are most influenced by what is presented to them first and secondly influenced by the most recent presentation. What happens in between is not so powerful. This is an important concept. When we want to persuade our audience, we should make our most powerful and credible presentations first and last. It is also important to make a general good impression first. There was a recent news report on ABC about a study that concluded we make conclusive psychological judgments about people within the first fifteen seconds of meeting them!

In the final analysis, leaders must be effective persuaders to be effective change agents. It is a psychological thing.

Fight or Flight & Stress Reduction

Schools are highly emotional places. Emotions run high in everything we do in schools. We are all emotional beings and we can never escape that fact. For schools to be healthy organizations and provide our students and adults with a nurturing climate conducive for learning and positive interaction between and among people, we must deal positively with emotions and stress. We have previously viewed the necessity of creating an "open climate" for discussion and debate so that every member of the school community feels free to voice his or her opinions on matters in order to ensure a positive climate. In the absence of such a supportive climate, the negative behaviors associated with stress infect the school climate and the primal emotional response of **"fight vs. flight"** characterizes interpersonal relationships and discussions. It is basic human nature.

Just the fact that we put hundreds, sometimes thousands, of people together in the same building creates a stressful situation. Everyone brings their stresses and problems with them to school. The challenge of keeping students orderly and on task in classrooms of thirty students on average is daunting itself. Overcrowded schools add to the stress by creating what can be called an "elevator effect"—when too many people cram onto an elevator, the situation is stressful in and of itself, tensions rise and negative behaviors ensue. Modern schools should be designed to provide more than enough space for everyone to spread out and feel comfortable.

The basic challenges of schooling combined with the pressure that is often put on educators and students to excel and the overload of tasks that must be accomplished in too short a time period creates an inherently stressful situation. Add to it strong personalities and strong yet differing beliefs and opinions of how things should be done and you have the conditions set for "fight or flight psychology."

Whenever we become angry, it is our basic instinct to either fight or flee. It is our primal response to anger whatever and wherever its cause.

The noted psychologist Walter Cannon (1929) first described the elements of the *fight or flight response* that can happen in either or both individual and group situations. It is a primal reaction to threats to our well-being that protects animals and humans from harm by eliciting the instinct to either fight to protect oneself or flee in fear and anger. It is a physiological response caused by a release of stress hormones such as *adrenaline* and *norepinephrine* from the hypothalamus into the blood (Morris, 2005). Cannon also observed that this physiological mobilization took the same form regardless of the threat. It can be triggered by physical trauma, fear, emotional arousal, or simply be caused by someone having a really bad incident happen at work or school. It can also be triggered by arguments, debate, emotional discussions, criticism, stressful events, or externally based psychological pressure. It is a primal and autonomous response that ensured the survival of early humans when faced with danger and it transforms to psychological situations when we are faced with emotional threats or confrontations. It becomes an ego defense mechanism when our selves and our belief systems are challenged or maligned.

The Canadian physiologist Hans Selye concluded that we react to physical and psychological stressors in three stages he called the **"general adaptation syndrome"** (1956, 1976). The three stages he observed were *alarm reaction, resistance and exhaustion.* When we receive a psychological or physical threat, we respond to the stress with a strong emotional response. We become more sensitive and alert, our heartbeat and respiration quicken and our muscles tense. Our coping behaviors and ego defense mechanisms kick in. During the second stage, *resistance,* we struggle against psychological disorganization and signs of physical strain emerge. If the stress becomes extreme or prolonged, desperation ensues and inappropriate coping mechanisms appear and we tend to cling to them rigidly. In stage 3, *exhaustion* and "burnout" ensues. We begin to feel hopeless, cynical, irritable, and begin to feel that nothing is worthwhile. Real physiological effects can emerge in the form of illness, stress disorders and substance abuse. **"Emotional burnout"** is a real phenomenon that often occurs in both teachers and school based administrators because of the emotional and psychic energy we must put into our work every day.

When schools undergo "restructuring" the fight or flight syndrome often emerges because of psychological realities. When teachers, parents and school staff members work hard to build their programs and initiatives and maintain psychological "ownership," and then they are told by outsiders that they must restructure their schools according to external mandates, stress inevitably ensues. **"Turf wars"** and **"territorial behaviors"** often characterize the discussions and debate and resistance occurs. **That is why self determined change through teacher empowerment works so much better than imposed reform.**

Schools, especially urban schools, are often riddled with stress factors. Schools, organizations and social systems can become overloaded with pressures and responsibilities. When a person is pressured with too much to do and too many pressures bear upon the person psychologically and emotionally, his or her psychological systems break down and the person's psyche becomes disoriented. That is known as **"cognitive overload"** and when a whole school is overloaded with stress factors, its systems become "overloaded" and its "collective ethos" suffers. That may very well be the precursor and cause for toxic school cultures to emerge. All of the schools I have observed that descend into toxicity were plagued by too many responsibilities with too few resources to effectively deal with them. That is when they become out of control.

The realities of stress and its negative consequences puts into question the whole concept of high stakes testing that plagues our nation's schools and reduces so much of the education of our children to test preparation. When principals and school staffs are threatened with removal from their positions and displacement by a state takeover and reconstitution, it causes inappropriate behaviors and extreme turmoil that is harmful to our children! When Philadelphia's schools were taken over by the state it was like a "corporate raid on our schools." The results were Faustian to say the least. It was very traumatic and the aftermath is very sad when we see what has happened in our schools **"first hand." Yes, some people should feel guilty.**

When I think how in Philadelphia, Pennsylvania, in America, it is the normal practice of our newly imposed centralized autocratic administration to remove principals and other administrators from their positions by sending the school police to "walk them out of their offices," it is Faustian in its reality. It is dehumanizing. They are not criminals. It is authoritarianism at its worst. **To see it happen in our schools and think about the history of man, it is chilling in its lunacy—it is hysteria. And to think that it is happening in Philadelphia, the seat of American democracy and the National Constitution Center, I can not help to think we need to collectively look in the mirror at what we have become as a people.** There are better ways to ensure that administrators who are removed from office do not trash their offices than to escort them out of their offices by school police officers like common criminals. It is called the civil suit and the criminal complaint.

We all better stand up for democracy if we want our American values and ideals to live in our schools. If our leaders were chosen democratically with term limits and constitutional procedures for early removal from office, there would never be a need for such disgraceful practices.

The Emperor's New Clothes

The story of the *Emperor's New Clothes* is a story that is oh so poignant when we talk about our leaders. It happens all the time in school systems. None of the Emperor's assistants have the courage to tell him or her that he or she stands in his or her underwear. Instead, we tell the CEO that his clothes are beautiful when they are not and they lack substance. It is a psychological effect and a reality of life in autocratic systems.

The phenomenon occurs when the leader, usually a CEO, regional superintendent, or a principal of a school sets the policies and programs for a school or school system. No one has the guts to say the truth and argue with the boss. The consequences are just too great. You may lose your job; you may be demoted; you may lose your opportunity for advancement; you will lose your favor; or you will at least be branded as a negative if you criticize or argue with the policies of the boss. It happens every day in America. Retaliation and retribution are institutional illnesses of the bureaucracy.

Here is good advice: If you want to survive and advance in the bureaucracy, this is what you say to the emperor. In Philadelphia, the last emperor was Paul Vallas who upon his arrival in Philadelphia after the state takeover, had bragged to the newspapers that "people are being **'jettisoned'** from their positions as administrators." It did not matter that they were outstanding administrators who dedicated their careers to the schoolchildren of Philadelphia. But anyway, this is what you should tell the emperor if you want to advance in our bureaucracy:

- Your one size fits all standardized curriculum where you tell all of us how and when to teach everything is just what we need. After all, all children are the same, they all learn at the same rate, teachers need to be told what to do, and no authority on pedagogy has ever advocated for that mechanism. Wow, you have saved our city.
- Yes, all children need test preparation every day in schools.
- Yes, the focus of instruction should be on what is on the state tests.
- It's great to see your loyalty to our clients—the corporations that hold themselves out as managers of schools and profit from our schoolchildren.
- You are so smart. You told the mayor and City Council that the budget was balanced, and after you got your contract extension and raise, you let it be known that we are $160 million in the hole. What a genius.
- It's really great the way test scores went up in elementary schools for the last several years even though it never shows up in our high school test scores.

- It was really good use of funds for you to divert to your self conceived standardized curriculum initiative the money the Federal government gave to Philadelphia's schools for use by our Small Learning Communities that existed before you came and stood as a model for school reform. It really doesn't matter that we already had a core curriculum when you came to Philadelphia.
- I would tell you more about how great you are and about how beautiful your clothes are but I am sure you know it already. Can I have that job now?

While I say this here satirically, it is exactly why we need democracy in education.

The Napoleonic Complex

Yes, the Napoleonic complex is a real psychological phenomenon that rears its ugly head in schools and school systems. It occurs when the need for power and ego gratification takes over the mentality of the leader. It manifests itself in the leader thinking that he or she is superior to others and must impose their views upon the follower. It results in excess authoritarianism and the acts of the leader are focused on the need to force submission of the followers. It most often results in the leader creating an adversarial climate with subordinates and over reliance on employee disciplinary procedures in a retaliatory manner. Such a leader often treats the employees like children. Whatever the psychological cause for this phenomenon, it always causes a feeling of helplessness and most often creates nothing more than dissension and toxicity in the culture of the community.

This is not the place to psychoanalyze those who are afflicted with the mentality, but we must recognize it if we are to guard against it. It is another argument for term limits and democracy in choosing our leaders, for in bureaucracies, those types of people are usually blindly supported irregardless of the destruction to the community of schools they cause. Blind support of such leaders is an institutional illness of bureaucratic school systems. Some psychologists believe such behavior is grounded in an "authoritarian personality" (Adorno, 1950). The authoritarian vs. democratic personality is a large area of psychology but there is good argument that many authoritarian behaviors are rooted in a weak self image and often results in bias and prejudice (Morris 2005, p. 573). The authoritarian type of leader often sees himself or herself as infallible (Haberman, 2005). Additionally, the authoritarian leader is more apt to dismiss alternative ideas and often attempts to stamp out dissent through punitive means and even Machiavellian exile by cutting the position of the dissenter. The dominating and overly directive leadership mentality is destructive to the community and causes an unwholesome environment for the workers, but in schools, it creates a climate that is not good for children or doing what we need to do for children.

Democracy in choosing our leaders is the purification process for such situations.

Group Dynamics

The psychology of group dynamics is at the heart of leadership and there have been thousands of research studies investigating the processes of groups. In Chapter 5, "Leadership for the 21st Century," we reviewed the findings of researchers on organizational dynamics which are in large part findings on the psychology of groups in the context of organizations. The dynamics of small groups is a complex subject and there have been thousands of studies. There is no way we can exhaustively summarize those findings here. However, there are some points that should be reviewed here about small group psychology since most of the work of educators is done in teams that are in fact small groups with tasks to accomplish.

When a group is formed and assigned a task to complete, and no leader is specifically appointed, a leader always emerges. That process usually occurs by the members of the group looking at each other until someone suggests that a specific group member take on the role. The other members will usually affirm the nomination unless someone sees that person as unfit in their eyes and then a discussion will ensue. If consensus does not follow, a vote is normally done. Or, a second scenario will probably happen: When the group members look around the group and no one appears to want the role, someone will usually say, "Alright, I'll be the leader." The group will usually defer to that person. In either scenario, a leader emerges!

Whether that leader is effective and whether the group effectively accomplishes the task, is dependent upon the dynamics that ensues. The question that always arises is whether autocratic leadership, democratic leadership or laissez faire leadership causes the group to be more functional. Situational factors always effect which leadership styles are most effective and the kinds of leadership behaviors that are most effective depends upon the situation in which the leader finds himself (Shaw, 1976). In crises situations that requires quick and decisive action, autocratic leadership is usually more effective because the followership looks to the leader to take charge and give effective direction. However, in settings where the group's task is complex and no immediate action is necessary, democratic leadership usually elicits more commitment to task. Non authoritarian leadership usually results in more satisfaction of group members than authoritarian leadership. In a pioneering study of leadership styles, Lewin and associates found that hostility and aggression was significantly far greater in autocratic groups than in democratic groups (Lewin, Lippitt, & White, 1939; Lippitt & White, 1943).

An interesting study that is on point to our discussion about school governance and democracy in choosing our leaders is one done by Mortensen who concluded that emergent leaders who are given recognition and support by group members show more acts of leadership than those who are not supported by the group (1966)! Outstanding leadership whether delivered in an autocratic or democratic manner may always be linked to the support of the followers. That is why, in a democratic governance scenario, the group may still choose a leader who is high on the scale of autocraticity if they feel the leader is effective in their situation. It depends on the situation and the interpersonal skill of the leader. This suggests that great leaders can not be appointed from afar because they can never see the situation as clearly as those from within. That is just physically impossible. Democracy is just an inherently better way of choosing our leaders than an autocratically appointed governance structure.

The bottom line is that the effective leadership style for any school community is dependent on the situation of that school community. The ability to gain trust in the competency and integrity of the leader is always a major factor along with the leader's ability to develop positive interpersonal relationships. It may very well be that outstanding leaders can and must adjust their style to the situation and task at hand. Flexibility may be the key.

Educational Psychology

This is not a book specifically about learning psychology, but everything discussed in this book is about educational psychology because it all is part of the psychology of schools and learning. Democracy in education is so important to effective learning psychology because everything we do in schools and everything we learn is dependent on the cognitive constructs our minds develop. John Dewey is widely viewed as the father of **"constructivist psychology."** His vision of constructivism is based on the view that learning is always dependent on the "mental constructs" the learner develops in his or her mind. Achievement in his view is based on the amalgamation of the mental constructs we make for ourselves from our experience and it is the task of instruction to set up learning experiences for students to investigate facts, draw conclusions, and develop cognitive constructs in the form of generalizations.

The concept of the requisite **"background of experience"** is basic to the development of comprehension ability, and it is a reality that unless leaders have developed a background of experience in the field they attempt to lead, they can not possibly comprehend the situation adequately to make good leadership decisions. That is why non educators do such a poor job of running school systems. Good decisions must be collegially based and made by those of us who actually work in school settings.

For all of us, learning is a life-long process. Piaget posits that all learning from infancy through childhood into adolescence and adulthood is based on assimilation and accommodation of external stimuli (Phillips, 1969). In the sense of community building and the development of achievement in children and the achievement of the adults who teach and raise them, effective assimilation and accommodation is all based on the democratic process. We must all get the facts in an open and honest climate based on the integrity of what we do and say, assimilate those facts into collective cognitive constructs, and act accordingly.

In Conclusion

All of psychology plays a part in what we do in schools, the achievement of children and the dynamics of school organizations. For great schools to emerge, we must all master the science and art of psychology. We, as professionals in schools must always have a psychological perspective on behaviors that occur in schools. It not only helps us to guide us in developing courses of action, but a healthy perspective that the behaviors of ourselves and others is controlled by the fact that we are all psychological beings allows us to accept the behaviors of others in a non judgmental and non condemning manner. After all, we are the professionals.

For all the reasons laid out here in "The Psychological Perspective" and the collective mission of schools to develop great school governance and great school leadership so our students and school communities may achieve to our highest levels—**the imperative for democracy will always emerge.** All the issues of mankind are found in schools and we must resolve all the issues through the processes of democracy.

Because of the "proximity effect" for ethical decision-making, it is clear that appropriate moral decisions for what we do in schools can not be made by bureaucrats who stand outside of schools. What has been imposed upon our children in the face of high stakes testing is incredulous to watch as it plays out in schools. While we speak about student centered education, what we so often get is adult centered education and power broker education that almost always results in the best interests of administrators being the focus of schooling, not the best interests of children. *For the interests of students to be in reality the guiding principle we live by in schools and education, we need to debate and discuss the issues and resolve those issues between and among those of us who* **"look into the eyes of the students we teach."** *Morality can happen no other way. There is also a moral imperative for our schools. That is it.* **The moral imperative for schools is also the democratic imperative for our schools!**

Finally, let us always remember, we do not need degrees in psychology to understand that happy, cared for, excited people who feel part of the community and have a sense of self fulfillment do a better job, do more, and learn more!

10

Our Unions & Their Potential Greatness

Professionals can choose their own leaders, govern themselves, and govern their schools better than anyone else in the world. Trust them and trust democracy—they are our hope.

The imperative for democracy does not require a sea change in the great professional organizations of our time. It only requires simple changes in the way we do business and recognize the need to empower our teachers and administrators to interact in a democratic and professional way. We must grow as a nation and an educational community and recognize that, **"We are all in this together."** That is all that needs to happen. We can do that if we so choose.

The most recent report from the *New* Commission on the Skills of the American Work Force, *Tough Choices Or Tough Times,* shared "one way" to create high performance schools and school districts everywhere (2007): They proposed that schools "be operated by independent contractors, many of them owned and operated by teachers" (Executive Summary: *Tough Choices Or Tough Times,* at p.15). The teachers of those schools would be "employees of the state" and so would the administrators. They could also be employees of the local school district, or they could just be employees of the individual schools. They would just have to be granted by the state the legal authority to run their schools democratically. It would be of little difference to how our Constitution grants Americans the rights of citizenry. That is all that needs to happen if we are to effectuate such a model.

The National Center on Education and the Economy is a not-for-profit organization created to develop proposals for building a world class education system. It engages in public policy analysis and development and works collaboratively with others at the local, state and national levels to advance its proposals in the policy arena. The National Center gathered together some of our nation's top leaders and thinkers to organize its "*New* Commission" and conducted a two year research study of the world's leading education and economic systems. The Commission engaged a professional staff of 19 researchers as well as many consultants. The Commission, in addition to studying the United States, conducted field research in other countries which are world leaders in education including Austria, Belgium, Canada, China, Czech Republic, England, Finland, France, Germany, India, Ireland, Italy, and New Zealand. Many of their reports can be found on their web site:

www.skillscommission.org. It was supported by The Annie E. Casey Foundation, the Bill and Melinda Gates Foundation, the William and Flora Hewlett Foundation and the Lumina Foundation for Education.

Nothing in their research and nothing in their proposals threaten the **"basic fairness and personal security"** that unions of men and women seek to protect. It is a **great fallacy and myth that our professional teaching organizations stand in the way of progress in education and progress toward new and innovative forms of school organization.** The only thing that stands in the way of such progress is the adversarial nature of union history that is historically forced upon our great professionals through the industrialized thought of an era that can no longer meet the demands of our modern times (*New* Commission, 2007). The professionals that are represented by our leading educators' organizations, the American Federation of Teachers and the National Education Association, are highly intelligent people with great character. They are professionals. They can and must be trusted.

Our professional associations are already governed democratically pursuant to their constitutions that create their organizational and governance structures so it would only logically follow that they would fully comprehend and embrace the thought of governing their schools through the processes of democracy. While most school administrators in the United States are not organized in unions with collective bargaining rights, there are some administrators' unions that exist in America. Most of them are found in large cities. An ironic and enlightening scene I once observed was a meeting of the union that represents Philadelphia's principals: It was a textbook display of democracy in action. Yet many of those very same principals go right back to their schools and declare to the teachers, "This is not a democracy!" Well, it should be! It would be a more effective school if it were governed as a democracy.

The *New* Commission recognizes the imperative to work with unions to effectuate change in our educational system and to empower teachers to take on the responsibility of educational accountability. In their recommendations for change, the *New* Commission states: "In states with collective bargaining laws, legislatures would need to work closely with the organizations that represent teachers to effect the kinds of changes we have in mind, for it is obviously easier to implement such changes with strong union support" (See, Executive Summary: *Tough Choices Or Tough Times,* at p.14). **In reality, it is impossible to effectuate systemic change without the support and empowerment of teachers.**

The *New* Commission advocates teacher empowerment through new types of organizations that enable teachers to take on the responsibility and accountability for education. They state: "In the new system, it would be relatively easy for teachers to reach out to other teachers and form organizations to operate schools themselves, much like doctors, attorneys, and architects form partnerships to offer their services to the public (at p. 14). In their eighth step for change, they assert: **"Too often, we have built a bureaucracy in our schools in which, apart from the superintendent of schools, the people who have responsibility do not have the power, and the people who have the power do not have the responsibility"** (Executive Summary at p. 14). They, too, recognize that the "problem is not with our educators. It is the system in which they work."

In return for taking on the challenges of this new paradigm and responsibility, they recommend that teachers be able to earn significantly more money without costing the country much more money. They argue that a new compensation system would allow beginning teachers to earn significantly more money and teachers at the top of career ladders to make significantly more money, too. Their starting salaries could be $45,000, which is now the median teacher's pay in America, and teachers could earn as much as $95,000 to 110,000.00 per year. They propose a compensation system that takes into account cost of living differences in different parts of our country and in different parts of individual states. They also predict that their plan would attract and keep the best teachers teaching in our most needy schools rather than the present scenario where our best teachers are "bought off" by higher performing suburban school districts.

Under their plan, states would qualify and license teachers through a comprehensive processes including demanding examinations. The states would create a statewide salary schedule that would be flexible and allow teachers to be paid more for teaching in remote or especially tough urban areas. They could also create incentives for teachers to move into shortage areas such as math and special education. The changes in collective bargaining practices would not be monumental and many of the protections bargained for by state and local teacher's associations could still be maintained.

Consistent with this new paradigm, would be a provision that, once a teacher is assigned to a school, that teacher would have the **"right to participate"** in the governance of his or her school. Integral to that right would necessarily be **"voting rights"** for the leaders of the school entity. The **"right to vote"** would at least extend to the board of trustees, and more democratically, to the principal, school council members and even other school leaders such as department chairs and small learning community leaders. There are several organizational structures that could emerge.

Such a system would also require a system to enforce those rights to participate and provide viable procedures to resolve conflicts. What would emerge within school systems, is a legal system within the larger legal system of our country. It is no different than what we already do in America. We now have our collective bargaining systems with arbitration systems in place that largely stand as the governance systems of schools and their bureaucracies. This adversarial system would be replaced by a non adversarial system more in tune with principles of our American constitutional democracies. School organizations and their founding documents would be living, growing, emerging documents just like our Constitution. This new system would be far better than the present adversarial system that now so often destroys the community of our schools.

The new paradigm also fits well with the imperative for democracy and is consistent with the democratic principles for choosing and changing school leaders through the processes of American democracy. The state can ensure competencies for prospective principals through certification processes and the creation of a **"pool of eligibles"** who then have the right to seek nomination and election or selection as principals of public schools. All states already require certification for principals.

The issue of **"job security"** for school principals who have taken the risk of standing and leading a school can be settled through the creation of **"career paths"** out of the principalship position. Some paths would lead to higher level administrative positions within the school districts or states, or could even lead back into teaching. That would be consistent with the concept of the **"lead teacher"** who takes on the leadership of the group of teachers for a year or two. There could also be a special pay scale for those who teach after assuming the role of the principal. There are many of us who are school administrators that would like to teach again, but do not do so because of the reduction in compensation or because we would go back into the present bureaucratic system that, in its uncaring lunacy, may force us into a terrible teaching situation.

A career path scenario would also allow principals to **"leave with dignity"** their present positions. Rather than being forced to desperately cling to their positions in the face of their declining chemistry with those he or she leads, they could move onward at the end of their term as a normal and credible process. Principals then could move onward and even seek another principalship elsewhere. A leader's chemistry with his or her followership rises at the beginning of the leader's tenure, peaks, and then falls off. That happens to every leader. **That is why leadership renewal needs to be a process—it is a process of democracy.**

That is certainly a far more dignified and far better way than we most often end a principal's tenure now. The present scenario usually is a process where the principal is determined to be unfit for the job. Where unions are involved, it becomes a legal process for declaring a principal incompetent or guilty of malfeasance. The present systems we use are often devoid of ethical merit. In Philadelphia, downtown administrators can unilaterally, and for any reason whatsoever, decide to remove a principal. When they do so, several school police officers are sent to physically remove the principal from their office by "walking them out" of the building. How authoritarian! How disgraceful to America and what we stand for.

We need systemic change. We need credibility in what we do. We need to operate with the mind set that we are all in this together. We can no longer cling to the adversarial processes of the past if we are to do what we need to for children. We must embrace many of the recommendations of the *New* Commission if we are to have a "world class educational system." That includes working together with our unions.

Look at our present adversarial bargaining system. Our school districts start off the negotiations by first "punching the unions in the nose" and then saying, "Now let's sit down and talk about how to change your contract to benefit the children." That is how we negotiate school systems for our children now. We effectively say to the unions, "We are not giving you a raise; we are taking your human rights away from you; we are making you work more hours; we are cutting your benefits to your families; we are going to dictate to you how it is going to be!" And then, they have the audacity to ask unions to change contract provisions for the benefit of children. What they really mean in today's realities is to change the contract to benefit the administrators, the politicians, and the power brokers. What a stupid way to be.

To change school systems we need to change the way we negotiate labor contracts with our professional employees. We need to change the administrative culture. **The unions are not the axis of evil. They are organizations of mostly dedicated professionals. The adversarial system has not worked, is not working, and will not work in the future. Open your eyes!**

We need to grow as an educational community, grow as a nation and grow as humanity! We need to grow as a democracy if we are to serve our children well and preserve America as the greatest nation on Earth.

Allowing, even demanding that our professionals who make up our professional associations rise to the potential of our collective greatness is part and parcel of the imperative for democracy. There is not only an imperative for democracy in our schools, but there is an imperative for democracy in America to go beyond our Constitution and reach into all that we do. We must renew and stand for what we profess to believe in—American constitutional democracy.

The welfare of our children and the welfare of our nation depend on it!

11

The Inherent Immorality of Bureaucracy

There are institutional illnesses that are inherent to the nature of bureaucracy and it is the "moral imperative" of us all to rid our most precious institutions of those diseases that infect the fiber of what we do collectively. Our most precious institution in America is our schools, not only because we raise our children in them, but because our America depends on them.

The charter school movement in America started because our leading thinkers in America recognized that our bureaucratic school systems were largely failing our young and our country. They realized that the large archaic institutions that grew out of another era were inefficient and produced poor results both academically and socially. Strict scrutiny of our system of education makes it questionable whether our bureaucratic system of school governance is inherently incapable of providing us with a world-class educational system. Our leaders promoted a new frontier of educational reform based on the belief that we must break down the present inefficient and unwieldy system to set the conditions for great schools to emerge.

Bureaucracy by its very nature is an inherently flawed system of governance. As long as we cling to it, we will continue to have less than satisfactory schools. It is our collective moral imperative to change the culture of bureaucracy. Bureaucracy produces the same result whether it is in Philadelphia, New York, Chicago, Miami, Houston, Denver, Los Angeles, Toronto or London. It also produces the same results in small school districts within our states. We have focused on Philadelphia for the purpose of highlighting what happens in schools and school systems all across America so we can improve our schools for all of our children.

We have previously touched upon the issue of whether bureaucracy is inherently incapable of producing a moral result? There is a moral purpose to what we do. Michael Fullan is one of our nation's leaders in raising the issue of this moral imperative. In his book, *The Moral Imperative of School Leadership"* (2003), he discusses the need to change the culture of our schools and the culture of our school systems if we are to effectuate a moral purpose for our schools. His words are particularly poignant: "You don't have to go very far into the question of the role of public schools in a democracy before discovering that moral purpose is at the heart of the matter. The best case for public education has always been that it is a common good. Everyone, ultimately, has a stake in the caliber of the schools, and education is everyone's business." (Fullan, 2003).

Philadelphia's public schools were taken over by the state pursuant to an agreement between Mayor Street and the governor of Pennsylvania. The school district did not have enough money to fund our schools, the tax burden on Philadelphians was prohibitive of new school taxes, and the state legislature was unwilling to put up new money for our failed system. The takeover of our schools was Faustian to observe and very demoralizing to those of us who have spent our lives working for our children. It was in actuality a corporate takeover mentality very similar in nature to the forced takeover of a city by an army. Prior to the takeover, then superintendent, Deidre Farmbry, tried to help those of us who were, in her words, only guilty of being "in the wrong place at the wrong time." Administrators, seeing the loss of their jobs as imminent, tried to help their friends by placing them in high positions throughout the school district including principalships. It was like, "Batten down the hatches the enemy is coming!" I wrote her a position paper that argued that our school system had become an **"unhealthy organization."** She quoted that concept in her subsequent speeches.

The sad thing is that we still are an unhealthy organization. The problem, you see, is in the nature of bureaucracy itself. Five years later we are still in the same position we were in then. In between, I have witnessed events that are just plain Faustian in nature and you would not believe that they happen in America unless you saw them for yourself. Paul Vallas came in with an attitude that he must clean house and actually bragged to the media, "I am 'jettisoning people' all over the place." Ironically, what he did was fill their positions with his own people, many of whom came from Chicago along with him. Just this past December, he started doing the same thing all over again. He had to cut the positions of dedicated Philadelphia educators because he mismanaged the budget. Philadelphia's schools are in reality $160 million in the whole. So much for the state takeover.

What I saw happen in Philadelphia was reminiscent of what I read in history books about World War I. It is of little difference. It was just sublimated aggression. Remember our chapter on the psychological perspective. What happened can be explained by the phenomena raised therein. **Especially remember the Milgram studies—if we do not see first hand the pain of those who are affected by our actions, we do not understand the consequences of what we do.** We can read about it and see it on television, but if we do not see its effects first hand, the impact is not real and we let it continue.

Yes, the School Reform Commission has effectuated many outstanding initiatives. Most of them are in the arena of charter schools that are independent of the bureaucracy and exempt from many of its mandates. There are also many individual initiatives throughout our system such as the Constitution School and the new High School of the Future founded in partnership with the Microsoft corporation. Where we have failed is in our bureaucratic schools. That is because as long as we cling to the mandates of bureaucracy, we will cling to the failure of the past. The problem is in the nature of bureaucracy itself—it is inherently flawed.

The purpose of this chapter is to highlight some of the institutional illnesses that arise in all bureaucracies. It is the nature of the beast. Nothing here is meant to condemn those of us who, on occasion, have lowered ourselves to bureaucratic behavior for we all have at one time or another. It is meant to recognize the flaws of bureaucracy so we may take caution in what we do. It is a moral imperative and it is one of the bases of the democratic imperative.

As Michael Fullan so adeptly points out, **"We are talking about system transformation." That is the mission of school reform.**

So in that vein, let us view some of the institutional illnesses of bureaucracy:

The King or Queen is in Charge Disease

That is the phenomenon where the leader, whether it be the chief operating officer, the superintendent, regional superintendent, or principal of an individual school takes on the mentality that he or she is the supreme boss. That is really the psychological basis for the adversarial nature of bureaucracy that permeates everything that happens in schools. Most of the bureaucratic schools I have been in are characterized by that mentality. It manifests itself in the leader ignoring procedures designed to elicit basic fairness. It creates negativity and in its extreme forms creates a toxic school culture.

The Aristocracy Disease—"We Are Better Than You!"

That is based on the dichotomy of labor and management. Managers believe they are better than those they manage. They believe they know more than their subordinates, are more intelligent and must tell or teach their subordinates what the subordinate does not know. It manifests itself in statements like this that are made by autocrats such as Paul Vallas: "We have to allow our principals to make decisions 'for' our schools." How condescending! It amazes me how one day a teacher is just a mere subordinate, and the next day when he or she is made management, they know everything! In bureaucracies, this becomes a collective mentality. It is the reason why, in Philadelphia, we have a standardized curriculum and mandated pacing schedule that tells teachers what to teach, when to teach it and how to teach it. It more often blocks good instructional practices and is advocated by no expert on pedagogy in America. It certainly is antithetical to the concept of "professional learning communities."

Whose School Is It?

The "Downtown" Disease—the Blame Game

The "Downtown" disease is how a social science teacher at Mastbaum A.V.T.S. refers to the mentality of the central administration in Philadelphia whose central offices are located at 440 North Broad Street. They have a collective mentality that the teachers and their union are to blame for the ills of the schools and the school system. In actuality, it is the central administration that fails the children so often. What amazes me most is how the teachers hold the schools together in spite of the lunacy that surrounds them and is foisted upon them from afar. At the last collective meeting of assistant principals that I attended, we spent most of our time talking about how bad the teachers were. It was reported to me that the same thing took place at the principals' meeting and finally one department head who attended the meeting stood up and said, "I haven't heard one good thing said about teachers. I don't know what kind of teachers you have at your schools, but at my school the teachers are willing to do anything we ask and do a great job doing it." Then, and only then, did some of the other principals say they had good teachers, too.

The "Axis of Evil" Disease

The union and the union's building committee is not the "axis of evil." They are an essential part of good organizational dynamics. They enhance the workplace by bringing problems, conflicts and issues to the attention of management and leadership. Under our labor laws, it is the legal duty of the administration to resolve those issues. The union, like anyone in America, only wants **"basic fairness."** Administrators in bureaucracies and the politicians need to stop blaming the union and the teachers and the negativity of our adversarial past must be eliminated from the culture of our school systems. The attitude that the union is the axis of evil creating all the problems of the world is counterproductive and often ruins the climate of our schools for children. We can not allow our children to live much of their lives in houses of hostility.

The "Write-'Em-Up" Disease

That disease inflicts bureaucracies because of the adversarial nature of labor relations and the grievance and arbitration procedures that require due process. It could very well be that it is the single most destructive practice of our school system. It is often used as a **modus operandi** of central administrators and many principals, if not most principals. It is the **"management by threat disease"** and is always counterproductive. It is not leadership at all. "Writing someone up" is the psychological equivalent of hitting them with a stick. What credible and competent psychologist do you know that advocates hitting someone with a stick as a good motivational practice? Yet we do it all the time in bureaucracies. It is a matter of course to many in power. I have never seen it yield a positive result. It always causes anger, animosity and fight vs. flight responses. It is totally destructive of what we want to accomplish in schools. It should only be used as a last resort to document serious inappropriate acts in schools or complete incompetence. If a principal has to "write people up" to gain compliance, that principal has totally lost his or her power to lead! In large school districts it is a serious and debilitating institutionalized illness that destroys the fiber of schools.

The Management By Memo Disease

Closely connected to the write-'em-up disease is the management by memo disease. In bureaucracies, so much communication from top to bottom is done through the memorandum that it becomes overly pervasive and replaces and destroys simple interpersonal interactions that are so important for good leadership. Now that we have e-mail, it becomes so much worse. We use both e-mails and memos in so many situations that we lose the interpersonal connectedness of what we do. Remember, Kouzes' and Posner's assertion: "Leadership cannot be exercised from afar." Well, it cannot be exercised by the memorandum either. It is one thing to communicate from downtown offices through memos, but is quite another for principals to communicate through memos. Principals who overly rely on memos and e-mails do so because they have poor interpersonal skills and wish to hide behind the distance that memos and emails create. That is not good for fostering synergy among people and is counterproductive to building the interpersonal relationships that are so crucial to good leadership.

The Retaliation Disease

That is close to the write-em-up disease. If a teacher or staff member speaks out against the leader or fails to be submissive, they are retaliated against in one way or another. A retaliatory measure that is often used is to give a disliked subordinate a terrible teaching assignment. Teachers are often given the worst teaching roster in the school to put them in their place. Many administrators retaliate by "writing up" underlings for ridiculous or made up reasons. It is blatant slander and defamation. That is why the present employee discipline system that makes principals and superior administrators **"prosecutor, judge and jury"** is so blatantly violative of the Bill of Rights and basic American ideals. It is a terrible practice that should be eliminated immediately. I have seen many of my colleagues railroaded out of schools by principals who abuse their power. We can not tolerate **"abuse of power"** in our schools. This is America folks!

The Blind Support Disease

That brings us to the "blind support disease." Principals' actions, whether right or wrong, ethical or unethical, are almost always supported by their supervisors. Why? Because that is the psychology of power within bureaucracies! Reinforcing the chain of command always trumps ethics in school bureaucracies. It is really the "keeping the chain of power" disease. That is always a paramount concern in bureaucracies. It is the bureaucratic power structure. Supervisors have a fiduciary duty to supervise competently and ethically. Their fiduciary duties lie to the school community, not to those they supervise who are in positions of power. In bureaucracies, that legal duty is breached regularly.

What would you say if we had a justice system where the appellate courts always upheld the lower court's decisions whether right or wrong, moral or immoral? What kind of a justice system would that be? Then why would we maintain such a ridiculous governance system for our schools? Appellate courts regularly overrule trial courts and lower courts for error in their decisions. Supervisors of principals must regularly overturn their decisions whenever they are questionable. Without that, we can not yield a moral result.

The Machiavelli Disease

The "Machiavelli disease" represents the philosophy of power where the leader destroys all threats to his or her power. This Machiavellian approach is named after the infamous Niccolo Machiavelli who ruthlessly ruled in Italy during the end of the fifteenth century and beginning of the sixteenth century. It happens in bureaucratic school systems more often than we care to acknowledge. It is done as a practice in Philadelphia whenever a principal wants to get rid of an assistant principal who is favored by the teachers. Or, it manifests itself when a specific subject, course or program is cut by the principal of a school to get rid of the disfavored person who teaches the course or runs the program. Allowing that to happen in schools hurts the children. I have personally witnessed that scenario several times in my experience.

The "Whose Friend Are We Putting In Today?" Disease

This is, of course, the ages old phenomenon that who you know is more important than what you know. It is a major reason why we have so many ineffective principals and bureaucratic leaders and a major reason why they are never removed from their position no matter how incompetent. It happens repeatedly as if it were an inalienable right of those in power to put their friends in high places. There is nothing more debilitating to those who work their way up the right way than to see that happen. There is nothing more destructive to organizational cohesiveness. There is nothing that causes "leadership brain drain" more than that. Some people go through processes like principal's intern programs that are supposed to be pathways to the principalship while others are just put in as principals by a person who has the unilateral clearance to get away with it. It is a prescription for mediocrity.

In Philadelphia, the reality we talk about in the trenches is, "They do whatever they want." The rules change every day. The cure for such ridiculousness is strict rules for choosing principals that are enforced vigilantly. That is why we have election laws in America. That is why we have elections of our president, governors, and mayors. Even when there is a selection committee, there is usually a powerful being on that committee who railroads his person through or has supervisory power to contravene what the committee wants. Because of the power games people play, there must be strict and transparent selection or election rules put in place if we are to have a credible system that works.

The Self-Dealing Disease

Self-dealing happens all of the time in schools. It is when a principal or superintendent acts purely for self interest and not for the interest of the students, parents, teachers and school community. A school leader of any kind is a fiduciary and has the same fiduciary responsibilities as the trustees and boards of trustees. They are a type of trustee. **Principals, superintendents and superiors of any kind have the same duty of care, loyalty and good faith as all trustees do.** The question then arises: What is the remedy for breach of trust? It is hard to prove damages so there really is no remedy at law through a civil suit. What happens when supervisors do nothing? The legal term for that is **"ratification"** and supervisors then also become legally liable under the legal theory of "respondeat superior." **So what is the remedy for self-dealing? The remedy is democracy.** When the followers see the leader self-dealing as their usual behavior, their course of action is to vote the bum out! Or, at least speak up to the supervisor, school board, or board of trustees who can remove the person from the position or has the authority to decline to rehire that individual. Democracy in its entirety is the only viable remedy for self-dealing and is a substantial argument in support of the democratic imperative for our schools.

An example of how self-dealing plays out that happens every day in schools is one I have recently witnessed: A student in a high school had a third grade reading level. In Pennsylvania, our schools use the PSSA standardized test mandated by the state for Adequate Yearly Progress assessment under *No Child Left Behind*. The principal used school district funds to hire a Reading Specialist to teach the student how to take the test. The specialist taught nothing but "test preparation." As soon as the PSSA tests were administered, the specialist was let go. The specialist was hired purely to make the principal look good on the PSSA test. How about the student's need to have remedial instruction for her Reading disability? Nobody cared about the student and her disability at all. The final result is that the girl will never learn to read adequately! If that were my child, there would have been a lawsuit! Everyone in our school knew the principal cared about nothing but making herself look good. Yet, in the absence of democracy, that principal will continue in her position indefinitely. Self-dealing like that happens every day in schools! It hurts children.

The Annual Fraud—Is it the School's Budget or the Principal's Budget?

In Philadelphia, an individual school's budget must be signed by the parent representative and the staff's union representative. The reason for that is that the parents and teachers are supposed be part of the budgetary process. There is supposed be a degree of democracy in the process. In reality, there is none. What happens every year in most schools, is the principal decides what he or she wants, for whatever reasons, and unilaterally makes the budget as if it were the principal's money. Then the principal calls in some unknowing and uninformed parent and has the parent sign the budget without any knowledge whatsoever of what it contains. The principal fraudulently represents that the parents had some knowledge and input into the process. Then the principal does the same thing with the union representative who unwittingly, and to be amenable, goes along with it! That is the standard practice within the School District of Philadelphia—what a disgrace!

The sad thing is that it happens all across America. Only in public school systems is public money handled in such an incompetent manner. Public money should never be placed in the hands of a single person. It is a prescription for impropriety. Budgets for all public organizations should always be placed in the hands of a committee that is organized democratically and required to proceed in a transparent, open, participatory manner, consistent with American ideals of due process. That is precisely why we have **"sunshine laws"—democracy is the purification process.**

In Conclusion

Yes, democracy is the purification process for the institutional illnesses of our bureaucratic school systems in America. That is a beauty of democracy. It allows those who live much of their lives and work in their school community; those who see "first hand" what is really happening in their schools; those who care about our children and look them in the eye every day, to stand and say, "What is happening is not the way it should be. It is not the way we want it to be. Let us stand in community and do it this other way instead because that is the right way to do it—the moral way." It is the moral imperative of democracy.

12

Hilltop Revisited
The Conclusion

Great schools for children are really simple things. A school is a group of people who gather together to provide instruction in the lessons of learning and life for our children that we raise. It is a community and the best form of governance for communities in America is still and will always be DEMOCRACY!

The imperative for democracy is clear when we look at all the issues of education and think of them in the context of the best interests of children, the human condition and the realities of organizational governance. We have visited many of the great issues of education. They are issues of education that are everywhere in America and everywhere in the world. There are no easy answers. There are only temporary resolutions of the issues and then we must resolve those very same issues again and then again. That is the inescapable process of governance. In the face of all we must face in America and the world, we must always remember the core of what we believe in as a nation that has always made us the greatest country on earth—governance of the people, by the people and for the people.

We cannot forget our basic values of governance when we cross the threshold of our schoolhouse doors. It is within those doors that we plant the seeds of our country's greatness and we plant the seeds of our future. In today's world of high technology and easy travel, the schoolhouse walls can no longer stand as walls. We must send our children out into the world both physically and intellectually to educate our children well and preserve our standing in the world. There is a high degree of consensus within our educational leadership that we must do things differently if we are to move forward and lead the world. We must grow as a total educational community for that to happen. We must grow as a nation above and beyond the adversarialism of the past and replace it with true collegiality. There is no other path to our continued greatness.

No matter how we structure the hierarchy of education, we are always hooked to the reality that education is always delivered to students within the confines of the local school community. Great teaching is always a face to face interpersonal relationship even when interfaced through technology and project based instruction. Man is a social being and we can never escape that fact. We can never escape that education, its leadership and its governance is always based on interpersonal relationships. It can never be well facilitated from afar and will always be tied to the local school community. Great schools are places where people work together in community and the governance structures we create must **"set the conditions"** for that greatness to emerge.

We know that good education depends on the school community working together for the benefit of the students, the school community and the larger community that is our America. That is why such concepts have emerged as the professional learning community, the small learning community, the common vision, the collective mission, collegialism, leadership and democracy in education. The bottom line is that we all must work together if we are to have great schools, and for that to happen we must govern ourselves together.

The word "accountability" is used so often in education today. But the reality is that you cannot hold a group of people accountable without first empowering the group to be accountable. In a democratic society, the people hold their leaders accountable. It is not the leader holding the people accountable. If we want our public schools to be accountable, we must empower the school community to be accountable. It is the only way to ensure a moral result in public education based on the true best interests of the children.

We have viewed most of the forms and issues of school governance. In the face of all the issues of school governance, the form of governance that always emerges and appears consistently as the one that is most likely to set the conditions for greatness in individual schools is the simple form of governance represented by "Hilltop Babe Ruth." That simple form of democratic governance is used all over America. It has been used to create all kinds of great communities from our towns and cities, to our libraries, to our youth organizations, to many of our most successful business organizations and to most of our outstanding schools and school districts. It just fits so well into all we know about schools, education and governance of people.

What is the answer to the question, "Whose school is it?" The answer is that it is everybody's school. The answer is that our public schools to be public schools must be the community's schools or our schools are no longer public schools. The deeper answer, when we look at the governance of individual schools is that it is the school community's school. It is the student's school and that is to whom we owe our primary fiduciary duties of loyalty, care and good faith. But is also the parents' school, the teachers' school and the community's school. School boards of any kind and of any name stand as trustees for our children in our schools but also as trustees for our parents and teachers who work in those schools. All of our school leaders are also trustees for the public trust that is our schools. They must serve the community that they lead and govern if we are to have greatness in our schools. There is no other way. Servant leadership is a must.

The imperative for democracy will always exist. We must embrace it. The form of governance represented by Hilltop Babe Ruth is essential for professional small learning community synergy. It is so very poignant and symbolic that the principal of the newest school in Philadelphia, the High School of the Future, calls herself **"the lead learner."** If she does nothing more than fulfills that role in its truest sense, instills that concept in the total school community of Philadelphia, and that concept is borrowed elsewhere and put into fruition in all of America, she will have served us all as a great leader—as a visionary leader.

The basic democratic formula for our schools that is so promising for our schools is so simple yet so powerful. It is the basic concept the fathers of our country embraced and instilled when they drafted our Constitution. Every member of the school community, once they sign up as a resident of that school through admission, has the rights of membership to participate in the governance of their school. Under democratic principals of equality, equal voting rights can be fairly apportioned in a number of satisfactory ways. One of those voting apportionment scenarios that has already been used effectively in schools is the one family one vote and one staff member one vote structure. Then, democracy dictates that the people vote for their school leaders. Whether they vote for their board of trustees alone or whether they vote directly for their principal is arguable. But I would argue for direct election of the principal. That is what our nation chose to do about our president because it is the best way of implementing the values of democracy.

If we allow our politicians to appoint school boards and school leaders, our schools then become the politicians' schools. If we allow founders of schools and coalitions of founders to appoint future trustees, the schools are then their schools and they have been granted ownership rights in our public schools. They are then no longer public schools. If we, as the *New* Commission advocates, create schools that are limited liability corporations owned by teachers, where do the parents stand? Even if that does happen, they also need to be governed democratically to ensure the stockholders of the limited liability corporations their participative due process rights to be part of the governance of their schools. We can not, in America, have selected leaders. We must have elected leaders.

Remember the analogy laid out in the introductory chapter: What would you say if the president of the United States of America said that he would choose the governors of each state and the mayors of our cities and our towns and impose them upon the people? What would you say if he declared he would choose our congressmen and senators? You would say that is crazy. You would say that is a disgrace in America. But that is exactly how many of our school districts in America are now governed. We must change that practice.

The *New* Commission raises what they say is an important truth: **"The problem is not the educators. It is with the system in which they work."** Implementing a new system will take courage and leadership. A new system must have integrity and professionalism.

Great schools for our children can only emerge if the total school community works together. For that to become reality we must work collegially, be led democratically and governed democratically. There is just no other way to develop the requisite excitement, energy and synergy that is necessary for an **"ethos of greatness"** in our schools.

Our leaders must be inspirational leaders—inspirational to the children; inspirational to their parents, inspirational to the teachers; inspirational to the support staff; and inspirational to everyone else in the community of our schools. For us to find inspirational leaders capable of instilling that passion and synergy in the local school community, we must do it through the process of democracy. **It is imperative if we care about children.**

The one thing that is for sure is that as long as we have caring, dedicated teachers, parents and others in our schools, we will always have the ingredients of great schools. We then, only need to set the conditions for them to find their inspiration, rise up, and stand as true professionals and parents in professional learning communities within a democratic society. **It is imperative for our schools, our America, and our children that we embrace democracy in all its essence to govern our schools.**

Every American has dreams and visions. Every American has dreams and visions for his children. We all have dreams. In honor of all of our hopes, dreams and aspirations, there are no greater words to conclude this book than the words of the great Dr. Martin Luther King, Jr. May we remember them here:

> *I have a dream that one day our nation will rise up and live out the true meaning of its creed: "We hold these truths to be self evident, that all men are created equal."*

APPENDIX

Figure 5.1

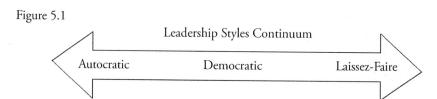

Leadership Styles Continuum

Autocratic   Democratic   Laissez-Faire

Figure 5.3

Martin Haberman's
Dimensions of Effective Urban School Leadership
Assessed by
Star Urban Administrator Questionnaire

I. Sensitive to Diversity_____Insensitive to Diversity
Does the respondent understand the pervasive importance of race, ethnicity, class and gender in the process of interacting with all constituencies involved in the school community, or does the respondent assume that these differences will not affect his/her leadership? This dimension predicts the respondent's ability to be perceived as fair and equitable in an urban school serving diverse children, parents and community in poverty.

II. Creates a Common Vision_____ Fosters Personal Preferences
Does the respondent have a strong and persisting commitment to creating a common set of goals and objectives for all school staff, or does s/he believe that it is best for each staff member to decide school goals for him/herself? This dimension predicts the likelihood that respondent will create the effective work teams and cooperative activities needed for the school to succeed, or simply seek to make individuals happy by following their preferences.

III. Develops Positive Working Climate _____ Enforces Rules
Does the respondent appreciate that the leaders' role involves dealing with a complex set of interpersonal relationships, or does s/he see the leader as the final authority in enforcing rules? This dimension predicts the respondent's potential for creating a positive working climate, or having the school function as a depersonalized bureaucracy.

IV. Instructional Leader _____ Building Manager
Does the respondent place a high priority on the leader's role in improving teachers' instructional effectiveness, or does s/he see the leader's role in controlling and maintaining the building as his/her highest priority? This dimension predicts whether the respondent will function as the school's leading educator, or as the overseer of the school organization and physical facility.

V. Data Driven_____Idiosyncratic
Does the respondent use data as the primary basis for setting school policies and procedures or does s/he use school traditions, personal charisma or pleasing staff as the basis for instituting school policies and practices? This dimension predicts the ability of the respondent to increase the effectiveness of the school in achievement, attendance, suspensions and in other critical areas where the data is readily available.

VI. Product Evaluation_____ Process Evaluation
Does the respondent focus on the results as the fundamental criterion of success, or does s/he believe that procedures followed can be used as the criterion of success? This dimension predicts whether the respondent will maintain a focus on improved learning as the ultimate value to be preserved, or whether the programs in his/her school will be evaluated on the basis of procedures followed and how the programs are implemented.

VII. Personal Accountability_____ Others Accountability
Does the respondent understand and accept the need for the school principal to bear personal accountability for student learning and other measures of school success, or does s/he believe it is the role of the principal to ensure that only others are held accountable for various aspects of the school's program? This dimension predicts the respondent's willingness to hold him/herself accountable for people and processes which s/he cannot completely control.

VIII. Responsible Leader _____ Delegator
Does the respondent understand the leader's role to be primarily one in which s/he will be the responsible authority for performing major functions, or does s/he believe that the leader's role is primarily one of delegating as much as possible to others and overseeing their work? This dimension predicts not only the respondent's leadership style but the degree to which s/he perceives the school leader as directly and personally responsible.

IX. Expanded Principal's Role_____Traditional Principal's Role
Does the respondent understand that the effective urban school principal is the leader of a community based, non-profit organization, does s/he see the role of principal as limited to his/her role and status in the urban school district bureaucracy? This dimension predicts the respondent's propensity to connect the school with the resources needed to serve diverse children in urban poverty, or to be limited to only the district's budget, personnel and resources.

X. Bottom-up Representative _____ Top-down Representative
Does the respondent perceive his/her role as primarily representing the needs of the school upward to superiors, or does s/he interpret the role of the principal as primarily representing the mandates and policies of the system downward to the staff? This dimension predicts whether the respondent will protect and enhance effective practices in his/her school or simply follow orders.

XI. Parents with Voice _____ Parents as Helpers
Does the respondent understand the need for parents, caregivers and community to be involved in the life of the school as participants with voice, input and even power, or does s/he see the value of these constituencies as essentially supporters of the school program? This dimension predicts the likelihood that the respondent will seek to involve parents and community as genuine partners, or limit them to homework helpers and visitors.

XII. Client Advocate _____ Staff Advocate
Does the respondent understand the principal's role as an advocate of children, parents and community, or does s/he see the "good" principal as one who only supports teachers and staff in problem and conflict situations? This dimension predicts the respondent's ability to implement the school's commitment to serve diverse students and families in poverty and simultaneously represent the professional staff.

XIII. Problem Solver _____ Reactor
Does the respondent perceive the role of school leader to be primarily one of active involvement in problem solving, or does s/he see the principal as the legal authority making final decisions from options presented to him/her? This dimension predicts whether the respondent will be a dynamic, creative leader, or whether s/he will passively wait for problems and solutions to be presented to him/her.

Figure 5.4

Local School District Leadership Competencies

These are the primary responsibilities of the principal as determined by the central administration of the School District of Philadelphia as of May 1, 2007. They were derived from a set of 37 leadership competencies that were originally formulated in collaboration with representatives from Microsoft Corporation. They were originally reduced to 16 because of the impracticability of trying to assess prospective principal candidates on so many criteria. Subsequently, they were reduced to the final 12 listed here. The issue is whether these competencies can be measured in any valid and reliable way through an interview or testing situation. They are most effectively gauged by observation in the field on a day to day basis. The only people who see the leader's behavior on a day to day basis are those who work in a school community every day. It is a tenant of democracy that the people see and the people judge. Leadership cannot be exercised from afar—neither can it be assessed from afar. Nonetheless, these are relevant competencies of effective principals and leaders in any professional organization and are representative of those efforts in many school districts throughout our nation.

Primary Responsibilities
- Serves as an instructional leader who can design and manage processes that improve the delivery of instructional services
- Able to confront and remedy inadequate teaching practice
- Creates and maintains safe school climate
- Sets expectations and effectively deliver results for academic achievement, climate safety, budget efficiency, and employee/student performance
- Serves as a role model to school community (students, staff, families)
- Identifies and engages community resources (public relations)
- Is accessible to students and community; establishes an inviting climate for the community to interact with the principal
- Is a visible force to ensure and advocate the health, safety, and welfare of students, staff, and community
- Listens and responds to concerns, questions and needs (emotional, social) of students, staff, families and community
- Possesses a passion for learning, growth, and people, recognizing both mistakes and success as learning opportunities
- Reads, writes and speaks with clarity, explaining expectations in a clear and timely manner
- Promotes a positive reputation of the school
- Orchestrates technology for purposes of instruction, communication, and safety
- Hires effective faculty and staff
- Organizes and budgets resources, being creative about budgeting and managing
- Motivates students, parents, and staff to do their best

Core Competencies
- **Functional / Technical Skills**—Possesses required functional and technical knowledge and skills to do his/her job at a high level of accomplishment.
- **Motivating Others**—Creates a climate in which people want to do their best; can assess each person's strengths and use it to get the best out of him/her; promotes confidence and optimistic attitudes; is someone people like working for and with.
- **Integrity & Trust**—Is widely trusted; is seen as a direct, truthful individual; presents truthful information in an appropriate and helpful manner; keeps confidences; admits mistakes; doesn't misrepresent him/herself for personal gain.
- **Valuing Diversity**—Manages all kinds and classes of people equitably; supports equal and fair treatment and opportunity for all; fosters a climate of inclusion, where diverse thoughts are freely shared and integrated.
- **Interpersonal Skills**—Is warm, easy to approach; builds constructive and effective relationships; uses diplomacy and tact to diffuse tense situations; has a style and charm that immediately puts others at ease and disarms hostility.
- **Managing and Measuring Work**—Clearly assigns responsibility for tasks and decisions; sets clear objectives and measures; monitors process, progress, and results; designs feedback loops into work.

- **Drive for Results**—*Pursues everything with energy, drive, and a need to finish; does not give up before finishing, even in the face of resistance or setbacks; steadfastly pushes self and others for result.*
- **Directing Others**—Establishes clear directions; sets stretching goals and assigns responsibilities that bring out the best work from people; establishes a good work plan and distributes the workload appropriately.
- **Managing Vision and Purpose**—Communicates a compelling and inspired vision or sense of core purpose; makes the vision sharable by everyone; can inspire and motivate entire units or organizations.
- **Priority Setting**—Spends his/her time and the time of others on what's important; focuses on the critical few and puts the trivial many aside; can quickly sense what will help or hinder accomplishing a goal.
- **Assessing Talent**—Is a good judge of talent; accurately projects what people are likely to do across a variety of situations; hires the best people available from inside or outside; assembles talented teams.
- **Managerial Courage**—Tactfully dispenses direct and actionable feedback; is open and direct with others without being intimidating; deals head-on with people problems and prickly situation.

These are leadership competencies that did not make the cut:

- Building Effective Teams
- Managing Through Processes & Systems
- Problem Solving
- Intellectual Horsepower
- Dealing with Ambiguity
- Creativity
- Learning on the Fly
- Organizing
- Developing Others
- Action Oriented
- Organizational Agility
- Presentation Skills
- Comfort Around Authority
- Negotiating
- Listening
- Managing Relationships
- Conflict Management
- Written Communications
- Customer Focus
- Planning
- Time Management
- Personal Learning & Development

School Council Model of School Governance
AKA The "Constitutional Model"

Judicial Branch—Board of Trustees

- Oversees the operations of the school
- Assures the school functions as envisioned in the organizational document
- Assures the appropriate interplay between the school council and the principal or lead teacher
- Assures participative due process
- Passes resolutions necessary to the operation of the school
- Resolves disputes between branches of governance and individuals or groups within the school community
- Makes final determination of disciplinary actions
- Members are elected democratically or appointed by a body that is elected democratically
- Term limits and reelection or reselection

Executive Branch
Principal, Lead Teacher or CEO

- Executes the mandates and policies of the board of trustees, supervening governmental body, and education laws
- Runs the daily operations of the school
- Does all executive acts necessary to fulfill the collective vision and mission of the school
- Presents recommendations to the school council for the educational plan
- Implements the final educational plan and school based policies
- Presents a recommended school budget to the school council for approval
- Supervises staff and executes student and employee discipline procedures
- Is elected by the school council, board of trustees or directly elected by the school community

Legislative Branch—School Council

- Develops the educational plan & local school policies
- Assesses, evaluates and revises the educational plan
- Implements participative due process procedures for involving all stakeholders in the decision-making process of the school and assures parents, teachers, staff, students and the community-at-large has an opportunity to be heard
- Participates in the budget-making process and passes the final approval of the budget after holding public hearings where all stakeholders have an opportunity to be heard
- Is comprised of teachers, parents, students (in high schools) staff members, and community representatives
- Representatives are elected directly or appointed by an elected body, or a combination of both

School Community

Teachers   Parents   Students   Support Staff   Community-at-Large

- Elects the board of trustees, principal & school council or has meaningful input into their selection through an open, transparent process; or elects those who are empowered to vote for officers and officials; and/or has meaningful input into who is on the "election" committee and who is chosen as the principal.

Note: It is important to note that under the "Constitutional Model" the principal, lead teacher, or CEO does not stand in a superior hierarchical position to the school council. They are equals. School councils that have been placed in a lower organizational position do not work because it creates a paternalistic relationship and renders the school council as a mere advisory group. There are many variations of this basic format that can be created. The powers of each branch must be formulated in the charter or constitution of the school, or in the mandates of law or the supervening school board. The school council has sometimes been placed in a superior position to the principal, but that organizational design changes the balance of power to a corporate design and the council becomes another form of board of trustees.

References

Adorno, T.W. Frenkel-Brunswick, E., Levinson, D.J., & Sanford, R.N. (1950) The Authoritarian Personality. New York: Harper & Row.

Antunez, B. (2000) When Everybody Is Involved: Parents and Communities in School Reform. National Center for Bilingual Education {Online}. Available:http//www.ncbe.gwu.edu/ncbepubs/tasynthesis/framing/6parents.htm.

Barth, R. S. (1991) Improving Schools From Within. San Francisco: Jossey-Bass.

Beck, L. G. (1994) Reclaiming Educational Administration as a caring profession. New York: Teachers College Press.

Bennis, W. (1989) On Becoming a Leader. Mass.: Addison-Wesley.

Brown v. The Board of Education, 347 U.S. 483, 78 S.Ct. 686 (1954).

Bruner, J. S. (1963) The Process of Education. Cambridge: Harvard University Press.

Caine, R. N., & Caine, G. ((1997) Education on the Edge of Possibility. Alexandria, VA: Association for Supervision and curriculum Development.

Caldwell, B. (1992) The Principal as Leader of the Self-Managing School. Journal of Educatinal Administration, 30, 6-19.

Cannon, W. B. (1929) Bodily Changes in Pain, Hunger, Fear and Rage. New York: Appleton.

Charter School Law, 24 Pa.C.S. §17, et seq.

Cheng, Y. (1994) Principal's Leadership as a Critical Factor for School Performance: Evidence From Multi-Levels of Primary Schools. School Effectiveness and School Improvement, 5, 299-317.

Chester-Upland Community Parents on the Move, Amicus Curiae Brief, In Support of Petitioner , Commonwealth of Pennsylvania, Department of Education v. Chester Upland School District Board of Control, __ A.2d __, No. 496 M.D. 2005, (Pa. Cmwlth. October 16, 2006)

Collins, J. (2001) Good to Great. New York: Harper Collins.

Comer, J.P. (1984) Home-School Relationships as they Affect the Academic Success of Children. Education and Urban Society. 16(3), 323-337.

Comer, J.P. (1988) Educating Poor Minority Children. Scientific American. 295(5), 42-48.

Comer, J.P., Haynes, N.M., Joyner, E.T., & Ben-Avie. [EDS.] (1996) Rallying the Whole Village. New York: Teachers College Press.

Commonwealth of Pennsylvania, Department of Education v. Chester-Upland School District Special Board of Control, Commonwealth Court of Pennsylvania, Memorandum Opinion and Order (October 16, 2006) No. 496 M.D. 2005.

Commonwealth of Pennsylvania, Department of Education v. Chester-Upland School District Board of Control, __ A.2d __, No. 496 M.D. 2005, (Pa.Cmwlth. October 16, 2006)

Conard, A.F., Knauss, R.L., & Siegel, S. (1977) Enterprise Organization. New York: The Foundation Press, Inc.

Cooper, J., & Croyle, R.T. (1984) Attitudes and Attitude Change. Annual Review of Psychology, 35, 395-426.

Cotton, K. (2003) Principals and Student Achievement: What the Research Says. Alexandria, VA: Association for Supervision and Curriculum Development.

Covey, S. (1991) The Taproot of Trust. Executive Excellence, 8(12), 3-4.

Covey, S. R. (1989) The Seven Habits of Highly Effective People: Powerful Lessons in Personal Change. New York: Simon & Shuster.

Covey, S.R. (1992) Principle-Centered Leadership. New York: Simon & Shuster.

Deal, T.E. & Peterson, K.D. (1999) Shaping School Culture: The Heart of Leadership. San Francisco: Jossey-Bass.

DiPilato, G. (1995) Handout provided to class in principalship program at Pennsylvania State University.

Education Emowerment Act, 24 Pa.C.S. §17-1701-B, et seq.

Engle, S. H., & Ochoa, A. S. (1988) Education for Democratic Citizenship: Decision Making in Social Studies. New York: Teachers College Press.

Festinger, L. (1957) A Theory of Cognitive Dissonance. Evanston, IL: Row, Peterson.

Finn, C. E., Jr. (1991) We Must Take Charge of Our Schools and Our Future. New York: Free Press.

Frankl, V. (1946) Man's Search for Meaning. Boston: Beacon Press.

French & Raven (1959)

Fullan, M. (2001) Leading in a Culture of Change. San Francisco: Jossey-Bass.

Fullan, M. (2003) The Moral Imperative of School Leadership. Thousand Oaks, CA: Corwin Press.

Fullan, M., Hargreaves, A. (1996) What's Worth Fighting For In Your School. New York: Teachers College Press.

Gill, B., Zimmer, R., Christman, J., & Blanc, S. (2007) State Takeover, School Restructuring, Private Management, and Student Achievement in Philadelphia. Santa Monica, Rand Corporation. RAND URL: http://www.rand.org.

Glickman, C. D. (1993) Renewing America's Schools: A Guide for School Based Action. San Francisco: Jossey-Bass.

Glickman, C.D. (1998) Education and Democracy: The Premise of American Schools. San Francisco: Jossey-Bass.

Goleman, D. (1995) Emotional Intelligence: Why It Can Matter More Than IQ. New York: Bantam Books.

Goleman, D. (1998) Working With Emotional Intelligence. New York: Bantam Books.

Goleman, D. (2000) Leadership that Gets Results. Harvard Business Review, March-April.

Goleman, D., Boyatzis, R. & Mckee, A. (2002) Primal Leadership: Realizing the Power of Emotional Intelligence. Boston: Harvard Business School Press.

Greenleaf, R. (1970) The Servant as Leader. Indianapolis: Robert K. Greenleaf Center for Servant-Leadership.

Greenleaf, R. (1977) Servant Leadership: A Journey into the Nature of Legitimate Power and Greatness. New York: Paulist Press.

Haberman Educational Foundation (2007) http://www.habermanfoundation.org. Houston.

Haberman, M. (1999) Star Principals Serving Children in Poverty. Indianapolis: Kappa Delta Pi.

Hall, C.S. Gardner (1985) Introduction to the Theories of Personality. Toronto: John Wiley & Sons.

Harlow, H.F. (1949) The Formation of Learning Sets. Psychological review. 56, 51-55.

Harlow, H.F. (1958) The Nature of Love. American Psychologist. 13, 673-685.

Harlow, H. & Zimmerman, R. (1959) Affected Responses in the Infant Monkey. Science. 130, 421-432.

Hirsch, E. D., Jr. (1996) The Schools We Need and Why We Don't Have Them. New York: Doubleday.

Hoy, W., Tarter, C. J., & Kottkamp, B. (1991) Open Schools, Healthy Schools. Newbury Park, CA: Sage.

Hunt, D. (2007) The Personal Renewal of Energy. Toronto: OISE Press.

Independent Schools Act, 24 Pa.C.S. §5-502.1 et seq.

Jacks, J.Z., & Cameron, K.A. (2003) Strategies for Resisting Persuasion. Basic and Applied Psychology. 25, 145-161.

Kouzes, J.M., Posner, B.Z. (1986) Eye of the Follower. Administrative Radiology, April 1986, 55-56, 58, 63-64.

Kouzes, J.M., Posner, B.Z. (2002) The Leadership Challenge. San Francisco: Jossey-Bass.

Kouzes, J.M., Posner,B.Z. (2003a) Credibility: How Leaders Gain and Lose It. San Francisco: Jossey-Bass.

Kouzes, J.M., Posner, B.Z. (2003b) Encouraging the Heart: A Leader's Guide to Rewarding and Recognizing Others. San Francisco: Jossey-Bass.

Kozol, J. (1992) Savage Inequalities: Children in America's Schools. New York: Harper & Row.

Levine, D.U. & Lezotte, L.W. (1990) Unusually Effective Schools: A Review and Analysis of Research and Practice. Madison, Wisconsin: National Center for Effectiver Schools Research and Development.

Lewin, K., Lippitt, R., & White, T.K. (1939) Patterns of Aggressive Behavior in Experimentally Created "Social Climates." Journal of Social Psychology, 10, 271-299.

Maddi, S.R. (1996) Personality Theories: A Comparative Analysis (6th ed.). Toronto: Brooks/Cole Publishing Co.

Marzano, R.J., Waters, T., & McNulty B.A. (2005) School Leadership That Works: From Research to Results. Alexandria, VA: Association for Supervision and Curriculum Development.

Maslow, A.H. (1943) A Theory of Human Motivation. Psychological Review, 50, 370-396.

Maslow, A.H. (1970) Motivation and Personality, 2nd ed. New York, Harper & Row.

Meir, D. (1995) The Power of Their Ideas: Lessons for America from a Small School in Harlem. Boston: Beacon Press.

Meir, D., Schwartz, P. (1995) "Central Park East Secondary School: The Hard Part Is Making It Happen in Democratic Schools." In Apple, M.W., Beane, J. A. (eds) (1995) Democratic Schools. Alexandria, VA: Association for Supervision and Curriculum Development.

Milgram, S. (1963) Behavioral Study of Obedience. Journal of Abnormal and social Psychology, 67, 371-378.

Milgram, S. (1974) Obedience to Authority: An Experimental View. New York: Harper: Harper & Row.

Morris, C, & Maisto, A. (2005) Psychology: an Introduction. Upper Sadle River, NJ: Pearson Prentice Hall.

Mortensen, C.D. (1966) Should the Group Have an Assigned Leader? Speech Teacher, 15, 34-41.

National Commission On Excellence In Education (1983) A Nation At Risk: The Imperative For Educational Reform. Washington, D.C.: Government Printing Office.

Noddings, N. (1992) The Challenge to Care in Schools. New York: Teachers College Press.

Nuguera, P. (2005) Address to the Haverford High School Faculty. Haverford, PA.

Perloff, R.M. (2003) The Dynamics of Persuasion: Communications and Attitudes in the 21st Century (2nd ed.). Mahwah, NJ: Lawrence Erlbaum Associates.

Petty, R.E., & Caciopo, J.T. (1981) Attitudes and Persuasion: Classic and Contemporary Approaches. Dubuque, IA: Wm. C. Brown.

Phillips, J.L. (1969) The Origins of the Intellect: Piaget's Theory. San Francisco: W.H. Freeman.

Piaget, J., (1969) The Origins of the Intellect.

Powers & Powers (1983).

Ratner, D.L. (1970) The Government of Business Corporations: Critical Reflections on the Rule of "One Share One Vote." Enterprise Organization. New York: The Foundation Press, Inc.

Ratner, D.L. (1970) The Government of Business Corporations: Critical Reflections on the Rule of "One Share One Vote." 56 Cornell Law Review 1. Cornell University Press.

Reichfield, E. F. (2001) Loyalty Rules: How Today's Leaders Build Lasting Relationships. Boston: Harvard Business School Press.

Report of The New Commission on the Skills of the American Workforce (2007) Executive Summary: Tough Choices Or Tough Times. National Center on Education and the Economy. Washington, DC: www.skillscommission.org.

Report of The New Commission on the Skills of the American Workforce (2007) Tough Choices or Tough Times. San Francisco: Jossey-Bass.

Rogers, C.R. (1959) A Theory of Therapy, Personality and Interpersonal Relationships. In S. Koch (ed.) Psychology: A Study of Science. (pp. 184-256). NY: McGraw Hill.

Rogers, C.R. (1961) On Becoming A Person. Boston: Houghton Mifflin.

Rogers, C.R. (1965) A Humanistic Conception of Motivation. In R.E. Farson (ed.) Science and Human Affairs. NY: McGraw Hill.

Rogers, C.R. (1977) Carl Rogers On Personal Power. NY: Delacorte Press.

Rutter, M., Maughan, B., Mortimore, P., Ouston, J., & Smith, A. (1979) Fifteen Thousand Hours. Cambridge, Mass.: Harvard University Press.

Sergiovanni, T. J. (2004) Building a Community of Hope. Educational Leadership, 61(8), 33-38.

Sergiovanni, T. J. (1992) Moral Leadership: Getting to the Heart of School Improvement. San Francisco: Jossey-Bass.

Shaw, M.E. (1976) Group Dynamics: The Psychology of Small Group Behavior. New York: McGraw-Hill, Inc.

Sizer, T.R. (1984) Horace's Compromise: The Dilemma of the American High School. New YorK: Houghton Mifflin.

Sizer, T.R. (1992) Horace's School: Redesigning the American High School. New York: Houghton Mifflin.

Sizer, T.R. (1996) Horace's Hope: What Works for the American High School. New York: Houghton Mifflin.

Skinner, B.F. (1938) The Behavior of Organisms. New York: Appleton-Century-Crofts.

Skinner, B.F. (1948) Science and Human Behavior. New York: McMillan.

Skinner, B.F. (1989) The Origins of Cognitive Thought. American Psychologist, 44, 13-18.

Smith, W,F., Andrews, R.L. (1989) Instructional Leadership: How Principals Make a Difference. Alexandria, VA: Association for Supervision and Curriculum Development.

Snyder, Susan. "Report: Managers Fall Short in Philadelphia Schools." The Philadelphia Inquirer, 1 February 2007, sec. A p. 1.

Sunshine Act, 65 Pa.C.S. §701, et seq.

Taylor, K. L., (2004) Through Their Eyes: A Strategic Response to the National Achievement Gap. Philadelphia: Research For Better Schools.

Waller, W. (1932) The Sociology of Teaching. New York: Wiley, 1932.

Warehime v. Warehime, 722 A.2d 1061 (Pa. 2000).

Wasley, P., Hampel, R., & Clark, R. (1997) Kids and School Reform. San Franciso: Jossey-Bass

Waters, J. T., Marzano, R.J., & McNulty, B. (2004a) Developing the Science of Educational Leadership. Spectrum: Journal of Research and Information, 22(1), 4-13.

Waters, J. T., Marzano, R.J., & McNulty, b. (2004b) Leadership that Sparks Learning. Educational Leadership, 81(7), 48-51.

West Chester Area School District v. Collegium Charter School, 760 A.2d 452 (Pa. Cmwlth. 2000), affirmed by S.C. of Pa., 812 A.2nd 1172 (2002).

Whitaker, T. (2003) What Great Principals Do Differently: Fifteen Things that Matter Most. Larchmont, NY: Eye On Education.

Whitehead, A.N. (1929) The Aims of Education. New York: Macmillan. (From) Wikipedia; (2006) http://wikipedia.org/wiki/Self-actualization

Woodall, Martha. "Nationally, Hired Firms Have Had Little Effect." The Philadelphia Inquirer, 1 February 2007, sec. A p. 10.

Index

Afterword—The Power of the People

Much has happened in America pertaining to our schools and their governance since the first words for this book were written. Our schools and school systems are dynamic organizations and change comes quickly as we find our way to effective school reform initiatives. It is a growth process for us all—everyone who has anything at all to do with education in America.

As I lay upon paper these final words before the final version of this first edition goes to press, there are many issues being raised across America from the fight in Washington D.C. over whether to keep the democratically elected school board or allow the mayor to take over the schools, to the teachers in Los Angeles, California, who have demanded and been granted the power to turn around their failing schools by determining themselves what to teach, when to teach it and how to teach it. They are two examples of democracy in action and we must acknowledge those examples of what can happen when the people are given a "true voice" in the governance and leadership of our schools.

Much of this book has focused on what has happened in Philadelphia, Pennsylvania, in the aftermath of the state takeover of our public schools so we can learn from our experience and apply it to all of America. It is only fair to acknowledge the outstanding progress our School Reform Commission has made in returning our school district towards the inclusive processes of democracy. In response to the many voices of the school community of Philadelphia who have called for a voice in the decision-making and governance of the school district, the School Reform Commission has embarked on an inclusive process for choosing our next Chief Executive Officer of the School District of Philadelphia.

Under the leadership of Sandra Dungee-Glenn, the new Chairwoman, and the addition of two educators to the SRC, Denise McGregor Armbrister and Heidi Ramirez, they have proceeded to gather information on what the school community wants to see in a new CEO for Philadelphia's public schools. They have held many meetings throughout the city to assess the views of the people and now seek to make their final choice based on much of what they have learned. They have also assembled a community advisory group of forty school system, parent, teacher and community group leaders to help them choose our next CEO. They should be commended for their efforts to listen to the people of Philadelphia and the educators within our schools.

But what is also of major significance is that Helen Gym, an Asian American who is leader of Parents United for Public Education, was selected by Philadelphia's leading newspaper, *The Philadelphia Inquirer* as "Citizen of the Year." She has been recognized as an "inclusionary leader" who has tirelessly worked leading and advocating for change and demanding a voice in the governance and decision-making of our schools. She has asserted poignantly: "If we are waiting for someone else to stand up and do what we know is right, then we will wait forever." She also has made another point that we all should keep in mind as we debate the great issues of our times: "Schools are where we institutionalize our love of our children. And why not invest in love and give our children all they deserve?"

She, like all parents, teachers, and citizens all across America who have stood up and participated in the progress of our schools, should be given a resounding standing ovation for their effort.

All of the examples mentioned above, are examples of the power of the people within a democratic society as we rise to be heard. The greatness of our schools depends upon the greatness of the people in our collectiveness. I hope that this book, which has already been presented to the SRC in Philadelphia and has helped influence that body to be more democratic in its leadership and governance, influences everyone in America to embrace the ideals of democracy our country stands for and make those ideals come alive in the governance of our schools.

About the Author

Rich Migliore has served the School District of Philadelphia and its school community for over thirty years as a teacher of Reading, English, Law and as a high school administrator. He has held numerous positions including small learning community coordinator, department chair, School Governance Council Chair, Principal and Assistant Principal. He has had the rare opportunity to provide leadership in seven different schools, spending twenty years serving the school community of University City High School and seven years as assistnat principal at Furness High School in South Philadelphia. He has also participated in two principal's training programs including the Academy for Leadership in Philadelphia Schools supported by the Broad Foundation.

Rich also practices law in Southeastern Pennsylvania with a focus on education law in the public arena. Since the Pennsylvania state takeover of Philadelphia's public schools and the onset of the charter school movement, he has intensively studied school governance and leadership as they pertain to the organizational dynamics and structures of schools and the constitutional issues they raise. Through all the controversy of the new frontier of education, Rich has always kept a keen focus on the children and their best interests.

His wide variety of experience and insightful analysis of the movements of education enable him to see so clearly the realities of the world our schoolchildren live in as we try to improve our schools for everyone. His knowledge, expertise and depth of understanding show through clearly and passionately in the pages of this book as he advocates for the children of America. I have known him for all of those years and have had the opportunity to see him in action and see his dedication first hand and the respect he always earns from his colleagues. The respect he earns is due to his personal credibility, integrity and sincerity in everything he does.

Joe DiRaddo, Reading Teacher
University City High School